STAKES IS HIGH

SUNY series, Critical Race Studies in Education

Derrick R. Brooms, editor

STAKES IS HIGH

Trials, Lessons, and Triumphs in Young Black Men's Educational Journeys

DERRICK R. BROOMS

Cover image: © Nathan Brown. Used with permission.

Published by State University of New York Press, Albany

Printed in the United States of America

For information, contact State University of New York Press, Albany, NY
www.sunypress.edu

Library of Congress Cataloging-in-Publication Data

Name: Brooms, Derrick R., author.
Title: Stakes is high : trials, lessons, and triumphs in young Black men's educational journeys / Derrick R. Brooms.
Description: Albany, NY : State University of New York Press, [2021] | Series: SUNY series, critical race studies in education | Includes bibliographical references and index.
Identifiers: LCCN 2021011015 | ISBN 9781438486536 (hardcover : alk. paper) | ISBN 9781438486543 (pbk. : alk. paper) | ISBN 9781438486550 (ebook)
Subjects: LCSH: African American men—Education, Higher. | African American men—Social conditions. | African American college students—Biography. | Education, Higher—Social aspects—United States.
Classification: LCC LC2781 .B759 2021 | DDC 378.1/982996073—dc23
LC record available at https://lccn.loc.gov/2021011015

10 9 8 7 6 5 4 3 2 1

This work is dedicated to our young people—
may you continue to become and pursue all your possibilities.

Contents

Part III: Lessons

Acknowledgments

First, to the men whose lives are the focus of this project, thank you for trusting me with your experiences, narratives, sense making, ideas, thoughts, and perspectives. I appreciate you sincerely. I look forward to continue bearing witness to your genius, intellect, resourcefulness, resilience, and beauty. You are royalty.

Love, blessings, and thanks go to Joseph McCoy. Thank you for believing in me, supporting and mentoring, pushing and calling me higher, and sharpening my iron. I am grateful every day. Thank you, Darryl Brice: your constant encouragement is a gift that I cherish deeply. To Arthur Davis and Reggie McClain, know that I continue to walk in gratitude. Special thanks go to Bianca Baldridge; I truly appreciate you and your friendship as well as all the ways you keep me accountable and how you both encourage and continuously inspire me. Thank you for our talking sessions, your feedback, and your critical insights, which helped me further develop this project and pushed my writing and analysis in so many ways. Collectively, you all keep me on my path, strengthen my resolve, and keep me grounded.

A sincere thanks goes to my scholarly community. Through individual relationships and connections as well as the collective, I remain energized and uplifted by every opportunity to be in community. Thank you James Moore III for your example and encouragement, for your graciousness, and for your ongoing support. I am grateful for your support of this project from its early beginnings; thank you for your invaluable feedback and the ways you pushed me to better appreciate what this project could entail. Thank you, Jelisa Clark; it continues to be both an honor and a privilege to work with you, to collaborate, to coconspire, and to bring work to life. Your brilliance is energizing. Sincere gratitude goes to Bros. Matt Smith and William Franklin; working with you all continually inspires me in so many ways, and I remain humbled by and excited about our collective efforts.

Thank you Courtney Bell for your friendship and for helping me bring Kwa Jamii into being; I look forward to our future work together. Special thanks go to Adrienne Paul; your friendship and support are blessings. You are truly appreciated.

As Audre Lorde attested, without community there is no liberation. I give thanks for my many communities—from students and coworkers to colleagues and coconspirators to family and the larger collective. Sincere thanks go to a collective of people who offer critical support in a number of ways. For believing in me, pouring into me, and supporting me through a number of professional endeavors, I wish to thank Yoshiko Harden, Bob Green, Earl Wright, Tanya Robinson, Gwendolyn Purifoye, Linn Posey-Maddox, Sandra Barnes, Marvin Lynn, Darrell Hucks, Joe Goodman, Lateefah Id-Dean, Deadric Williams, Reuben Miller, Chris Jett, Marcelle Medford, Jerlando Jackson, Jamie Patton, and Eligio Martinez.

A very special thanks to Regina Dixon-Reeves for your early guidance and support in helping prepare me for the profession and in welcoming me to ABS. Those early sessions, both formal and informal, helped me better envision and define my path. It is indeed an honor to be your colleague and collaborate on joint and collective efforts. A special thanks goes to Armon Perry for your collegiality, your commitment, and your friendship. Thank you for teaching me, being an example, and providing me with opportunities. I will continue to pay it forward. To Theresa Rajack-Talley, thank you for your leadership and your ongoing support and encouragement. I appreciate our connection, and I've truly enjoyed and learned a great deal from our collaborations. To Kenneth Hutchinson, know that I miss you and our bond every day; thank you for shining your light on me. Please know that your legacy lives in me—and in us.

To Ayana Karanja, thank you for master teaching and mentoring, for your guidance and wise counsel, and your ongoing support. To Andre Phillips, thank you for your support and always making space for me; your office was my refuge and sacred space. To Maxine Proctor, thank you for advising and guiding me on my path; and a special thanks goes to Neal Bailey El for believing in me, giving me a chance, and encouraging and supporting me to strive for excellence. Thanks go to several teachers and staff who contributed to my development: (at Hirsch) Ms. Adams, Ms. Lee, Ms. Walker, Mr. Rogers, Mr. Smith, Mr. Bush, Mr. Watson,

Coach Thomas, Mr. Beverly; (at Horace Mann) Ms. Williams-Bey, Ms. Williams, Ms. Jones, Mr. Green, and Mr. Whitfield; (at Kenwood) Mr. Stevenson and Mr. Fraser.

To Mary Pattillo, Alford Young Jr., Reuben May, Ray Reagans, and Mignon Moore, thank you for your examples.

I am grateful to be connected and in community with the following colleagues and friends, all of whom I wish to thank: Daphne Watkins, BarBara Scott, Elighie Wilson, Lionel Howard, Jarrod Druery, Ruby Mendenhall, Frank Tuitt, Milagros Castillo-Montoya, Ted Thornhill, Dwayne Compton, Ernesto Mejia, Samantha Ellert, Roderick Carey, Daphne Chamberlain, T. Elon Dancy, Veronica Newton, Cam Williams, Felix Kumah-Abiwu, Brian McGowan, Paul Harris, L'Heureux Lewis-McCoy, Rabia Khan Harvey, Emily Ignacio, Sam Adams, Greg Thompson, Dion Steele, Richard Glass, Terrell Strayhorn, Ebonie Cunningham-Stringer, Thomas Calhoun, Zandria Robinson, Onnie Rogers, John Eason, James Jones, Mauriell Amechi, Stevie Johnson, Lisa Covington, Ahmad Washington, Torie Weiston-Serdan, Brian Burt, George Wimberly, Odis Johnson, Bianca Williams, Adrian Huerta, Derrek Griffith, Tim Eatman, LaVar Charleston, Danny Malone, Siobhan Smith, Courtney Luedke, Chance Lewis, Antoinette Hudson, Erik Hines, Elsa Camargo, and Antar Tichavakunda.

I give thanks to several people in my community of scholars who have taught me a great deal by their example, leadership, and commitment as I read and engaged with their work; attended conferences and heard their words, perspectives, and analyses; and engaged in conversations and in bearing witness: Walter Allen, Phillip Bowman, James Earl Davis, Leslie McLemore, Charles Payne, Janice Johnson Dias, Ivory Toldson, Lori Patton Davis, Cheryl Matias, Wizdom Powell, Jamal Eric Watson, Tobin Miller Shearer, J. Luke Wood, Sean Joe, Eduardo Bonilla-Silva, Sydney Freeman, Whitney Pirtle, D-L Stewart, Eboni Zamani-Gallaher, Michael Cuyjet, David Pate, and Shawn Anthony Robinson.

I send a shout-out to several University of Cincinnati graduate students whom I've had the privilege to work with in numerous ways: Shaonta' Allen, Curtis Webb, Chad Sloss, Shobha Kansal, Ayesha Casie Chetty, Faisal Alsenea, Nola Almageni, Amaha Sellasie, Kierra Toney, Anthony Stone, Brittney Miles, Marcus Brooks, Juliana Madzia, Kamonta Heidelburg, and Marcus Smith. I also send acknowledgments to a number of undergrad students: Tim Davis, Emil Howard, Krishyra Mitchell, Ariel Boughman, Zaire Parrotte, Sachika Singh, Deondre Hunt, Briana Young,

Jared Knight, Changa Johnson, LaVonne Heisser, Trey Snoddy, Jordan Dunnigan, Imani Coleman, Meleea Giordano-Briggs, Johari Jackson, and Tyla Thompson.

Thanks go to a community of folx: Michele Page, Chris Hall, Ms. Patton, Mrs. Burton, Hank Rich, Dave Ramsaran, Booker Whitt, Jimmie Wells, Ted Richards, Broderick Hawkins, Eric Smartt, Nate Wautier, Ted Richards, Addison Jackson, Dwayne Morrow, Arin Gentry, Devon Jackson, Parnika Patel, Kala Brown, Bryson McGuire, Eric Jordan, Kent Pugh, Chad Caldwell, CJ Harmon, Liane Hypolite, Brandon McReynolds, Jamar Montez, Elizabeth Roberts, Brandon Joseph, Isaac McCrimmon, Bridget Parler, Sendi Estrada, Juwan Bennett, Emmanuel Tabi, Robin Högnäs, Greg Quick, Matt Limegrover, Cynthia Doyle, Jenny Snyder, Nate Byrd, Gloria, Mike, Gabe Draper, Lamar Morris, Bamba Ndiaye, Joey Brown, Curtis Spencer, Victor Jones, Jake Rugh, Charles Gidney, James Bernard Pratt Jr., Tiyah Western, Donna Miguel, Jeff Kolnick, Kevin Jarbo, and Mr. Mack.

Thanks go to my collective: Kaveh Haerian, Dave Ferguson, Brandy Woods, Craig Alexander, Dwayne Maddox, Khirsten Scott, Mike Wolfolk, Divya Muralidhara and Ed Knoll, Greg Seaton, Kobena Osam, OT Mahone, Eric Smith, James Snowden, Royel Johnson, Sheeba Jacobs and Anay Shah, Alexis Mack, Jolie Sheffer, Cameron Khalfani Herman, Emily Ignacio, Jeff Maxwell, Shaun Cole, Chris Posey, Ardell Buchanan. Thanks also go to my MSA community: Vince Flowers, Leonidas Sloan, JC Lugo, Sean James, and, to name a few young brothers, Rob Head, Jonathan Henderson, Frank Rojas, Makonnen Tendaji, Muhammed Hassan, Alex Guerrero, George Parker, Justin Blakely, Bryan Cantero, Angel Roman, Steve Walton, Francois, Efrain Vidana, James Harris, Vontress Atkins, Gabriel Ezechukwu, Nick Hidalgo, Ramiro Acebedo, Terrence Andrus, and Kevin Fuentes.

To the members of my RES Community, who are a breath of life and a reflection of so much of our collective possibilities: Raquel Wright-Mair, Johnny Ramirez, Sylk Sotto, Lucy LePeau, Marc Guerrero, Chrystal George Mwangi, Yannick Kluch, Mo Moagisi, Kaifa Roland, Maria Salazar, Steven Asei-Dantoni. Many thanks go to Mary Tupan-Wenno for hosting us and Pravini Baboeram for teaching us and offering us your gifts and brilliance.

Thanks go to Juan Carlos Rivera, Bannon Stroud, Eric Boria, Cori Farmer, Arlen Wiley, Leon Gordon, Millan AbiNader, Josh Magallanes, Rob Shelby, Vanessa Lillard, Vince Welch, Bennie Williams, Doris

Martinez, Noory Lee-Kim, Keisha Wint, and Ijeoma Opara. I send blessings and gratitude to LaSaundra Hutchinson and family; thank you for keeping me (and us) in your community. Much love and appreciation go to my GetUP Community and all of who you are, what you represent, and what you've contributed and accomplished thus far, in addition to all that is on your horizons: Darion Blalock, Jamil Boldian, Rayvaughn Hines, Marlon Marshall, Anthony Ponder, Byron Caulton, Eric Charles, Anthony Hubbard, Bryant Alexander, John Warren, Cameron Barnes, Tyler Beck, Smith Francois, Robert Henderson, James Reed, Nigel Bruce, Matt Williams, Jonathan Holmes, James Cole, Eric Brown, Ed Green, Rafael Wordlaw, David Peake, Malik Battle, Rashid Williams, Jabrice Reese, Israel Durley, and Jermaine Taylor.

I hold space for Sherman Galbreath, Phillip Coleman, Devon Reavley, Wendell Jackson, Leon Donaldson III, Devon Wade, and so many more of our young people. And I send love to and hold space for Savannah Walker and her family.

I wish to recognize my connections to several professional entities who have been vital to my intellectual and professional growth and development. I give special thanks to the Association of Black Sociologists, the Scholars Network on Black Masculinity, the International Colloquium on Black Males in Education, and the *Journal of Negro Education* Editorial/Advisory Board. Though they are all different, each of these associations has served as a homeplace where I have been immersed in critical conversations about research, current events, and issues specifically related to Black communities. I have received tremendous support and I have been able to learn and grow both intellectually and professionally in extremely meaningful ways. Additionally, my thanks go to the Research Focus on Black Education SIG (AERA), the Council on Ethnic Participation (ASHE), and the Racial Equity Summit, all of whom, in their own ways, provided me with multiple communities in which to be immersed, supported, and maintained. I also appreciate being afforded great opportunities to connect with students and scholars at various stages of their careers and journeys and my own.

I'm grateful for the research support I have received, including grants, funding, and professional opportunities that all contributed to this project specifically, from the Midwest Sociological Society and, at the University of Cincinnati, the Taft Research Center, the Kunz Center for Social Research, the Black Faculty Association, and the Sociology Department. I also send thanks to the Fannie Lou Hamer Institute at

Jackson State University for facilitating opportunities for me to present work from this project and support for some of my other research work. Thanks also go to Rebecca Colesworthy: it is a pleasure to work with you; I appreciate your leadership and support and I'm honored by what we've accomplished together thus far.

To my family, I hope that my efforts and whatever it is that I might accomplish along the way reflect my appreciation. To my grandmothers, Vivian Covington, Anne Richardson, Lucille Brooms, and Helen Graine Faulk, thank you for helping me understand and pursue my possibilities. To Wilma Bell, I love you and appreciate you deeply; thank you so much for your othermothering. I send love and thanks to Wendy Fuller, Gran Rufus, Art Richardson, Granddaddy Scott, and Ray Covington. Thanks go to Dee, Mario, Andre, and Reisha; to Jeff, Lenora, Andrease, Lydia, Matthew, Jerome, JJ, Kim, Nicole, and Leon; to Jerry and Helen Brooms and family, Maine and Terina Brooms and family, BJ and Eddie McCoy and family, and Jamenda McCoy and family. Thanks go to Christine Brooms, Rebecca Edmond, and Vincent; and to Veda Hudson and Steve Richardson. Thanks go to Debbie and Chrystal. Blessings go to Ashton and Keyshawn as well as all my cousins, uncles, and aunts; and I'm holding space for Lil' Mario. Thanks and love go to Jah Breeze, Dianne Thomas, Camy and Paul Sundberg, Aisha and Kelton, Katilyn, Selah, and the Gummer and Peterson families.

I send love and blessings to DJ, Caleb, Duff, Mike, Langston, Quentin, Amari, and Ryan, trusting that each of you will continue to grow into your brilliance; and I send love to Lexi, Deanna, Quentin and Jordyn, Charleigh, Ari and Amaya, and Nia and Mike. I hope that each of you continues to pursue the best and highest versions of yourselves.

A special thanks go to my father, Rufus Brooms Jr.: thank you for your love, support, guidance, wisdom, and encouragement.

Love, thanks, and appreciation go to Natasha Burrowes. Thank you for your prayers, positivity, uplifting, ongoing support, and championing of me and my efforts.

To Danielle, Camille, Gabrielle, and Amina—you are the legacy; continue to shine your light even as you continue to become. You are a force, both individually and collectively. I carry you with me and you inspire me every day.

Preface

Dear Black boys and men, we love you. Thank you for all of who you are and all the gifts that you offer to us. You are radiant, and I truly hope that you'll continue to shine and embody your light in all the ways that you are called and desire to do so. I am writing this book for you. I am truly grateful for all the ways you've invited me into your spaces, the ways you've shared with me here and elsewhere, the ways you've listened to me and allowed me to share, and the ways you pour into me and us. As you move forward, into each of your tomorrows, please know that we hold space for you; we lift you up and affirm you. We appreciate you. We know the challenges are real and continual; we also know that there is great strength in the collective and we know that you continue to accomplish many of your dreams, goals, and aspirations—and on your own terms. Please know that you are never alone and that my greatest hope is that you can walk into and be free in all your possibilities. Let us all be the authors of our own stories. We celebrate your joy, your brilliance, your triumph, your becoming, your being.

Much Love,
DB

an invocation . . . for Black young men

by D. Brooms

we are the roses
we spring in the dawn
like carefully gardened possibilities
we are poetry
in motion
defying gravitation odds and laws
we float on
we touch the sky
we Black boy fly
we write litanies for survival
like morning devotionals
and invocations of becoming
we write rhythms on blue notes
bang buckets like wisdom
raining down from elders
feet racing toward promises
and sing prayers over sampled beats
beautiful struggles that remind and inspire
we are light
we call on innervisions
to channel our prospectives
we rise
stepping and marching in tune
ascending like a new moon
we jazz june

we are reflections and inheritors
knowing ancestors and foreparents carried us
we speak to those who are hearing us
we search for ourselves
we are bridges
we connect like quilts
let our efforts be undeterred
let our lives and realities be heard
and let us craft author and tell our own stories
in our own words

Introduction

> [College graduation] will mean a lot [brief pause] I think about it every day, ever since I started college. Just being the first generation not only to go but also to finish. It's a good feeling; thinking about all of the things I had to go through until now. It's going to be a bittersweet feeling because of all the great people that I met along the way.
>
> —Jamal

> If I don't graduate from college, the relationships I built, what is that gon' say to my son? What is that gon' say about me? Who's to say I don't start questioning myself like that? It's not the end of the world. Might be the beginning of hell [laughs in amusement], but it's not the end of the world.
>
> —Michael

Stakes Is High is about a select group of young Black men's educational experiences, their lives, and how they make sense of their pathways to and through college.[1] The eight young men whose lives make up this book all attended Ellis Academy (pseudonym), an all-male college preparatory secondary school located in a major urban city in the United States. My seven-year longitudinal study, which I began during the summer prior to when they started college, includes a retrospective view of their secondary school years and their meaning making throughout their postsecondary experiences.[2] In this multiphase study, I began by investigating their pathways to college, from their aspirations and the messages they received to their secondary schooling experiences, which laid the groundwork for contextualizing and understanding their postsecondary schooling experiences.

During their secondary school years, the majority of these young men resided within or in close proximity to the school neighborhood. They primarily relied on public transportation in traveling to and from school and, as I have discussed in other published work, their secondary school years were complicated by interactions and challenges with people in the neighborhood. As one of the young men noted, in reflecting on navigating the neighborhood, "It was tough, it was difficult, it was a tough neighborhood—everybody don't make it out. You have those that make it out, they come back and don't make it out again. And you have those that make it out and don't ever come back."[3] In addition, the secondary school they attended can be described as a counterhegemonic space where the culture of the school was centered on affirming Black boys.

Regarding the young men's backgrounds, six young men lived with their mothers as the primary caretaker and adult in their household, one lived with both his parents, and one lived with a great-aunt and great-uncle who served as guardians. All the young men have siblings, ranging in number from two to seven; seven of the young men self-identified as low-income; and seven were first-generation college students (based on their parents' degree attainment). I spent nearly 150 hours formally interviewing these eight young men over the course of this study and countless hours more communicating, checking in, and continuing conversations about a range of topics. As shown in their narratives in the previous epigraphs and the chapters that follow, all the young men thought about college to some extent, whether they aspired to go to college prior to attending, considered pursuing their athletic interests during their future college years, or devised strategies for completing college once enrolled. Their early thoughts about college were grounded in their lived experiences and the knowledge they developed during their adolescent years.

The stakes for Black boys and young men are both paradoxical and complex. Given the ways in which young Black men are repositioned in wider US society—namely, being marked as problems, considered to be in crisis, projected as oppositional, and relegated as disposable—they often are deterred from and placed at odds with educational success. At the same time, given the general and government-supported importance placed on college degree attainment (e.g., which endorses "college for all"),[4] they are pushed to achieve educationally while also being systematically blocked from what is held up as the ticket to long-term success in the United States. Whether through instructional design and curriculum, teachers' perceptions and beliefs about their abilities, or school-based policies and practices (e.g., discipline or selections for gifted education), Black boys and young men enter school buildings at risk of stereotyping, profiling, and being in trouble. They bear the brunt of generic educational expectations and are accosted by ideologies of meritocracy that both suggest and presume that they don't care about education. Too often, they are placed out of relationship with many school personnel and positioned beyond the school's caring networks. Moreover, they often are buried under the weight of a single story, a homogenized narrative, that predicts and expects educational failure.[5]

In this research project, I wanted to learn how these young men made sense of getting to college. Once they were in college, I talked with them at multiple points across their years there to explore their academic, social, and personal experiences. I explored their perspectives and experiences in real time, allowed them to lead the direction of various portions of our conversations based on some of their experiences and what they offered, and, as can be seen from the statements by Jamal and Michael, which open the chapter, I asked them to look forward and offer their point of view about future experiences and events, such as college graduation. Most importantly, in the chapters that follow, I situate my conversations with these young Black men with respect to their Blackmaleness—the combined impact of their racialized and gendered identities. Blackmaleness reflects the gendered racism that Black boys and men experience because of the ways that they are repositioned into the lower rungs of society, considered and treated as disposable, constructed as a perpetual threat, misread and misperceived in intentional and unforgiving ways, are susceptible to heightened levels of surveillance and secondary policing, and simultaneously experience hypervisibility and invisibility.[6] In other words, I take account of how their Black male racialized-gendered identities matter in their social relations, interactions, and representations—in their lived experiences in general and, more specifically, in their "desire to achieve against the odds," which education scholar Heidi Safia Mirza refers to as *educational urgency*, in their schooling efforts.[7]

Jamal, as he looked ahead to his anticipated educational accomplishments, considered and thought about his college years and future graduation through the lens of his lived experiences—"all of the things

I had to go through until now." Throughout his college years, Jamal experienced frustration and anxiety due to academic challenges, had to contend with several instances of overt and passive anti-Black racism on campus, and battled with racial microaggressions and disparaging stereotypes specifically because of his Black male identities. These experiences, which were both consistent and ongoing, shook his academic confidence and undermined his sense of belonging in college. Thus, Jamal's point that he had thought about college graduation "every day, ever since I started college" speaks to the range of these experiences (and others), provides insight into his sense of educational urgency and offers a glimpse into the potency of these young men's narratives. Jamal was both tired and determined. He felt burdened by the lowered expectations placed on him and the stereotypes held about him—and other young Black men. At the same time, however, because of the wealth of his community, he received significant positive support along the way and felt empowered to accomplish his educational goals.[8]

Both similarly and differently, Michael's educational urgency is evident in how he thinks about his ongoing efforts and educational focus. He thought about his educational endeavors and potential future graduation as testimonies to his sense of worth that not only mattered to himself, especially given the trials and tribulations he experienced through his educational journey, but also to his family because of his first-generation college status, and in particular to his son. In one of our conversations, Michael shared his belief that going to college could help change the history and trajectory of his family—both economically and in future opportunities. Given this heightened importance of college and what it could mean, he had internalized familial pressure and responsibility for attending college and also hoped to count graduation as one of his educational accomplishments. For each of the young men in this study, education was valued highly and their sense of its value was rooted deeply in their families and communities. As I show in the following chapters, in fact, the value they placed on education escalated through their experiences, the support and messages they received, and the educational investments they made as well. As a result, educational attainment mattered greatly to how they thought about themselves. Additionally, they calculated their future college graduation as an accomplishment that was both for and attributable to their families and communities. That is, the importance of education in these young men's lives and narratives encompassed a drive for cultural, generational, and social change that was inseparable from their Blackness.

Stakes Is High relies on the authentic lived experiences, choices, decisions, and meaning making of young Black men to understand their lifeworlds, especially in relation to education. I use the phrase "Stakes Is High" as the title of this text for a number of reasons. First, and importantly, this phrase comes directly from these young men's sense making. Second, as we discussed in a number of our conversations, they shared that they personally had a lot invested in and depending on their educational attainment, of which completing college was paramount. Third, and relatedly, stakes are high because of the ways that their aspirations and goals were embedded in their relationships; they discussed education as a shared value and something of collective importance to their families and communities. In addition, beyond their own desires, I use the phrase in several other ways: (1) to call attention to the daily realities of these young men's lives; (2) to connect these realities to the choices and decisions they make and to some of the decisions made and perspectives held about them; and (3) to acknowledge the range of their knowledge and understandings, all of which can contribute to their current and future experiences, challenges, opportunities, and life outcomes. And, finally, I use the phrase to register the high stakes of research in helping to recognize these young men as experts and counter detrimental narratives about them, with researchers as fellow stakeholders in their representations and success.

These young men's narratives help to reveal their experiential knowledge and serve as powerful counternarratives regarding how young Black men value education, the critical importance of their goals and efforts, and the worth they see and appreciate in their own selves and their lives. I use the young men's narratives and experiences to ground each chapter of this book, primarily because I see these young men as experts on their own lives and experiences. That is, I wanted to provide space to help bring these young men's narratives forward and allow them opportunities to make sense and meaning from their own experiences and perspectives. Some of the questions that guided this study included: How do these young Black men account for their pathways to college? How do they make sense of their secondary schooling experiences in relation to their aspirations and expectations for college? How do their Black male identities impact their educational journeys and experiences? What challenges have they experienced, how do they make sense of these, and what efforts did they undertake in trying to respond to or overcome them? Finally, in what ways do education, in general, and college, in particular, matter to their lives, their families, and their futures?

I pay particular attention to the lessons these young men extract from their efforts, decisions, trials, and triumphs during their educational journeys from secondary school to college. This research is set in the United States, and it is concerned with how these young men aspire to, prepare for, navigate, and negotiate college through critical personal strivings. I use a critical race methodological approach in this study to present research and findings grounded in young Black men's experiences, knowledge, and worldviews.[9] This research is not simply about pushing back against the oft-cited and misguided perspective that prescribes deficits to Black youth. In this approach, I use these young men's experiences and stories as counternarratives that powerfully affirm their lives and humanity. I describe and examine the resourcefulness and commitment of these young Black men in forging their futures and demonstrate how their aspirations, communities, and efforts help keep them on their pathways to and through college. These young men's narratives must be presented as counternarratives because they run against the dominant stories often told about Black boys and young men and their education. In relying on and interrogating these young men's narratives, I aim to reveal their self-empowerment, sense of agency, and growing clarity about the role of education in their lives.

Counternarratives are an important element of critical race methodologies, as they are grounded in experiential knowledge. According to critical race theory (CRT) scholars Daniel Solórzano and Tara Yosso, CRT "recognizes that the experiential knowledge of people of color is legitimate, appropriate, and critical to understanding, analyzing, and teaching about racial subordination."[10] In this book, counternarratives are employed to serve three key functions. First, they are critically useful as a way to expose and disrupt dominant racial ideologies. Second, they can be understood at multiple levels: the individual, the institutional, and the societal.[11] Importantly, in this realm, they can extend the understanding of personal or individual experience, such as Black boys' and young men's experiences, and help examine how racism operates through systems of privilege and power, especially in educational domains. Finally, counternarratives also provide an opportunity to interrogate the status quo and privilege that lie at the heart of dominant narratives, especially when juxtaposed with counternarratives.[12]

In giving name to educational urgency and explicating the ways in which it appears, is nurtured and pursued, and is deployed and revealed in the young men's narratives shared throughout this book, I underscore a critical heuristic lens—that is, how these young Black men discover and learn for themselves—through which to both view and understand their lives and their pathways to and through college. The narratives offered throughout this book help exhibit young Black men's knowledge and help recenter and give voice to their epistemologies and ways of knowing. As Solórzano and Yosso contended, "If methodologies have been used to silence and marginalize people of color, then methodologies can also give voice and turn the margins into places of transformative resistance."[13]

Focusing on Black Boys' and Young Men's Education—and Lives

Success is often held up as the goal of education, though what success is supposed to entail can vary. In this research project, I wanted young Black men to define and characterize their own understandings of "success," to narrate their experiences through their own interpretative lenses (as I generally followed their lead on where their narratives took us during our conversations), and to make sense of their decisions, choices, and experiences along the way. Overarchingly, I wanted success to be determined in their own terms and through their own lives. My understanding of my own success as a researcher was centered on trying to discern what these young men thought about themselves personally and also what they wanted to achieve educationally and in their professional pursuits postcollege. That is, I wanted to get a deep sense of what success meant and looked like and how it mattered in their lives. I also wanted to understand how education mattered in their lives by using college as the primary focus. Thus, it was integral to the research design and focus to rely on young Black men's sense of empowerment and allow space for them to be experts about their own lives and educational experiences.

There are two discernible, and disturbing, patterns in ongoing conversations about Black youth's schooling experiences.[14] First, there is a hyperfocus on those students who do less well in school as it relates to outcomes (e.g., graduation). For instance, a range of conversations center on Black men's departure from college as a basis for projecting their lack of educational seriousness and abilities. Some of this focus relates to oppositional culture, "cool masculinity," and academic deficiencies. Second, for those young people who do perform well, stories and discussions about them often rely on exceptionalizing their experiences. For instance, in a recent story about Hazim Hardeman's educational accomplishments and resilience in becoming a Rhodes scholar, reporter Susan Snyder noted that his path "was sinuous, improbable, the kind of story usually reserved for Hollywood scriptwriters."[15] This characterization of Hardeman's experiences can, in some cases, be likened to the ways in which Black youth's aspirations and achievements are narrated in ways that are "unseen" or more of the daily unexpectedness.[16] Instead, I affirm and echo sentiments asserted by education scholar Ivory Toldson: "When you truly know Black males, you expect their brilliance, rather than be surprised by it."[17]

If Black boys and men's educational accomplishments are "improbable" and attractive as Hollywood scripts, then by contrast their lack of achievement seems both expected and normative. This "normativity" or expectation of failure informs too many narratives that are peddled constantly about Black boys' and young men's lives and experiences, reinforces the status quo and the same old stories about them, and simultaneously neglects their needs and denies them educational opportunities. Instead of focusing on an individual undertaking as *the* story, what is more remarkable, exceptional, and overwhelmingly unnamed and underexamined in their experiences is the staunch anti-Black racism that confronts them in multiple facets of their lives. By anti-Black racism, I mean the numerous ways in which racial oppression against Blacks is both systemic and central to the US social order, being carried out in both logic and ideology as well as within and across social institutions (e.g., schools, criminal justice, etc.). The brutalities inflicted upon Black life stem from the violence and terrors in both the historical and present record, from colonization to enslavement to the present, that informs the condemnation and subjugation of Blackness. Further, anti-Blackness is predicated on Blacks' structurally antagonistic relationship with humanity as they constantly (and seemingly perpetually) are rendered as both "other" and nonhuman.[18]

As opposed to supporting such dominant narratives regarding Black boys' and men's "improbable" accomplishments, which are inherently anti-Black, we must ask: What barriers exist that delimit their achievement at higher levels? And why are people continuously surprised by their educational achievements and accomplishments and their intellectual and personal brilliance? Unless we're willing to ask these kinds of questions, Black boys will continue to face significant and undue inequities in their educational experiences. Likewise, if we are not serious about improving their educational opportunities and life experiences, then the dominant narratives about and framings of them and the "surprise" about their accomplishments will continue to persist. As opposed to hailing the exception and pitying (or punishing) those who do not achieve at such levels, greater interrogations and analyses are needed of the ideologies, policies, and practices that (re)produce the status quo, limit their opportunities, and increase the stakes of their educational experiences. Moreover, given their firsthand understanding that "stakes is high," the young men whose narratives comprise this book are living testaments to their hopes, aspirations, resistance, resilience, brilliance, and transformation. While they represent themselves as individuals, they are also representative of the type of knowledge and understanding we can gain when we center, listen to, and learn from Black boys and young men as they make sense of their own lives—as opposed to relying on the same old stories to tell us, and them, who they are.

Scores of Black men and boys are quite aware of the deficit-laden narratives that surround and delimit not only their educational opportunities but also their lives. I stand with education scholar Bianca Baldridge in the need for "relocating the deficit" and others who see, understand, and appreciate the brilliance and gifts of Black youth.[19] During various conversations, each of the young men in this study discussed how they were confronted and accosted on numerous occasions, in their youth and young adult years, by anti-Black racism, symbolic and structural violence, and other people's projections and denigrations of them and their possibilities. Thus, from an early age these young men had to develop a variety of skills and rely on various forms of knowledge and capital in order to manage and negotiate miseducation, negative messaging, stereotypical projections, and spirit murder (the general and specific disregard for their lives and the psychological trauma it produces), along with misrepresentations of them in their local communities, in educational settings, and in the media.[20] Importantly, then, the resilience, aspirations, determination, and resistance that these young men developed, sharpened, and called on over the course of their schooling did not simply occur in schools but also through their lives beyond school. That is, their lived experiences in general undoubtedly shaped their schooling experiences. In addition, their sense-making ability and the lessons that they deduced from their lived experiences in and beyond school also helped them develop and enhance their educational urgency.

Part of the motivation in writing this book is to allow space for young Black men to offer their own narratives about their lives and education—their aspirations, experiences, missteps, triumphs, and lessons. Core to my effort is focusing on Black boys' and men's *possibilities*—which centers the promise and potential of Black youth as learners, doers, and achievers and as individuals who are capable of accomplishing their educational and personal goals. The idea of possibilities also honors their resistance, recognizes the beauty and brilliance of who they are already, and appreciates and celebrates their becoming.[21] The basic premise of this study is centered on the question, Who would know or articulate young Black men's educational journeys and experiences better than themselves? Thus, like other CRT scholars, I see and understand these young men's narratives to be born out of their experiential knowledge, simultaneous forms of resistance and affirmation, and the centrality of race and racism within their experiences. As Hazim Hardeman, the recent Rhodes scholar from Philadelphia, discussed in an opinion piece, one's knowledge of their experiences is a powerful tool that can inform their educational trajectory. In reflecting on his life and experiences, he explained, "This awareness has caused me to be sensitive about how I narrate my story. What I seek to reject, at every turn, is a narrative in which my individual success magically alchemizes into the dissolution of the barriers that makes my story the exception to the rule."[22]

Similarly, my inquiries into these young men's lives, thoughts, and educational experiences are neither simply concerned with nor solely informed by schooling. As a way to honor and in an attempt to understand these young men's educational narratives, it remains important for me to "know" them. By "know," I mean to consider their educational experiences beyond school walls and understand that knowledge is developed and harbored significantly through one's life experiences. By "know," I also mean to spend time with, develop relational proximity with, be willing to both listen and hear, and, just as important, seek to understand their lives and experiences through discerning and reflecting on my own. Several aspects of my own identities and experiences are prominent in this research as well. I approached my study as a youth worker, as a former secondary school history teacher and athletic coach, as an individual who continues to serve and volunteer in Black communities in several locales, and as a Black man who mentors and works with many Black boys and men and other young adults of color. The position I hold, then, is based on my own lived experiences inside and outside the classroom in addition to my experiences teaching, coaching, mentoring, learning, and interacting with Black boys and men in this manner over the course of my professional career.

It is important to note that I took a longitudinal approach in this study because I wanted to learn about these young men's experiences over a course of time that allowed space for critical reflections, sense making, and understanding—all through multiple experiences. That is, the narratives that these young men offer are dynamic and were collected over numerous conversations. In getting to know them, I spent time with them in their own domains even at times when I did not "interview" them, I did not ask questions about their schooling experiences, and I did not ask them to make sense of their experiences and decisions. As a result, even as I discuss what they shared and what I learned from them, this is all within a broader context of developing deep relationships and connections and a meaningful knowledge.

In considering the multiple (potential) contributions that Black youth offer us, counternarratives provide important and much needed space for their own truths, reasonings, and accounts. Indeed, what we must ask and reckon with is twofold: What is lost? And what are the costs of continuously silencing, denying, and ignoring Black life, Black struggle, Black triumph, Black progress, Black narratives? As the preeminent scholar W. E. B. Du Bois pointed out more than a century ago, the global history of Black people is one of strife.[23] And, as we connect this strife to the educational realm, all too often education is and continues to be a site where Black youth suffer from anti-Black racism and anti-Black state violence. Whether the speakers describe being subject to miseducation, whether they "wanna holler and throw up both their hands," whether they imagine school is "like being a soldier in Iraq," whether they feel as though it is them "against the world," or whether they use resilience and capital to "transform school failure" into success, Black youth's narratives about their schooling experiences offer rich and critical insights about the conditions of education and the need for fundamental change and improvement.[24] More specifically, in this work, there is a great deal to learn from Black boys and young men as they counter, resist, and recover from the conspiracies and attempts to destroy them.[25]

In many ways, some different and some similar, as it relates to their knowledge and epistemologies and other ways of knowing, the narratives of the young men in the current study are powerful, insightful, and necessary to be heard. These young men have learned valuable lessons about loving and valuing themselves, leaning on their communities for personal and educational support, and trusting their experience to make sense of their lives. The struggles that the young men discussed throughout our conversations are academic, personal, familial, and communal; at the same time their struggles also are intergenerational. All too often Black boys' and men's lives, opportunities, and possibilities are limited on a continual basis across an array of social institutions (including schools) and public spaces. These realities make Black boys' and men's narratives that much more necessary and valuable in discerning and understanding how they think about their lives, themselves, and their experiences. Additionally, their narratives serve as much needed tools that can help dismantle and resist anti-Black sentiments, deficit-laden inquiries and ideologies, and lowered projections and underappreciation of who they are. As I discuss throughout this book, for the young Black men included in this study, their educational pursuits and experiences provided them with valuable lessons about their lives, livelihoods, and futures.

Overview of the Book

This book investigates three core issues regarding young Black men's pathways to and through college and their educational experiences. Black young men's educational experiences are a major area of research focus, given what they reveal about institutions and Black boys' and men's possibilities. Chapter 1 serves three primary purposes. First, I examine several critical reflections from the young men in this study to provide insight into their meaning making, theorizing, and interiorities. These reflections are related to their sense making about recent and ongoing events (such as the police killings of Black boys and men) and their Black male racialized-gendered identities. Second, I very briefly explore some of the salient literature on Black boys and men's educational experiences, with primacy given to their college years. This portion is offered as a way to contextualize their educational experiences. And, finally, I use the last portion of the chapter to detail how these young men's lives and narratives inform the theoretical approaches used in the study, which include critical race theory and the concept of educational urgency. I blend these two constructs to analyze these young men's experiences and meaning making and to provide new narratives about young Black men and education.

In discussing their educational experiences, I divide the following chapters into three parts. Part 1 (chapters 2–4) focuses on their secondary schooling experiences. Chapters 2 and 3 investigate the young men's precollege years and their pathways to college. Chapter 2 explores the young men's educational aspirations in the context of challenges they faced within their own and the school's neighborhood. Most prominently, the young men discuss their college aspirations as being motivated by trying and wanting to get out of the neighborhood. In this realm, some of their college aspirations align with what education scholar Tara Yosso conceptualizes as aspirational capital (the ability to hold onto hope in the face of structured inequality).[26] In discerning and discussing their pathways to college in chapter 3, the young men give tremendous credit to their families and communities as driving forces for their aspirations and critical hope. In this chapter, I examine experiences that sparked their sense of empowerment and agency in addition to various messages they received and internalized about their potential. These young men give credence to various family members for their ongoing words of encouragement and high expectations for their educational pursuits. Also, they speak to the power of their community, especially their peers and school personnel, in supporting and encouraging their college aspirations. In discussing their reflections across these two chapters, I lay the groundwork and provide a context for these young men's educational urgency.

Chapter 4 focuses on the young men's reflections about attending a college preparatory secondary school. The goal here was to understand how they made meaning from various school- and academic-related experiences. In a sense, I focus on what the young men identify as most salient in supporting their aspirations and college going. Across their narratives, they discuss the strategies they developed and deployed, the support and messages they received, and how they internalized some of the lessons learned from and through their experiences. This chapter helps show the bridges between their aspirations and ideas about college with specific information, knowledge, and preparation they received.

In part 2 (chapters 5–8) I focus on these young men's collegiate experiences. Chapters 5 and 6 pay particular attention to a range of challenges that the young men experienced during their early college years. In chapter 5, I hone in on their academic struggles and the ways in which their academic confidence, sense of belonging, and sense of self were shaken, undermined, and strained. By exploring their early experiences, I uncover their transition strategies and their efforts to meet the academic demands of college. Through these experiences, I also shed light on their mindsets and sense of self. Chapter 6 examines how the young men pursued their educational and personal goals, even as they faced a number of unforeseen challenges. Some of these challenges are related to race and class, while others are much more personal and social. The challenges discussed across both chapters help provide a context for better appreciating the young men's various forms of capital as well as their resilience and educational urgency.

Chapters 7 and 8 build on the discussion from the previous two chapters and amplify the young men's pursuits and self-learning through their college experiences. Primarily, I investigate their notions of success, how they account for the successes they achieved during their college years, and what these experiences mean for their sense of self. I discuss the young men's interiorities to provide greater depth and insight into who they are, and I examine their sense of self-empowerment, which is birthed in and matured through their experiences. I connect this discussion to these young men's educational urgency and also tie their educational desires to their families and communities.

In part 3 (chapters 9 and 10) I hone in on the major themes and critical takeaways from this project. Chapter 9 summarizes the major findings offered within the book and considers how Black boys' and men's educational narratives matter. In this chapter, I revisit and give considerable attention to their collective discussions of the stakes of their educational experiences and their meaning making. In doing so, I bring together some parts of their narratives discussed throughout the book into a concerted focus, place them in conversation with each other, and relate them to the trials and concerns that proved prominent in their experiences. This discussion amplifies their theorizing and sense making and allows for understanding their educational desires with greater precision and insight. Through it centers on some of the more salient challenges of their educational journeys, chapter 10 serves as the conclusion and offers several recommendations. I combine micro- and macro-level views of the young men's efforts and discuss the need to restructure conditions and opportunities for greater successes.

Chapter 1

"They don't give us a chance to be us"

Black Boys' Sense Making and Theorizing about Their Lives

> Man, LaQuan McDonald, sixteen shots, that stood out to me. They don't value us! . . . [long pause] Sixteen shots, and he was walking away [takes a deep breath and shakes head side-to-side in disbelief]. . . . Mike Brown, that one hit close to home. . . . That hits close to home because that could've been me! I think about Trayvon and they say he wanted to be an astronaut, I think they said he wanted to fly planes. Just what could he have been? Just so much loss . . .
>
> —Chauncey

The Black young men whose narratives comprise this book are extremely insightful and have a great deal to offer about their lives and experiences in pursuing their personal and educational goals. Without doubt, their lives intersect and connect with those of other young Black men in the United States and abroad in a multitude of ways. Moreover, as I discuss throughout this book, their discernment and meaning making offer fertile ground to learn from them how we might better understand and theorize about their lives and experiences and how we might better support, nurture, love, and care for them as well.

As revealed in Chauncey's statement opening this chapter, where he offered some reflections on the recent and ongoing killing of Blacks in the United States during one of our conversations, young Black men see and hear, pay attention to, and are cognizant of the lives of other Black boys and men. Chauncey's reflection is related to the Movement for Black Lives (M4BL), connects with the ongoing #BlackOnCampus movement within higher education, and also highlights an element of what Frantz Fanon identified as the "fact of Blackness."[1] Fanon articulates the struggles and constraints that Blacks experience in trying to rationalize their Blackness in relation to an irrational system of racism and race prejudice. In contemporary times, this "fact of Blackness" is evident in the ways in which Blacks continue to endure anti-Black racism and hypersurveillance in various spaces—whether it be through actions of "concerned citizens" or encounters with police or within educational spaces. These forces coalesce to overwhelm Blacks, keeping them under the watchful eye of society, and they further demonstrate the societal acceptance and rationalization of policing Black bodies. Scholars note that the growth of social media platforms has played a prominent role in providing outlets for Black people to share their experiences in general and as they relate to racism, hostility, violence, discrimination, and anti-Blackness in particular.[2] Similarly, the use of social media (e.g., Twitter and Facebook) has helped spread awareness about various encounters and experiences that threatened the lives, health, and well-being of Blacks throughout the global north, in places including the United States, Canada, and the United Kingdom.[3]

In our conversation, Chauncey, one of the young men in this study, discussed the recent police killings of Sandra Bland, Tamir Rice, and Eric Garner. In the statement that opens the chapter, Chauncey also expressed an embodied proximity with LaQuan McDonald, Mike Brown, and Trayvon Martin. These incidents stood out to him precisely because of his proximity in age, where and how the killings happened, and the ways in which they reminded him and made him reflect on the lack of value for Black life in the United States. His points echo those of education scholar Darrell Hucks, who argued, "Historically, African American males bear the weight of timeless atrocities, experiencing a painful history of discrimination that continues to influence their marginalization in society."[4] Even more pressing, though, given the ways in which Black boys and men routinely are imagined and projected as threats and criminals, Chauncey's attestation that it "could've been me" is connected to and situated within his Blackmaleness. In some ways, Blackmaleness speaks to the devaluing of Black men and boys, is based on a very particular gendered racism related to their Black male identities, and, as a result, demonstrates the ways in which Black men and boys are subjected to stereotyping, profiling, and anti-Black male violence.[5]

As we continued our conversation, Chauncey explained his sentiment that it "could've been me" in the following way:

> Like man, they was just, regular Black men doing nothing wrong. I wear a hoodie every day, I had a hoodie on yesterday. That make you a threat? I heard there's some places where they don't want you to have a hoodie on. Jordan Davis and his friends were at the gas station, the white dude felt threatened? They get to say what they want to say; they say they feel threatened but how can they say that? It's a joke . . . it's a joke!

In this conversation Chauncey expressed frustration, anger, and disbelief regarding both the lack of value for Black life, as well as the significant human losses that Black families and communities continue to endure, particularly because of anti-Black racism and violence. Some of his "frustration" can be understood as righteous indignation regarding practices and policies that continuously devalue and criminalize Black people, Black lives, and even what might be considered Black cultural styles. Many people interpret these practices and policies, whether in schools or social settings or in the workplace, as continuous campaigns to police and surveil Black bodies—and Blackness. Simone Browne, in her recent study on the surveillance of Blackness, argued that surveillance technologies are informed by the enduring history of racial formation in the United States (and abroad) and by the methods of policing Black life under slavery.[6] More pressing, though, is the historical and ongoing legacy of white supremacy that presumes, suggests, accuses, and stamps guilt onto Black people regardless of their actions; that constantly punishes and terrorizes Black people for their existence; and that continuously denies Black humanity.

It is significant that, in varying ways, the young men in this study asserted that these incidents and experiences matter to them greatly. As Elizabeth Alexander contends, they are part of the "Trayvon Generation."[7] Each of the young men, in their own ways, shared personal experiences and proximity to violence, physical attacks, or threats to their own lives, well-being, and safety as well as to their family, friends, and associates. This speaks most prominently to some of the trials and challenges of their everyday realities. These young men know and are familiar with loss—human, material, resources, and opportunities. These young men know the devaluing of Black life as children, learners, leaders, brothers, uncles, fathers, husbands, and family and community members. Chauncey's reference to Trayvon Martin's potential ambitions sparked uneasiness and urgency in our conversation. He imagined and wondered "what could have been" for the lives and futures of Trayvon Martin, Mike Brown, Tamir Rice, Sandra Bland, and the many individuals he named specifically, as well as for members of his own family and community.

Regarding my positionality, I see my life as intricately tied to these young Black men, not simply through our conversations during this research or through my teaching and service but through our lived experiences, educational desires, and sense of self. As a result, my use of "we," "us," and "our" in my written work (throughout this book and elsewhere) is used intentionally to communicate our connections and linked fate. That is, the notion that "they don't give us a chance to be us" is inclusive of my life as well; additionally, as discussed later in this chapter, even as these young men are theorizing about their own lives, they are theorizing about my life as well (e.g., the section later in this chapter entitled, "Theorizing Our Lives through Our Lives"). Similar to Chauncey, and to all these young men, I think about and reflect on what could have been for Daunte Wright, My'Khia Bryant, Ahmaud Arbery, Breonna Taylor, George Floyd, Tony McDade, and Botham Jean, to name just a few individuals, as well. I also think about and hold space for *what is* for Jamal, Michael, Chauncey, Chris, Paul, Malik, Julius, and Edwin (the eight young men who are the primary focus of this book), for all the individuals and communities who contributed to this study and other projects, and for all those to whom I am connected to in various ways. My writing is intended to reflect our connections and realities.

"Black males are seen as statistics and bound by our social conditions"

The young men whose lives and narratives comprise this book described experiences from their middle and secondary schooling years that easily undermined, ignored, and denied their educational aspirations and possibilities. In some ways, several young men felt and experienced educational neglect most prominently because they lacked support, guidance, and investment from the schools they attended and the personnel there. Some young men discussed the ways in which they were denigrated by adults from various backgrounds, not all of whom worked within a schooling context, simply because they were Black boys who lived in or traveled in particular inner-city neighborhoods that were economically deprived, underresourced, and suffering from institutional and systemic racism. As an example, Chris shared the following reflection about his experiences, meaning making, and learning about being young, Black, and male:

> The only thing I can think about, but I wouldn't call it a lesson, but just being a Black male from the inner-city . . . not necessarily having to be tough but knowing how to stand your ground when going home and stuff like that. I had one incident with a public transit employee; you know, like the people who sit in the booth. You can't let someone else use your bus pass and give it to someone else. One of my friends didn't have a way home and I let him use mine. I remember the guy saying I wasn't going to be anything except like those guys who were hanging out [on the corner] or in gangs. I said, "What do you mean? I have a 3.5 [grade point average] and I'm about to go to college." He laughed and said, "College, right!"

These types of interactions and other related experiences in both his home and the school neighborhoods helped impress Chris with the need to understand and protect his sense of self-worth and value his own education. On a routine basis, Black boys are accosted and confronted by other people's projections about them; and, importantly, these projections often are laced in deficit rhetoric and anti-Blackness and can delimit their potential. In the US psyche in particular, Black males constantly are rendered as "boyz in the hood" and "menaces to society," to borrow from films and narratives of the 1990s that continue to help popularize and simultaneously stigmatize some of their lived realities, especially in urban environments.[8]

In reflecting on this interaction specifically, it's clear that the idea that being Black and male delimited how others viewed him inspired Chris's educational aspirations and fueled his educational urgency. As I discuss later in this chapter, the local environment played a critical role in how many of the young Black men in this study thought about themselves and their futures. In continuing to discuss this experience and interaction, although initially he had not cited it as a lesson, Chris reflected:

> It just stood out to me and made me realize that there were going to be people that look like me trying to stop me from moving forward—or just not to think that I could be something different than what's in my environment. It was frustrating. That was one of those events where I realized that this is what people might think, and they didn't even know me. It highlighted to me that Black males are seen as statistics and bound by our social conditions.

Chris's interaction with this public transit employee, who had absolutely no insight into his educational engagement, performance, or aspirations, revealed how his Blackmaleness and connection to particular neighborhoods, even just as a traveler, rendered him both invisible and marginal. In similar fashion, Chris's intent to ensure that his friend was able to secure transportation so he could get home also was nullified, given how the transit worker disparaged and belittled him. In interactions such as this and too many others, Blackmaleness serves to misrecognize and distort Black boys and young men, rendering them invisible and serving as a way to nullify and deny their actions and intentions together with their innocence and humanity. In concert with education scholar Roderick Carey and others, Black boys and young men often are confronted by other people's denigrating views that promote their marginal mattering—a "minimal recognition that implies their insignificance."[9] Chris's insignificance was made clear through this transit employee's complete dismissal of his individuality, to the extent that he was repositioned as both a problem and a derelict ("I wasn't going to be anything except like those guys who were hanging out or in gangs") and because his educational aspirations were seemingly misplaced, misguided, and not conceivably possible ("College, right!").

The response to Black boys' aspirations to and plan on attending college as unimaginable, or even to respond with grave doubt simply because of their home neighborhoods or the neighborhoods they happen to be navigating, shows some of the ways in which they are negatively constructed and perceived in their everyday lives. Experiences like these demonstrate how Black youth are maligned and considered disposable simply because they live in or have to travel through the hood (or other ghettoized communities). These experiences also reveal how people who live, work, or attend school in these environments are saddled with the burden of rising above the peril, yet the structural racism and institutional betrayal that allow for the hood's existence and continuance are routinely ignored. Additionally, what these types of experiences and interactions make clear is that how Black boys and young men present themselves (or perform) has no effect on the daily denial, disregard, and dismissal that they face. Even further, the penetrating impact of doubts, lowered expectations, and dismissiveness violates their humanity and their possibilities and can limit the opportunities they are afforded. As researchers note, even Black boys and young men who are high achieving and high performing still face negations, discrimination, and anti-Black oppression.[10]

These types of interactions and experiences were critical learning moments for a number of the young men, which helped to raise their awareness about their lives and worth and, according to several of them, helped to inform and inspire their educational urgency. For Chris, although he experienced frustration, this particular interaction pushed him into deep introspection about how he needed to value himself and resist other people's projections of him. The fact that the individual "didn't even know" Chris, the "guys" who were "hanging out or in gangs," or his schoolmates and peers who were from or had to navigate these neighborhoods—any or all of whom may have held similar types of aspirations, who had achieved a number of accomplishments during their youth, and, even more importantly, who even through trials, tribulations, and possibly questionable decisions still were full of potential, felt comfortable and confident in denigrating him—speaks to the lived realities of too many Black youth. Critical in the mattering of Black boys and young men are the ways that they think about, see, and value themselves. Developing a healthy sense of self is important to Black youth's futures, as this interaction shows; it also can serve as a buffer and form of resistance against both micro- and macro-assaults on their value, worth, and humanity. What has been clear, overwhelmingly, is that if Black boys and men have to depend on others to learn of and appreciate their sense of self, then they will continue to be betrayed and neglected.[11]

Because Black boys' and young men's lives do not matter and can be relegated to insignificance, then they will live in environments, be confronted by social institutions, and interact with adults in ways that persistently reinforce that they are the problem and should make peace with mediocrity.[12] Because Black boys' and young men's lives do not matter, they are shot and killed by police officers, as in the case of Tamir Rice, who was shot in the park for his imaginative playfulness. Because Black boys' and young men's lives do not matter, they are shot and killed by private citizens for playing their music "loud" at a gas station, as was Jordan Davis. Because Black boys' and young men's lives do not matter, they are hunted down and killed by individuals who claim to be public or neighborhood safety officials because they are wearing a hoodie, "looking" suspicious, and trying to defend themselves from physical assault, as in the case of Trayvon Martin. Because Black boys' and young men's lives do not matter, they are assumed to possess superhuman characteristics and strength, they are shot and killed in their communities, and their bodies lie in the street for hours as if they were roadkill, as with Michael Brown. Because Black boys' and young men's lives do not matter, they are arrested, accused of stealing their own bookbag, jailed because they cannot pay bail, and forced to endure three years of imprisonment without being convicted of a crime—with two of those years in solitary confinement—even though charges were never levied against them, as in the case of Kalief Browder.[13] Because Black boys' and young men's lives do not matter, there have been too few inquiries into schools and schooling systems that continue to fail them, deny them educational opportunities, miseducate them, and kill their spirits.[14]

Too many people continue pouring poison in the lives of Black boys and young men; and, even more problematic, too many people, institutions, and agencies profit from their struggles, challenges, and demise. In some ways, a "pathological condition" continues to be thrust on Black families and communities, which renders their lives unworthy, and for Black males, the societal jury has already cast the verdict that they should be bound by their social conditions and even doomed.[15] These cultural messages about Black boys and young men reveal the constant and ongoing threats to their character and humanity that they endure. Others of us—too many of our Black boys and young men, too many of our Black girls and young women—have had our development arrested; been shot, maimed, wounded, or denied: been hypercriminalized and neglected; and been spirit-murdered specifically because of our Blackness.

At the same time, even as they are faced with these windfalls of challenge and problematization, it is precisely because Black boys and young men do matter that we must create space to hear and listen to their experiences, amplify their voices, and value and appreciate their humanity—even as they still are surveilled, remain under constant and persistent assault, and continue to be devalued across a number of social institutions. It is because Black boys and young men do matter that we need to reshape our schooling environments into spaces that support their possibilities and create stronger pathways for their educational and personal successes.

Black boys' and young men's interactions with adults, school personnel, and individuals connected to various structures, institutions, and organizations continue to relegate them to marginality. According to the participants in this study, young Black men often interpret these interactions and experiences as cautionary tales of "negative possibilities" and "negative circumstances" that could entrap their lives. Research continues to show that Black boys and young men must navigate racial microaggressions, hostilities, and marginal mattering in and beyond school settings; importantly, these experiences reveal the multispatial dynamics that encapsulate their lives.[16] Many of these Black young men were accosted in the street by people in their age group who held quite different aspirations and experienced different realities and by community members who scoffed at them, and some experienced educational neglect from teachers, staff members, and schools that failed to invest in their possibilities. Nonetheless, some of them identified and activated their achievement efforts in order to resist some of the challenges in their circumstances and lived experiences.

Taking a panoramic view of these interconnected experiences and spaces (such as neighborhoods, schools, and other social institutions) provides a more robust view of these boys' lived experiences and sense making. It is important to note that not only does Black boys' out-of-school time play a significant role in their educational experiences, but also that multidimensional racial discrimination impacts the lives of Black youth on a daily basis.[17] As a result, the actions and strategies in which they engaged and the resources and support they called on in order to pursue their educational goals should not be viewed as a singular instance or happenstance. Instead, I argue that much of these young men's choices and decisions were made on an ongoing basis through conscientious measures to deflect and resist negative messaging, weave through and around potential pitfalls, respond to and rebound from challenges and setbacks, revisit and lean on lessons from their families and communities, and stay on the path toward their educational and personal goals.

Even as they shared negative experiences, some of which were quite disheartening, at the same time the majority of these young men also spoke of receiving critical support and guidance for their academic aspirations, educational goals, and personal development. Additionally, they were connected to family members who believed in and supported their possibilities, they were embedded in a secondary schooling environment at Ellis Academy that focused on and contributed to their college going, and through various testimonials they revealed that they believed their personal ambitions, motivations, and character all contributed to their educational pathways and their educational urgency.

In the next section, I turn my attention to some of the pertinent research literature on Black boys and young men's lives and schooling experiences that also helps provide a context for my study. The literature review here is brief because I also engage with literature throughout each of the chapters when discussing and analyzing these young men's experiences.

Black Boys and Young Men's Lives and Schooling Experiences

> "What does it mean for me to be a Black man?" . . . for me, I guess showing, for me to be a Black man, I'm the type of person I'm determined to show people that Black men aren't the savages or the type of Black man that gets displayed through media messages or things like that. Me being a Black man with a [college] degree, I think it shows that we can just be whatever we want to be. That sounds so cliché [laugh]; getting that from Nas. I think about all the scrutiny we get from being a Black man from everyday situations and things like that . . . that makes it hard to be a Black man in society. People aren't letting go of what they see in the media or tv and they don't give us a chance to be us.
>
> —Malik

I use Malik's words to speak to the current literature on and realities of Black boys' and young men's educational experiences, their positioning in US society and abroad, and the narratives that dominate their lives. Malik begins by emphasizing his determination not to be reduced by other people's projections and misrepresentations; at the same time, inherent in his statement is the need to reimagine Black boys and men and their possibilities. He contends that Black boys and young men are afflicted by stereotypes and denigrating views that attack and deny their humanity. These projections necessarily marginalize their gifts, talents, and assets. In the extant literature, as it relates to education, researchers contend that Black boys are troubled, problematized, stereotyped, and failed in schools across educational contexts from the United States to Canada, the Caribbean, and the United Kingdom, to name just a few locales.[18] As Malik notes, these viewpoints restrict the lives of Black boys and men and ultimately "don't give us a chance to be us." This critical consciousness is crucial to understanding how Black boys and young men think about themselves and make sense of their lives. In important ways, Malik's statements about his determination, coupled with his degree attainment, are consistent with the ability of Black boys and young men to routinely shatter stereotypes about and denigrations to their lives and character through their brilliance, determination, and achievements.

Researchers maintain a need for understanding and viewing the lives of Black boys and men within a historical context, one that allows us to appreciate the enduring struggles they have faced within local societies. For instance, Toby Jenkins argued that the challenges of educating Black males in the United States started with the ways in which Black disenfranchisement was ingrained intentionally in the very structure of the early colonies through laws, legislation, and de facto practices. The gripping lock of oppression disempowered Blacks legally, politically, economically, and socially, all of which has continued through the present day.[19] Within the educational arena, scholars note that Black boys are not being served adequately in schools, regardless of locale.[20] Multiple studies show that Black boys face various forms of exclusion, neglect, and denied opportunities in schools across the United States, the United Kingdom, Canada, and the Caribbean.

In response to these schooling conditions and experiences, Black boys and men continue to persevere and pursue their own measures of success. Many of these efforts are marked by these students' resilience, their ability to achieve in spite of the conditions they face or experiences they endure, and their high personal and academic self-expectations.[21] The next section explores research literature on Black boys' experiences in secondary school.

Black Males, Secondary Schooling, and Educational Pursuits

There has been extensive research and discourse about the troubles and challenges that confront Black males in schools and educational spaces, in both traditional school settings and community-based education spaces. Research has shown that Black males continue to encounter and endure inadequate educational contexts, especially in urban environments. These challenges include disproportionate discipline, unsupportive and uncaring schooling environments, stereotypes and multiple forms of anti-Blackness, and exclusion.[22] A number of researchers make explicit the ways in which Black males' educational experiences are connected to both their in-school and out-of-school experiences.[23] Thus, attempts to understand Black males' success must be sensitive to the academic and personal spheres of their lives, as each impacts the other.

For instance, education scholar Pedro Noguera contended that a number of environmental and cultural factors trouble Black boys and undermine their schooling experiences. These factors include social and economic hardships, cultural pressures, and educational discrimination, as well as the behaviors that some individuals adopt and perform in response. As Noguera discussed (and a score of sociologists have argued as well), environmental and cultural factors have a profound influence on Black males' identity development, peer associations, and behavior, including academic performance.[24] In fact, in studying the lives of Black men, several sociologists raise questions about and detail how they are repositioned in US society, such as Alford Young's book *Are Black Men Doomed?* and Elijah Anderson's edited volume *Against the Wall*. These works build on and connect well with others, such as Jawanza Kunjufu's inquiry and analysis about the conspiracy to destroy Black boys, which was published over three decades ago. Noguera astutely observed, "Interestingly, we know much less about resilience, perseverance, and the coping strategies employed by individuals whose lives are surrounded by hardships than we know about those who succumb and become victims of their environment."[25]

A critical factor that continues to complicate Black youth's educational experiences and development is the context of the urban neighborhood. For Black boys and young men in particular, research demonstrates that residing in economically deprived, disadvantaged urban neighborhoods has a significant impact on their general health and well-being and also on their psychosocial, socioemotional, and identity development. Living in these environments exposes these youth to a range of disadvantages due to high rates of impoverishment, familial and communal stress, limited social supports, acts of violence and crime, gang activity, and sociopolitical and financial suffering.[26] Studies have found that when youth are exposed to these negative circumstances, they experience high rates of developmental disruption, mental and emotional stress, and threats to physical health, all of which disrupt and interfere with their educational endeavors.[27] As an example, sociologist Robert Sampson found that neighborhoods influence a wide variety of social phenomena, including civic engagement, health outcomes, and opportunities—both personal and professional.[28] Thus, the neighborhood effect plays a vital role in people's lived experiences, especially those who are disadvantaged, as it impacts their health, development, behaviors, and values—such as jobs (and job types), educational engagement, and participation in law-abiding or deviant activities. Along the same lines, previous research found that Black boys' and men's experiences in their community and school contexts affect their reactive (or proactive) coping strategies, which influence vulnerability and resilience in school, and research has also found that the concentrated neighborhood disadvantage exerts a significant influence on Black youth's college aspirations.[29]

Further, researchers contend that the way in which Black males define and pursue their educational goals can provide important insights for how to support them in their educational journeys.[30] As an example, in an ethnographic study of high-achieving Black male students at a racially and economically diverse suburban high school, Quaylan Allen used an antideficit approach to highlight students' resilience despite structural, cultural, and personal barriers. In examining academic expectations and parental support, Allen found that students "understood and worked to satisfy the academic expectations of their parents, adopting relatively meritocratic views of schooling while attempting to use academic success as means to college attendance and social mobility."[31] Allen also found that these Black male students enacted agency in their academic pursuits, drew on parent and teacher systems of support, and succeeded despite pervasive deficit perceptions of Black male education. Furthermore, studies show that Black male students' academic identity and achievement can serve as acts of resistance against white hegemony, emancipatory acts of racial uplift, and collective consciousness.[32] Along the same lines, in their study of Black males' schooling experiences in the United Kingdom, Cecile Wright, Uvanney Maylor, and Sophie Becker focused on how students attempted to recover from school "failure"—as measured by either permanent or temporary exclusion from school. Wright and colleagues found that students made significant efforts to transform their negative schooling experience, were determined to succeed, and used different forms of capital, such as aspirational capital and social capital, to navigate and negotiate their schooling experiences and pursue success on their own terms.[33]

In summary, as the literature reviewed here reveals, Black boys are routinely repositioned in educational contexts because they frequently face disproportionate discipline, assumptions about their perceived lack of interests in high academic achievement, and an environment of negative stereotyping. These experiences create hostile, inequitable, and exclusionary environments where their identities as Black males remain central to their miseducation and mistreatment. More than just considering resilience, research is needed that explores how Black boys and young men make decisions and take actions on an ongoing basis, think about education and themselves at different points of time in their educational journeys, and pursue their personal and educational goals.

Black Men in the College Context

Over the past fifteen years, increasing numbers of studies focused on Black men's higher education experiences have emerged. Within the college context, this research has two main threads. On the one hand, a good deal of this research continues to point to the challenges that Black men experience in college, such as racism and racial microaggressions, hostile campus climates, and college environments rife with anti-Black policies, practices, and racism.[34] For instance, in a qualitative study of thirty-six Black male students attending seven "elite," historically white institutions (HWIs), William A. Smith and colleagues found that these students experienced hypervisibility and were targets of hypersurveillance. These experiences, which included racialized stereotyping, Black misandry, and increased surveillance on and off campus, resulted in psychological stress and racial battle fatigue, which made their college experiences much more challenging than for other students.[35] Along the same lines, other studies show that stereotyping, anti-Blackness, and even racial violence are factors that marginalize Black men during their college years.[36] Also critical are the ways in which anti-Blackness and racial violence are perpetuated in higher education as well. On the other hand, several researchers have explored Black men's success, or success pursuits, by focusing on their strong academic performance, the importance of peer relationships, benefits they accrue from mentorship and relationships with faculty, and their engagement experiences in student activities and organizations as well.[37]

Even as Black male students face a number of challenges during their college years that can create conditions of isolation and alienation, researchers still have found that Black men continue to identify, create, and pursue ways to persist in college. One particular area that continues to prove important is Black men's own sense making and experiential knowledge, which is the focus of this book. As an example, in a qualitative study investigating eleven Black men who successfully completed their baccalaureate degree, Bryan Warde identified four critical factors that supported their staying on course to degree completion: (1) having an epiphany about the importance of higher education; (2) having access to the resources needed to attend and persist in an institution of higher education; (3) having a mentor; and (4) being resilient when faced with obstacles. Warde contended, "There was a general consensus among the participants that as critical as having resources and mentorship was to their academic success, none of it could have happened without the desire and drive to stick it out when things got rough."[38]

Similarly, in a qualitative study of fifty-nine Black men across three historically white institutions that I coauthored with my colleague Arthur Davis, we found that specifically because of their racialized-gendered identities as Black males, these students experienced lowered expectations and racism, which negatively impacted their academic strivings and social integration on campus. In responding to these challenges, these men benefited from close peer bonds with other Black male students on campus along with mentoring and support from Black faculty.[39] In like manner, in my previous work, which examined the collegiate experiences of forty Black men at two HWIs, findings revealed that students were confronted by Blackmaleness in both academic and social spaces on campus and benefited significantly from their engagement in a Black Male Initiative program. This program helped establish a counterspace on campus, which provided the men with opportunities to be embedded within a micro-community with their Black male peers that provided holistic support, enhanced their identity development, bolstered their sense of belonging, and supported their academic drive as well.[40] Other studies confirm the importance of Black men's personal characteristics and attributes (e.g., ambition, determination, and maintaining a sense of focus) as factors that can contribute to their success, especially when combined with being in a supportive college environment, engaging in male-centered programs, and developing critical relationships with peers and institutional personnel.[41]

What complicates Black men's college successes are the campus environments and cultures that they have to navigate, together with their interpersonal interactions and associations with faculty, staff, and peers. Within these contexts, and based on these complications, attention must be given to Black college men's socioemotional wellness, mental health, and well-being. Researchers should pay greater attention to education and to health and wellness. Daphne Watkins has provided some critical research in this area by focusing on Black college men's mental and emotional health. For instance, in a study of forty-six Black college men at two different institutional types, a historically Black college (HBCU) and a predominantly white institution (PWI), Watkins and colleagues found that discussions with students who attended the PWI were dominated by conversations about "acceptance, or 'fitting in'; cultural conflict; racism/discrimination; social support; and (overall stressors)" while those with students at the HBCU focused on "their image, their lack of resources for advancement, and (overall) stressors."[42] Along the same lines, research shows that Black students' college experiences are impacted by minority status stress and imposter feelings (which involves feeling a sense of intellectual deceit or phoniness); in addition, the pervasive stereotypes and stereotype threat they face can undermine their academic engagement and adversely impact their socioemotional health and well-being.[43]

The findings from the literature reviewed here speak to the complexity of Black men's college experiences. Beyond the "same old stories" that continue to accost Black boys and men as always already in danger and that popularize their pathology, more research is needed to create a new narrative about Black boys and men.[44] Investigating how Black men make meaning from their college years and identifying the experiences that they identify as salient to their success is critical. These investigations have the potential to (1) deepen our understanding of Black men's assets and skills that they bring with them and develop in college, (2) enhance our endeavors to support these students and their efforts and goals, and (3) create environments and conditions that empower Black men and better position them for success, both academically and personally. In the next section, I discuss my theoretical approach and the frameworks that inform my analysis.

Theorizing Our Lives through Our Lives

> We [Black males] are held to a higher standard than any other race because of the stereotypes out there against us, the statistics that most of us are supposed to be in jail, not in college, and things of that nature. You know, like not living past twenty-one and things like that.
>
> —Paul

In this study, I use critical race theory (CRT) and educational urgency as tools to analyze the perspectives and experiences of young Black men in their educational journeys. I mainly focus on their experiences and meaning making regarding their pathways to and through college. Paul pointed directly to the challenges Black boys face as they navigate their lives. As his statement makes clear, Black boys and young men continue to be accosted by other people's projections, deficit perspectives, and (mis) perceptions. The types of stereotypes, statistics, and narratives that are called on to depict the lives of Black boys and men contribute to Black suffering. By "Black suffering," I am speaking specifically of the denial of and attacks on Black humanity and life; this suffering pertains to the physical, psychological, and psychosocial pain that Blacks endure precisely because of anti-Blackness. Indeed, Black suffering relates to what can be considered a lineage of the Black structural condition, which identifies death, both social and physical, as a core feature of Black subjectivity.[45]

Further, the stereotypes, statistics, and narratives are often used as weapons to delimit Black people's goals and aspirations, rationalize the lack of opportunities and resources provided to them, and undermine and deny their humanity. Given the histories of Black education in general, and Black boys and men's educational experiences more specifically, CRT is an important framework for analyzing these young men's lives and experiences. A number of scholars have used a CRT approach to investigate various facets of Black men's college experiences, ranging from navigating race and racism on campus and in a number of institutional spaces to discerning the ways in which Black men cope with institutional culture and climate as well as interpersonal interactions, lowered expectations, and deficit-laden stereotypes and projections. In addition, CRT is instructive in investigating how institutions act on Black students as well.[46] Given the permanence of race and racism in these men's lives, I couple CRT with a focus on educational urgency to make sense of and analyze the various ways in which they pursued their educational goals and their own possibilities.

Critical Race Theory

Critical race theory allows for essential attention to race and other intersecting identities, such as class and gender, as centerpieces of academic and social experiences for students of color.[47] Deriving from critical legal studies, CRT is based on a number of themes that have been used to guide the work of scholars, researchers, practitioners, and community members. First, CRT begins with the notion that racism is "normal, not aberrant, in American society"; it is, thus (as a number of scholars have argued), a permanent fixture in US society and institutions.[48] Second, CRT identifies interest convergence as a mainstay of societal reform. According to legal scholar Derrick Bell, interest convergence helps reveal that "the interest of blacks in achieving racial equality will be accommodated only when it converges with the interests of whites."[49] In particular, critical race theorists argue that whites have been the primary beneficiaries of civil rights legislation.

Third, critical race theorists maintain a social constructivist view whereby race and racism are seen as products of social relations and social thoughts. This approach challenges claims to objectivity and acknowledges how the concept of race is created, sustained, and manipulated to serve particular interests and only as convenient. The social construction of race reaffirms the racial hierarchy and keeps Blacks as faces at the bottom of the well.[50] Fourth, critical race theorists take an intersectional approach to analyze how various social identities, such as race, sex, class, gender, and sexual orientation, impact people's lives differentially. Additionally, this analysis allows for broader understandings of these constructs.[51]

Fifth, CRT is interdisciplinary and leans on a broad spectrum of knowledge bases (e.g., ethnic studies, women's studies, sociology, history, humanities, and the law) to better understand the experiences of students and communities of color.[52] And, finally, CRT uses storytelling (or counterstories) to "analyze the myths, presuppositions, and received wisdom that make up the common culture about race that invariably render blacks and other minorities as one down."[53] A key component here is integrating experiential knowledge, often drawn from individual and collective histories as "other," with ongoing struggles to transform institutions and society from racial hegemony. A significant portion of CRT scholarship focuses on the role of "voice" to learn more about how structures, institutions, policies, and practices act on people and impact their lives, especially those who have been oppressed. These counterstories provide a way to communicate both the realities and the experiences of the oppressed. According to education scholar Gloria Ladson-Billings, "The voice of people of color is required for a deep understanding of the educational system."[54]

Ladson-Billings outlined the benefits of a CRT approach to qualitative research in the following way: "The 'gift' of CRT is that it unapologetically challenges the scholarship that would dehumanize and depersonalize us. . . . CRT helps to raise some important questions about people and communities of color."[55] Thus, CRT serves as a powerful analytic tool to investigate Black males' status, positioning, and schooling experiences.[56] It is important that critical race theorists seek to offer a counterperspective to the denigrating and deficit-oriented narratives about marginalized groups, such as Black boys and young men, to advance racial justice. Using CRT, this study relies on Black young men's experiences and narratives as important and valuable knowledge to help understand and appreciate how they navigate and negotiate challenges to pursue their educational goals.

Educational Urgency

I combine CRT with educational urgency to analyze and make sense of these Black young men's lives, experiences, and meaning making. According to Heidi Safia Mirza, educational urgency relates to an individual's "desire to succeed against the odds."[57] In examining Black females' educational experiences in Britain and the ways in which they maintained their aspirations, she further noted that this "desire" is related to the context these women were in (as it is for individuals in other environments). Thus, as shown by Mirza's work and that of a number of other education scholars, the valuing and appreciation of education are rooted in Black communities—and are tied to Black liberation, agency, and consciousness.

First, educational urgency affirms the "desire" for education as a value and passion for Blacks throughout the African Diaspora. For instance, in their study of Black education in the United Kingdom, Mirza and Reay contended, "Evidence of educational urgency within the black community can be mapped at every stage of the educational process," and it helps inform students' focus and efforts through the lens of their goals and aspirations. Second, educational urgency takes account of agency enacted by individuals and groups.[58] This agency can be identified as an attempt to transform some of the traditional structures of education.[59] In this way we can better understand educational urgency as encompassing resistance and achievement.[60] Third, educational urgency informs the importance of educational attainment in both a current and future context; that is, educational urgency is relative to students' determination to persevere in pursuing their educational goals within their current schooling context and connects to their future educational goals as well. And, fourth, educational urgency can be encompassed by the compounding effect of students' determination, resistance, and resilience.

An important point as I extend Mirza's conceptualization is that educational urgency also can be connected to individuals' hopes, dreams, aspirations, and refusal to accept being labeled in negative and denigrating ways.[61] The current study examines a selected group of young Black men's educational pathways to and through college. In developing the study, I also paid attention to these young men's lived experiences, including their home neighborhoods, messages they received about college, and their educational efforts. That is, they share parts of their lives as a context to understand their decisions, choices, and educational experiences. To that point, I want to understand educational desires in the context of the high-stakes challenges these young Black men know they face: knowing that anti-Black racism persists in addition to understanding that they face very real devaluations of their lives, knowing they and others in Black communities have taken many losses, and knowing that "Black males are seen as statistics and bound by our social conditions." Thus, in line with previous research and connected to their efforts, these Black young men continue to see a need for "making space" for themselves as they respond to their marginalization.[62] Additionally, as discussed throughout this book, the young men's educational urgency also reveals their self-determination, agency, critical consciousness, and future orientation. Thus, I explore educational urgency at the micro-level, examining the ways in which these young men thought about, imagined, developed, made sense of, and pursued their educational aspirations and goals.

Given how Blacks in general, and young Black men more particularly (given the focus of my study), experience educational neglect, are miseducated, and are failed by schools, investigating the ways in which they transform and overcome some of their experiences to pursue their educational goals is important.[63] In this book project, I examine how a select group of Black male students enact, embody, and narrate educational urgency in their schooling efforts and experiences. This undertaking is critical as it relies on and amplifies young Black men's experiential knowledge and contributes to moving Black males from the margins of educational discourse to the center. Allowing space for these young men to share and make sense of their experiences, especially through a longitudinal approach, has the potential to create new narratives about Black boys and men and can provide fertile ground for (re)theorizing their own ways of knowing. These young men asserted their self-determination and educational urgency to succeed within education, meet the academic demands of schooling, respond to and overcome a number of challenges and setbacks they faced, actualize their agency, and reach some of their educational goals.

For too many of us, when they see us, we often are the faces at the bottom of the well—rendered as undeserving and unworthy. Of course, as W. E. B. Du Bois, Ida B. Wells-Barnett, Frantz Fanon, James Baldwin, Nikki Giovanni, Ta-Nehisi Coates, Michelle Alexander, and others have articulated, this is the fact of Blackness. Given this context and these realities, we need theories—new theories—to help us understand our lived realities. We must be the authors of our own lives, which also means that we must see ourselves. Here, we must bridge the potential and promise of our experiences.

The Need for Black Boys' and Men's Educational Narratives

What we have heard, from scores of students across a broad range of colleges throughout the United States, Canada, the United Kingdom, the Netherlands, South Africa, and other nations as well, is that too many of our college campuses are rife with anti-Blackness, undermine Black students' sense of belonging, disrupt their educational goals, and can be both toxic and hostile to them.[64] Allowing space for students' expressions, experiences, and narratives is important so that we can better understand how institutions act on students and inform the ways that we might create change on campus and across institutions to improve students' experiences and outcomes.

Traditionally, according to mainstream and dominant narratives, and especially because of their family dynamics and neighborhood contexts, too many Black youth, especially Black boys and young men, often are described in ways that reposition them away from schooling success. For instance, a March 2019 news story about Michael Love, then a twelfth grader at Cornerstone Health and Technology High School in Detroit, Michigan, noted the negative messaging he received consistently about his personal and educational possibilities. In response, and based on his academic aptitude and personal fortitude, Love gained acceptance to forty-one colleges and earned nearly $300,000 in college scholarships. He shared his perspective: "I got told a lot when I was young—I couldn't do this, I couldn't do that. So I just wanted to show people I'm better than what they think I am." More fundamentally, however, based on his own educational and personal desires, Love acknowledged, "I just wanted to improve myself because I didn't know what I was going to do after high school."[65] In alignment with the argument I offer in this book, Love simply wanted to accomplish his educational goals and (continue to) pursue his promise and potential. A number of scholars have noted that Black boys and young men often rely on drive and determination in their schooling efforts in order to achieve despite the odds or circumstances they face and overcome some of their school-related challenges.[66]

Similar to Love, scores of Black boys and men are accosted by a frenzied focus on notions of "underachievement," "lack of achievement," and "too little" educational seriousness. A good portion of this discussion is centered in anti-Blackness, cultural racism, and other pathologizing "rationalizations" that blame Black boys and men for their lack of educational achievement and ignore their actual achievements, showing little or no consideration of their lived experiences, their access to resources and opportunities, and the efforts they engage in when trying to accomplish their goals. For instance, education scholar Darrell Hucks found that Black boys and young men use resiliency as a way to navigate negative incidents with teachers and in response to threats of racism, both inside and outside school.[67] As opposed to such notions as the achievement gap, Ladson-Billings suggested the term "education debt" to more accurately describe the disparities in opportunities afforded to Blacks, which is a result of the historical legacy of educational inequities in the United States that were formed around race, class, and gender.[68]

For Blacks, education was forbidden during the period of enslavement, and afterward, starting in the Jim Crow era, Blacks attended public schools that received a pittance of school funding and resources from state and local allotments up through the late 1960s.[69] It is important to note that much of this systemic underfunding and underresourcing of Black education was based on ideas of Black inferiority and resulted from anti-Black policies and practices.

In offering the educational journeys of these eight young men, I caution against reading these narratives as stories about grit, "me against the world despite the odds," or "pulling yourself up by your bootstraps." While there are numerous elements of these young men's lives that may connect to such stories (or mantras), their lives and experiences are so much more. First and foremost, though, a "pull yourself up by your bootstraps" ideology not only ignores the racial realities in the conditions of their lives but also spares whites and whiteness of any accountability. This prevailing narrative also ignores interrogating how institutions act on Black students to understand factors such as institutional betrayal and structural racism. Second, and most prominently, perhaps, a significant portion of their narratives is about agency and self-determination. These are young Black men who are taking into account the various stakes at play in their lives and in their families and communities; they are making decisions rooted in their lived experiences and conditions and they also are trying to pursue their possibilities, with education and their future selves as primary anchors of these decisions. The efforts of these young Black men, and other Black people, to contextualize their lives with race, racism, and even pathological aversions toward Black boys and men, facilitate self-determination. As bell hooks explained, "For it is that discourse [self-determination] that allows African Americans to recognize our complicity, our need for an ongoing process of decolonization and radical politicization, while remaining steadfastly clear about the primary role the vast majority of white Americans play in perpetuating and maintaining white supremacy."[70]

The narratives of the young men presented in this book are critical testimonies about who they are, the complexities of their lives and pathways, their educational experiences, and their possibilities. The experiences and narratives that Chauncey, Chris, Malik, and Paul raise in this chapter and that the young men with whom I spoke reflected on, made sense of, and offer collectively throughout this book speak to their educational urgency and forge new (or renewed) identities and possibilities. The seeds for these young men's educational urgency were sown well before they transitioned to college campuses. Yet the dominant narratives that typically and routinely surround Black boys and young men and their pursuits continue to map deficits onto their bodies and into their identities.

Without a doubt, the ways in which these young men make sense of their postsecondary experiences and pursuits is tied integrally to their families, their lives, their communities, and their previous schooling experiences. Thus, in analyzing these young men's educational narratives, I pay attention to the multiple contexts of their lives that helped shape their aspirations, strategies, and efforts. The young men's narratives and educational urgency are also grounded in critical consciousness (of who they are and who they can be), agency (to choose and decide or even to produce particular results), resistance (to dominant narratives about them, lowered expectations, and repositioning because of Blackmaleness), resilience (their ability to overcome adversity), and hope (their dreams and aspirations—even as they developed them). In many ways, these ideas, expressions, and characterizations overlap, are interconnected, and build on each other. In the chapters that follow, I dig deeply into these young men's lives, experiences, and thoughts to uncover and share their educational pathways, pursuits, meaning making, journeys, interiorities, and sense of self.

PART I

SECONDARY SCHOOL EXPERIENCES

Chapter 2

"I needed to get out"

Educational Desires and the Urban Neighborhood

> I'm trying to think about how to say this because I don't . . . I needed to get out, that's what was keeping me motivated. At some point, I know I thought that I didn't think I would make it to eighteen [years old]. Not because I was engaged in illegal or illicit activities, but you just didn't know if you would make it there in environments like those. So, that's what motivated me.
>
> —Chris

There are an overwhelming number of ongoing conversations *about* Black boys and young men, which suggests that almost everyone has an opinion on what they should do as it relates to education—and their lives. Those conversations usually follow a predictable pattern: if they, Black boys and young men, would just care a bit more about education . . . ; if they would just try harder—and be more focused on their studies . . . ; if Black boys and young men cared as much about their education as they did about sports . . . ; if they would just care. . . . These "messages" and pseudo-inquiries have been spread across popular discourse and educational contexts and, in many ways, also have been used in attempts to admonish, reprimand, redirect, guide, tell, and supposedly "mentor" Black boys and young men.

The idea that Black boys and young men don't care about education is a hallmark of much education and popular discourse.[1] In effect, many Black boys and young men are indicted for their supposed "lack of caring" for or about education based on perceptions of their attitudes, (dis)engagement, and academic seriousness (or lack thereof). This narrative is especially prominent for many Black boys and young men from urban environments, such as Chicago, Detroit, St. Louis, Milwaukee, Los Angeles, New York City, Atlanta, and Washington, DC, to name a few, and even more so in neighborhoods that are economically deprived.[2] This is not simply a sentiment held by a few people or that exists purely in an abstract sense. The idea that Black boys and young men don't care about education is concretized in people's ideologies to the extent that some teachers weaponize these ideas in their teaching approach and praxis.[3] Too many teachers position themselves outside a relationship with Black male students and at a distance from them, while at the same time they claim that Black boys and young men aren't motivated, can't learn, or harbor low educational aspirations simply because "they don't care." Clearly, there are young men who do not have high educational aspirations; however, too often, the views and ideologies held by adults in addition to the material conditions of schools and communities also distance Black boys and young men from critical forms of support, resources, opportunities, and educational success.

Working at a school or in another educational context where Black boys and young men are students does not automatically equate to caring about their success or, what is even more fundamentally important, caring about them as people. Even further, being an instructor (or another type of school personnel) does not automatically equate to helping to empower and support Black students. As opposed to wagging fingers at Black boys and young men about what they should do, it is clear that more care, attention, and investments are needed for learning who they are, understanding how they think about and see their educational opportunities, and building on their promise and possibilities. It is short-sighted, demeaning, dispiriting, and antieducational to project onto Black males what they ought to do, especially for those who are out of or have no relationship with these youth, with little regard for knowing who they are as people or a solid understanding of their lifeworlds.

As stated by Chris in the epigraph and discussed briefly in the previous chapter, there are a myriad challenges that too many Black boys and young men face in their neighborhoods that literally threaten their lives and livelihoods ("I know I thought that I didn't think I would make it to eighteen"). The point here is not that they suffer from nihilism, but rather that many Black boys and young men are highly cognizant of the threats that they must navigate and negotiate, sometimes on a routine and daily basis. Too often in these settings, and more generally, across various social institutions, Black boys and young men remain undervalued simply because of the threats they face, which results in their being pathologized, written off as undeserving, and even repositioned as subhuman.[4] Additionally, there is a need to appreciate the agency that Black youth call on in trying to make sense of their lived realities and their decision making; as much as they are denigrated for "falling into traps" or "becoming products of their environments," neither of these sentiments explore or recognize the tremendous pressures these youth face and endure on a daily basis. Thus, for some young men like Chris, and for many marginalized youth whose lives are confronted and constrained in a variety of ways, educational urgency is expressed through their motivations, aspirations, and efforts because sometimes they cannot know if they "would make it there in environments like those."

Aspirations toward College—and Self

Black boys and young men's pathways to college and the messages they receive along the way play a role in their aspirations and early college experiences, especially for those who matriculate to higher education immediately following completion of secondary school. In addition, their messages and pathways also can inform their transition experiences, the ways in which they feel they belong, and the strategies they may employ during those early years.

In my efforts to develop a deep understanding of students' college experiences and how they developed and tried to pursue their educational goals, I spent a considerable amount of time talking with them about their precollege experiences. While most of these conversations focused on their secondary schooling experiences, which I have written about extensively, I also inquired about supports, messages, and guidance beyond school as well.[5] In particular, I wanted to learn what they knew and thought about college prior to starting secondary school and how they thought about college during their secondary school years.

Most importantly, I wanted to learn about their college aspirations and what factors motivated them toward college. All these inquiries regarding their thoughts about and aspirations toward college were open-ended so as to provide a broad canvas so these young men could share their thoughts, perceptions, and reflections through their own lenses. For instance, I asked, "What were your thoughts about college prior to starting high school?" I then asked follow-up questions based on what they shared in an attempt to gain greater clarity and specificity about their responses. What I found was a complex interplay of aspirations and desires that informed their educational and personal aims.

CHRIS: "FIRST AND FOREMOST, I NEEDED TO GET OUT OF THE NEIGHBORHOOD"

Chris revealed that he often sported an Ohio State University hoodie during his high school years. He wore it to school during the winter months or in cooler weather and sometimes after an athletics contest. Chris was a two-sport athlete in high school; he was a member of the football and the track and field teams and was a solid contributor on both. To Chris, Ohio State represented an aspirational institution, and the aspiration was informed entirely based on the prowess of their football team. In reflecting on his earliest thoughts about college, Chris explained, "I didn't really know anything about college outside of athletics like football and basketball. I just knew I had a couple of relatives on my dad's side who I see every few years that were going to college but I didn't know anything about it." And given his overwhelming interest in football in particular, he recalled, "I remember thinking that if I go to the NFL [National Football League] then I have to go to college. But, not about anything academic."

Beyond these thoughts that were focused on athletics, which were still underdeveloped and abstract, like many of his peers, Chris knew relatively little about getting to college. From the standpoint of athletics, an early consideration about possibly pursuing a professional career still relegated college as a waystation to higher pursuits. Harboring such aspirations often can reveal how athletic dreams (sometimes dubbed "hoop dreams" or "gridiron goals") inform the efforts and attention of Black male youth—as well as the support and praise they receive.[6] During their secondary school years, each of the young men in this study continued to develop and sharpen their thoughts and perceptions about college and their aspirations for college going. A critical component of these aspirations was centered in their lived experiences.

Chris's pathways to college were bolstered by motivation that he drew from his own lived experiences and family history. Notably, he pointed to the combined peril and challenges of his home and school neighborhoods, which presented a constant threat to his safety and well-being.

> So, for me, first and foremost I wanted to get out of the neighborhood, out of the area just based on what my perception was at the time. It didn't seem like there were many opportunities for folks just looking around my neighborhood or the city, especially for folks who were low-income. At the time [I thought], you get a bachelor's [degree,] and this can lead to better opportunities. My goal was really never to earn the amount of money of my parents or less—or any other relatives who were in the area. So, ultimately, not wanting to be impoverished.

In elaborating on what made him want to get out of the neighborhood, he explained:

> Just the, uh, the level of poverty, the level of violence and illegal activities. In particular, I remember when it came time for me to start high school or sometime in the summer before high school, at that point in time it was the highest number of public school students killed in the news. So, in my mind, why would I want to stay in this environment? For youth in [my hometown], and many people in [my hometown], bullets don't have names. In addition, it wasn't just that I saw news reports, I was seeing friends and even classmates who were in gangs and I didn't want that! There was one particular time when I was twelve or thirteen, I was in sixth grade, there were elementary schools that were school rivals. I saw eighth graders jump on another eighth grader from another school and then he pulled out a knife when he got up and chased them. The awareness of those types of things happening just made me realize that this wasn't the space that I wanted to be in long term.

The young men's experiences of navigating various neighborhoods, witnessing interpersonal crime and violence, and understanding how they could get "caught up" all converged to inform their educational urgency. Being able to get out and away from environments where they could face physical harm was cited as a motivator for a number of young men precisely because they saw how interactions within the neighborhood impacted people's lives. Throughout the larger study, the young men reflected that various neighborhoods they lived in or traveled to were "dangerous," and they often tried to limit their interactions so as not to draw unwanted attention to themselves. Further, when talking about their secondary school's neighborhood, they noted, "There were always issues with neighborhood guys" and "There's violence and drugs [there], but it's not an area that I'm visiting unless I'm visiting [or attending] my school." Researchers have identified a number of neighborhood elements, from interpersonal associations and relationships to interactions with police or the criminal justice system, that can threaten the lives, well-being, and opportunities of Black youth.[7]

I began this chapter with another quote from Chris regarding his motivations during his secondary school years. In his narrative, Chris made a distinct point about fearing how his life could be impacted negatively, or even ended, by violence ("At some point, I know I thought that I didn't think I would make it to eighteen"). Thus, the young men's points here about the dangers of the neighborhoods they navigated serve as a critical context for their college aspirations. The young men's desires to "get out" or use college as "a way out" were connected to some of the daily perils and negative possibilities they faced. At the same time, as Chris explained, the idea of "getting out" was complex and nuanced; he also stated, "For me, providing for my family and getting out, I thought that getting out was my way of providing for my family. I thought that getting out was what I needed to help change my trajectory."

CHAUNCEY: "THAT WAS MY WAY OUT AND I TRIED TO GET THE BEST GRADES POSSIBLE"

Similar to Chris, Chauncey shared that he translated his schooling and living experiences into significant motivators for his academic performance and educational aspirations. One of his main motivators during his secondary school years was trying to get out and leave his home city. Early on, though, Chauncey had "hoop dreams"—with strong desires to play professional basketball in the National Basketball Association (NBA). He poured his energy into his budding athletic identity, and he recalled spending countless hours playing basketball in the neighborhood with other male youth, including friends and his brothers. The oldest of five siblings, he invested heavily in learning about NBA players such as Derrick Rose, Kemba Walker, and Kobe Bryant and identified himself solidly as a "basketball player."[8]

Chauncey's athletic desires were developed and cemented prior to attending high school. In reflecting on his thoughts about college prior to his secondary school years, he acknowledged, "To be honest, I just knew I wanted to be a college basketball player. . . . That's all I was thinking at all. I wasn't thinking about college, I just wanted to be a college basketball player." His desire to be a college basketball player was filtered through the lens of eventually making it to the NBA. He made this point clear as he explained, "If you wanna think about it [college] from an educational standpoint, I definitely wasn't thinking about it. I was listening to people talking about the NBA and that was my focus. So, going to college was just to help me get there [to the NBA]."

As we continued our discussion, Chauncey elaborated on his athletic desires in one of our conversations and shared how this informed his thinking about colleges that he might consider attending. He stated, "I wanted to go to like North Carolina, Connecticut, or Georgia Tech. I was trying to get to the NBA, so I was just thinking about which team I needed to go to. I wasn't thinking about demographics and stuff like that, I was just thinking about sports and who [which NBA players] went to which school [college]."

Given his secondary school experiences, which included several personally tough interactions that threatened his physical well-being and undermined his schooling, Chauncey's focus and awareness shifted slightly regarding college. To be sure, he still held high athletic desires, and at the same time, he realized that different secondary schools afforded very different opportunities. At the first secondary school he attended, Arnold High (a pseudonym), which was a predominantly white private school, he was forced to finish the last two months of his second year at home because of an altercation on school grounds that transpired after another schoolmate was expelled. Chauncey surmised that the schoolmate and a number of their friends held him responsible for the expulsion, especially since he had not received any punishment himself at the time.

> So, they decided to come back up to the school and they came in cars about 30 [people] deep—I've never seen anything like that! I knew what was going to happen. I got into a fight right outside the school. I got kicked out because of

> the fight. The thing was I knew he was coming [back] and they said I endangered other students in the school. I knew he was coming but I didn't know he was coming deep like that! He came up with a bunch of guys and that was a wrap. They told me that I had to finish the rest of the school year at home and that was like the first week of March. So, I had a whole lot of time at home to finish the school year.

As he reflected on his experiences, he shared feeling denied and cheated out of his educational opportunities, "I felt cheated; I felt so cheated. . . . I felt so cheated, especially at the time because I couldn't figure it out." Finishing the school year at home was both lonely and deflating. Chauncey experienced some mental anguish as he revealed, "I almost felt depressed sometimes because your parents gone to work all day and you're just sitting in the house." At the same time, this experience sparked his educational urgency, "It just made me want to get back into school; I literally wanted to be in school."

Chauncey's schooling experiences at Arnold High negatively affected his mental and emotional health and well-being; he was disturbed, confused, and frustrated by the school's decisions to punish him. His "depression"-like feelings resulted from the school's decision to deny his educational needs as they punished him as the individual solely responsible for the altercation and relegated him to isolation, given that he had to finish the rest of the school year at home. In many ways, rendering this decision against Chauncey was a clear form of educational denial and institutional betrayal. Richard Lofton and James Earl Davis contend that institutional betrayal occurs when "social actors in an institution perpetrate harm on an individual who needs their services."[9] This decision also raises critical questions for Black students' lives and livelihoods in various educational spaces, and particularly in contexts of white schooling. For instance, given the history of racial strife and institutional racism in US education, scholars have levied questions raised much earlier by W.E.B. Du Bois in the early twentieth century, such as, "Does the Negro *still* need separate schools?"[10] Additionally, beyond a matter of schooling, prominent among potential questions is: What alternatives exist for young Black men in their efforts to secure their own safety? In Chauncey's case and that of too many others—a group in which Trayvon Martin is one of the more egregious and well-known examples—even when young Black men attempt to defend themselves from physical threats and violence to their personhood, they still are perceived and repositioned as threats to others, even those committing the violent acts against them. As a result, they are betrayed through both accusation and implication; in like manner, they also are betrayed because they are positioned outside the institution's caring network.

As a result of these experiences and the ways that he felt marginalized in and by Arnold High's schooling environment and punishment, Chauncey decided to change schools. After starting the next school year at the neighborhood school, Chauncey felt as if he were being denied again. "Like the first week of school was terrible. The learning environment at Monroe [High School, a pseudonym] couldn't be compared to Arnold High." He had transitioned from an academic environment where "I was fighting to pass every class. I had tutoring but that didn't help; I was doing everything" at Arnold High to Monroe High School, where "everybody was going in the same direction, they were trying to be the same." He felt that the neighborhood school, or at least the classes and students he shared those classes with, lacked any real academic seriousness; he did not believe he would be challenged academically and did not think he would be fulfilled. As a result, he transferred to a third school early in the school year and selected the school primarily based on his association with a peer from his home neighborhood.

> I was sixteen, [and] there was a guy who went to Ellis Academy named Curtis Hill. In my neighborhood, they used to call him "preacher man." I cried when she [my mom] mentioned it [me attending that school] because it was all boys; they wore uniforms and Monroe was my neighborhood school. I was trying to be like everybody else. At Monroe, everybody was going in the same direction, they were trying to be the same. I went and found the Curtis guy and I asked myself, "Man, what I gotta do to get in that school?" I told my mom about going there. After I cried about going there, I told my mom I wanted to go there. I figured that might be a way out.

Chauncey identified attending Ellis Academy as a fresh start, as a way to distance himself from some of the challenges he faced during his first two years of secondary school, and as an important opportunity, as a way to continue pursuing his athletic goals, as a way to get to college, and as a way out of the city. He translated these experiences and opportunities as motivators that inspired his academic efforts and educational urgency. Given these collective experiences, he spoke about his motivations to succeed in secondary school in the following way:

> Really just wanting to get away. Once I like . . . when I was at Arnold, I was just in the mix; I wasn't really seeing stuff. When I got to Ellis Academy, I saw a lot of stuff, like tuition. You can get there [to college], there's not too many barriers; the only real barrier was paying for it. So, that got me focused on getting scholarships, no matter how far away I had to go. At Ellis, that was my way out and I tried to get the best grades possible. And, I wanted to get out of the city.

It's significant that even as he talked about pursuing opportunities for playing college basketball and wanting to "get out of the city," Chauncey's ideas were nuanced. In realizing the financial costs of higher education to his family, given that his parents paid tuition for him to attend Arnold High, and reflecting on his experiences there where he felt that the school, "Believe it or not, wasn't big on trying to get people to college—unless you were big on sports or something. So I'm glad I got up outta there anyway." He recognized the financial investment his parents had already made to his secondary schooling experiences and the multiple ways in which they supported his efforts. Given this context, he also identified attending college as a way to actualize the many contributions that his family made on his behalf and as a way to honor his parents' actions, investments, and support.

Julius: "Everybody in my family went to college"

While several of these young men have similar backgrounds, such as their family's economic status and growing up in economically distressed neighborhoods, their backgrounds also are dissimilar in a number of ways. For instance, Chris specifically identified the neighborhood as a pivotal motivator for his college desires, while Chauncey's aspirations were informed by his athletic desires. Several other young men connected college-going aspirations directly to family accomplishments and expectations. Here, I examine the messages Julius received about going to college, the ideas about college that he harbored, and how he made sense of these thoughts. During his secondary school years, Julius noted that he was motivated to achieve academically by both his Black male friends and his lived experiences: "My support group, hands down! And I wanted to get out of my situation. I really wanted to get out of my situation and was willing to do whatever I could to get out of my situation, which was go to college."

Even though Julius experienced stress and strain in his family relations and said his situation was "unhealthy, it was violent, it was poor; there wasn't much love there," going to college also was connected to the messages he received and interpreted from his family history. One of the major factors that contributed to his decision to attend college was the realization that attaining a college degree is "the standard to succeed. If you want to succeed, then what are you going to do?" Julius's positioning of education as the "standard to succeed" aligns with the "college-for-all" message that was prominent during his secondary school years.[11] At the same time, however, he and other young men in this study critically analyzed their family histories, accomplishments, and current lives to make sense of their lifeworlds and their possibilities.

Julius participated in a number of youth football leagues, where he developed his athletic talent and homed in on his athletic identity. This participation informed the secondary schools that he considered attending and, at the same time, also helped him realize why he did not want to attend any secondary school in his neighborhood. He reflected:

> They suck. They were too violent! I was trying to go somewhere that wasn't violent. I was trying to go somewhere and ball. The only reason why Covington Hills was an option was because I had a guaranteed spot on the team. I know three schools that wanted me to come and play ball was Brooks Park, Covington Hills, and Faulk [high schools]. Ironically, all the coaches who coached the Panthers [a youth football team] were coaches at all of them and most of the team went to those schools.

Prior to his secondary school years, Julius made participating in football his main focus for college. "I always wanted to go to college and play football. And that was all that I thought about, it was just to go to college and be an athlete."

Julius credited his mother with discussing the pursuit of higher education with him and demonstrating the importance of college degree attainment in her own life. A mother of four with three children under age seven, Julius's mother worked full time and started and completed her master's degree during his secondary school years. Julius identified this accomplishment as a significant effort because he saw his mother still pursuing her own educational goals even as she managed family obligations and a full work schedule. He also credited his mother with prioritizing his education, as she offered clear and consistent messages about the importance of college to his life and career. In reflecting on the role that his mother played in his college aspirations, Julius quickly responded, "My mom went to college and it was like, everybody in my family went to college, so my mom was like, 'College is not an option. College is the next step, period.' It was a standard."

As can be gleaned from his narrative, Julius relied on, benefited from, and internalized a college-going ethos from his family. These conversations with his mother reaffirmed the importance of attending and completing college. As we continued in our conversation, I asked Julius about which schools his parents encouraged him to apply or attend.

> **Julius:** My momma didn't really. . . . I was just told to go to a university. HBCUs in life don't really mean anything—unless you're going to Morehouse. So, it was like, go to a university, period. And you'll be fine later.
>
> **Derrick Brooms [DB]**: What did you think about this encouragement?
>
> **Julius:** Um, it was cool. I never really thought about it. I'm going to go to college, I'm going to have fun and meet some girls. I'm going to go to college, make some money so I'm not in my parents' situation and be rich. That's all I thought about really.

A critical aspect of attending college centers on the college selection process. The message that Julius received about which colleges to consider pointed him to universities, which, in his estimation, was primarily because they reportedly have the most material resources to offer students. Similar to Michael and several of the other young men, the family's lack of familiarity with historically black colleges and universities (HBCUs) likely influenced the comment that they "don't really mean anything" in life.

Education scholar Krystal L. Williams and colleagues (2019) argued that HBCUs have rich histories that continuously are ignored and, as a result, too often they suffer from perceptions that overemphasize challenges and depict them from a deficit perspective.[12] There is a grave need to contest whiteness, and white institutions, as normative, proper, and best for all students or as ideal in their "representation" of real life. All too often, individuals criticize and steer individuals away from HBCUs by pointing to the predominantly Black population at these schools and suggesting that this "is not a reflection of *real* life." Obscured in this message is the long history of challenges, racial battles, and violence that Black students and families have endured at predominantly and historically white institutions.[13] Inherent in such denigrations of HBCUs and overinflations of predominantly and HWIs is ignoring the racial strife and hostilities that Black students continue to face and endure in their aims to secure and pursue educational opportunities. For instance, research shows that Black students continue to be saddled with racial battle fatigue, violence, and various racial hostilities, which contribute to physical, emotional, and spiritual suffering of students at some of these institutions.[14]

Besides his conversations about college types, Julius also recalled conversations with his mother about managing college experiences. He recalled being told that college "is fun," and that he should "enjoy it while it lasts." Julius was excited about getting to college because he imagined that he would have more freedom and would enjoy the social atmosphere. His mother also told him, "Make sure you get there but don't give up on it, don't get side-tracked with any of the things that you're doing. Stay focused."

Jamal: "Knowing I had the potential to be something"

As Jamal reflected on his schooling experiences and years as a youth, he credited his mother and grandmother for instilling a sense of self-value in him that both informed and inspired his motivations and aspirations. Even as Jamal recalled and thought about his home neighborhood, he expressed conflict on how to describe it. In one sense, he pointed out the economic and relational stress that poverty created for individuals and families in the neighborhood and how many of their critical needs went unmet. In another sense, though, he felt that this was a place where people nurtured his growing development and supported him and his aspirations. In describing his home neighborhood, he shared:

> The neighborhood where I lived, it was bad, but it wasn't bad. It was only bad during certain parts of the year. It was still people I grew up with and they always had my back. So, just knowing people in the neighborhood, I talked to them all the time; they'd tell me to stay in school. They had a lot of the fancy cars and flashy things but they'd tell me that it's not for everybody. They'd say, "You're in school and you play sports, find another way, don't try to be like us."

Thus, although he had a great level of comfort in the neighborhood and acknowledged receiving support from a variety of individuals within the community in addition to his family, Jamal remained subject to a number of challenges: "I seen [people in the neighborhood] doing a lot of things that they shouldn't be doing; like, I saw them shooting at people and stuff like that. But they always told me that this wasn't stuff that I should be doing."

These interactions with community members push back against deficit-laden narratives that individuals in many economically deprived neighborhoods are self-consumed and do not care about others. For instance, researchers contend that many such communities are resource rich, with inhabitants who act in ways that show their linked fate and to whom personal relationships matter a great deal, which can provide positive support.[15] Thus, the idea that all the individuals living there are bad people who are up to no good is both neglectful and an attack on Black humanity. While they themselves may have been in negative situations or lacked educational experiences that could lend support to others, these community members were clear in their suggestions that Jamal should stay focused on his school and athletic participation. In fact, Jamal felt a sense of security in knowing that these individuals "always had my back"; they acknowledged his potential, affirmed his interests, and suggested that he find his own way forward. Their encouragement for him to focus on his school efforts resonated with his own aspirations and goals.

He also reflected on some of the challenges of the neighborhood he lived in, which, in some ways, served as push factors for him to continue planning his future. "I think my least favorite part [about the neighborhood] was having police around there, harassing people—especially kids. They got me like three times; they got me when I was walking through the alley to take a short cut to get to the store. They shined the light in my face and asked me where I was going. They think just because you live in that neighborhood then you're up to no good." As evident from his narrative, Jamal received a range of messages about his possibilities. Among some community members, his focus on his education was supported and encouraged; however, simultaneously, he felt that he was stereotyped by police officers (and others) simply because of the neighborhood he lived in. As he made meanings from the activities he witnessed on the part of people in the neighborhood and, in particular, his interactions with police officers, he acknowledged his feelings:

> **Jamal:** It made me upset just because you think just because someone else is doing something that you hang around them you're going to end up doing it. It just makes me feel like you can't do anything without being stereotyped. You can use it as motivation; I used it as part of my advantage to not do those things, to keep going to school and not sell drugs or anything like that because I didn't want to be like everybody else.
>
> **DB:** What made you not want to be like everybody else—or like some of the people you saw in the neighborhood?
>
> **Jamal:** The main reason was because I kept seeing them getting locked up or going to jail. Going to jail was like, basically, being dead but you're alive. You can't do anything, you're restricted. They tell you when to eat, they tell you when to sleep—they tell you who can visit you and things like that. I saw people gambling. I didn't want any of that. You see that in movies too, but I didn't want to do it. It took me a while to realize that. I don't think I'm better than them, I just think I made better decisions than they did. I just want to do things the right way and not the wrong way.

Important in Jamal's experiences were the ongoing, daily decisions needed to make sense of his neighborhood and some of the activities that community members engaged in regarding how he thought about himself and his future prospects. Part of his motivation to avoid and resist stereotypes and not engage in illicit activities was to "keep going to school." While focusing on his educational aspirations could differentiate him from others in his neighborhood, he also held a critical view of how people's lives could be limited by engaging in such activities. Although this realization took him a while to acquire, Jamal maintained his focus on engaging in activities that could provide him with broader future opportunities, such as his educational and athletic pursuits.

Identifying the context regarding Jamal's background and home neighborhood environment is important to help better contextualize his educational focus and efforts. These experiences and realities both informed and inspired his sense of self and sharpened his educational urgency at the same time. Jamal internalized and reframed many of his challenges, which he used as motivation. This motivation was supported by messages he received from his mother and grandmother about college and careers. He explained, "I was told that college would be hard and it's hard to get a job in this world without having a bachelor's degree—that's what I was told when I was like fifteen or sixteen. They said to try it. They said you can't get a stable career without a college degree; that's what I learned from my mom and my grandmom."

Although I discuss messages from family in the next chapter, I mention the messages that Jamal received here because they also are part of the broader set of messages he received and the meanings he crafted from his lived experiences. A number of the interactions and encounters that he experienced in the neighborhood challenged his educational focus. At the same time, they informed his aspirations and how he thought about himself. Messages from his mother and grandmother were interpreted as "lessons" that he could pursue and activate in the future. He continued and discussed his motivation as well: "I think the number one thing is that knowing I had the potential to be something. My track coach always said, 'Don't talk about it, be about it.' I take that with me even today. I don't talk about it, I just try to do it. I surprised some people in high school and I surprised myself sometimes too. It's almost like the Nike commercial, 'Just do it.' I just try to do it." Through the multiple types of support he received as well as his exposure to and awareness of various elements within his neighborhood, Jamal determined that education and participation in basketball were his primary focus. Although it took Jamal "a while to realize" that he did not want to engage in many of the activities he saw in the neighborhood, he received positive messages along the way from the very people who were engaged in illicit activities. Jamal believed that these individuals "always had [his] back" because they discouraged him from engaging in similar activities and also provided him with a consistent message for him to stay in or focus on his educational endeavors. Jamal internalized and interpreted these experiences and interactions as a testament to his own potential, which also provided him with clarity and guidance for finding his own way and creating his own path.

Summary

First, and importantly, all the Black young men in this study, in their own ways and on their own terms, had some form of aspirations for college. For those who work closely with Black male students, this point comes as no surprise; for those who have less proximity to and knowledge about the lifeworlds of young Black men—and who have invested little time in learning about their goals and aspirations—several points are critical to learn and understand. Part of these aspirations are relative to the current "college-for-all" mantra that runs rampant throughout education and popular discourse. This message is powerful precisely because it often is tied to social mobility, financial gains, and career opportunities. At the same time, what often is obscured in the college-for-all mantra is exploring what not going to college means for young people, from those who are unable to afford college to those whose college opportunities are limited severely. Even further, what does college-for-all mean for youth at a school that "wasn't big on trying to get people to college," as described by Chauncey in his discussion of the private secondary school he attended initially. While the ideal of getting "all" students to college may have some merit, more focus is needed on the differential social, cultural, and financial resources, capital, and opportunities that students need in order to make this a reality, especially those from economically depressed neighborhoods or underresourced schools (and school districts) and those with little to no access to information on and resources needed for higher education.

Second, critical for each of these young men was the neighborhood context that they had to navigate and negotiate on a daily basis. I also contend that in their own ways, these young men felt confined by these neighborhood structures and some of the negative interpersonal dynamics they produced. Getting out of the neighborhood allowed these young men to reclaim themselves and their possibilities. In some ways, the neighborhood represented confinement and constraint—it represented limitations. Their desires to and eventual success in getting out of the neighborhood reflected their agency, and at the same time, getting to college speaks to their fugitivity.[16] These young men counted getting to college as a success for multiple reasons: it allowed them to resist having their lives narrowed, it reflected their agency, and their movement and ability to get to somewhere (college) was liberating. That is, many of the struggles that the neighborhood represented and posed could deny their lives, limit their future selves, and diminish their well-being. Their desire to get out of the neighborhood, even in its infancy, was based on their visions for new possibilities—for themselves and their families. Collectively, these young men's aspirations to attend college are reflective of their firsthand experiences, family and community-based support, experiential knowledge, and educational desires.

As demonstrated in this chapter, Black boys' and young men's educational aspirations often are impacted by their familial background, their environmental and neighborhood context, and the structural conditions where they attend school. Even as attaining a four-year college degree has been heralded as a great equalizer in US society, these youth's family histories, experiences, and cultural knowledge make this narrative contestable. On the one hand, they often feel challenged because of their lack of cultural capital in knowing how to "get to" college, and what is even more burdensome, the costs of college creates a sticker shock effect because parents and guardians cannot foresee paying for college based on their incomes and access to financial resources. Thus, given the limitations of their capital, both cultural and financial, making it to college is not simply an academic venture but also one that seems less attainable because of their backgrounds. Additionally, students' lack of social capital also compounds the points made here and the challenges they may face on their potential pathways to college. As a result, a significant barrier to students' trajectory to higher education is envisioning a pathway that accounts for and allows them to overcome these challenges and limitations.

Chapter 3

"I always knew that I was smart"

Personal Perspectives and Educational Pursuits

> High school was literally the best time of my life; I know people say that college is supposed to be the best time but I reminisce on high school all the time. You grow and learn from your classmates, teammates, administrators and teachers; you just grow and learn. I remember my best experience was going to the inauguration [of Barack Obama]; if I didn't go to that school, I know I wouldn't have experienced that. Just seeing Obama's inauguration just showed me that I can do whatever I want to do. Yeah, high school was the best time of my life.
>
> —Jamal

"It just made me feel like I can do whatever"

Critically important to these young men's sense of self as well as their educational aspirations and educational urgency was the combination of messages and support they received and their schooling experiences, personal efforts, and exposure. Latent in their narratives were ways in which they saw, learned about, and felt affirmed in regard to their possibilities. This point is clearly represented in Jamal's statement that he appreciated the social capital and relationships he developed that helped him enhance his awareness, growth, and maturity. Overwhelmingly, these young men pointed to specific experiences that served as pivotal moments in their development and sense of self. Some of these experiences were school related, such as garnering an academic, athletic, or personal achievement; others arose in lessons they learned in school, meaningful relationships they developed during their secondary school years, or ways in which they learned more about themselves as young Black men. I take a moment here to discuss this learning because these young men indicated on numerous occasions throughout our interviews and conversations that these were valuable and important events, experiences, and life moments. This learning was necessarily relational, as it connected these young men to each other and helped them learn more about themselves.

At various points during our interviews I talked with students specifically about what they had learned about themselves. For me these questions were essential because they allowed opportunities for students to reflect about themselves and their self-perceptions. Additionally, given the longitudinal focus of this study, such questions also allowed me to track students' reflections and learning as an ongoing process and across our conversations. Critically important to my methodological approach and the longitudinal design of this study was paying close attention to these young men's reflections and thought processes. This approach is central to my work here and elsewhere as the overarching goal is to allow space for Black boys and men to share through their own experiential knowledge and to learn from them as experts about their own lives. Such an approach, I and others argue, honors the sense making of Black boys and young men and gives them opportunities to gain greater insight about their interiorities. Moreover, this approach also keeps Black boys and young men's humanity intact by demonstrating that they are constantly evolving, continually becoming who they are, and unlike the overwhelming majority of negative media projections and portrayals, they are active agents in their own lives.

During my interviews with these young men, I engaged them in conversations that asked them to draw meanings from their secondary school years. In particular, a portion of our conversations asked them to reflect on what they had learned about themselves based on their secondary school experiences. In responding to my question asking him to describe his overall high school experience, Jamal evinced great admiration, in line with his statement that high school "was literally the best time of my life." He specifically referred to his learning and growth, his relationships, and the activities that he engaged in as critical to the quality of his experiences. For a number of other young men in this study, most prominent in their recollections was the 2008 election of Barack Obama as president of the United States. Much like Jamal, Chauncey also foregrounded Obama's election as a pivotal movement of his adolescence and, like several others, he portrayed the election as a testament of his own possibilities. He explained:

> I think I was in high school at the perfect time. Right when I got to Ellis Academy [Barack] Obama was running to get elected [for US president]. That was powerful! [My history teacher] Mr. Dorsey was like, "There are certain things in life that you can't get back, so if you want to go down to [the inauguration] you should go." Being there, seeing Obama get elected, and how people reacted was powerful! It just made me feel like I can do whatever and really we can. Just that happening at the time it had an impact on me and it probably had an impact on everybody at Ellis too. They're telling us all these things throughout the day, they're talking about "We believe in you" and a Black president getting elected! It was like, "Wow!"

Across both educational and political discourse, conversations abounded regarding the cultural, social, and historical significance of Barack Obama's presidential election. For some, this was articulated as the "Obama effect," a term describing the effects of his election and subsequent presidency on various populations in the United States and globally.[1] Several of the young men's reflections identified a clear message that they extracted and articulated related to their feelings of connection to Obama's election, his presidency, and their futures.

For several of the young men, Obama's election served as an embodiment of their own desires and ignited their resilience and aspirations. Their lives and efforts were living testaments to hope and possibilities. That these young men maintained hope and persevered to pursue and reach college is important because these efforts both reflect and affirm their agency and educational urgency. Central to these young men's efforts as well is activating and embodying resistance and resilience. A number of these young men saw college as a pathway to their futures and even their possible selves. These young men—who achieved and struggled, who held high self-expectations and were in the process of developing and refining their self-expectations, who felt constrained by neighborhood dynamics and yet harbored dreams and goals beyond realities present in their own families, who knew through experience that their Blackmaleness delimited some of the opportunities that they might be extended and still believed in and pursued their own goals—they represent, in their everyday lives, hope, resilience, persistence, and possibilities.

Additionally, even as symbolic representations such as Barack Obama's presidency created a very real presence in the lives of young Black men (among many others), their sense of empowerment was not just relegated to elected officials or highly visible public figures. A great deal of these young men's sense of self and self-efficacy also was related to what they battled through, navigated, negotiated, endured, overcame, and accomplished themselves. This point is critical for at least two reasons. First, it is noteworthy because it runs counter to the prevailing images and stories that circulate constantly in media outlets and educational discourse. And, second, the reality that Black boys and young men continue to defy the odds and racist ideologies held about them and continue to pursue success on their own terms needs greater attention. Even while I explore how the young men in this study made sense of their lives and experiences, there is a dire need for changes across multiple institutions (e.g., schools, media, criminal justice). That is, if we truly care about the healthy development of Black boys and men, greater efforts are needed to eradicate the various forms of institutional neglect and structural racism that constrain their lives.

Messages and Pathways to College

All the young men recalled receiving strong and supportive messages from their parents, family members, and community, including their school, about aspiring to and attending college. Across the young men's academic backgrounds, this message also aligned with a larger national narrative within this college-for-all era. Suggesting to youth that they were going to college occurred with increased frequency during this period and supported micro-messages that students received regarding what ought to be their educational goals and expectations. In fact, when youth suggest that they will not or may not attend college immediately following the completion of secondary school, their assertions are sometimes interpreted as resistance and dismissiveness toward education.

These young men held and developed aspirations for college that were birthed out of their personal goals. In this chapter, I pay particular attention to both the messages offered to several of the young men and their pathways to college. In detailing these messages and pathways, I also examine how the young men made sense of them and I then offer a critical analysis. For instance, I point out that some of the messages are rooted in family history and clear values concerning education while others involve career prospects. In addition, an important discussion in this chapter describes analyzing how these young men tried to develop and pursue the knowledge necessary to actualize their aspirations and the encouragement they received.

As researchers have argued, a key contributor to Black and Latino students' educational trajectories is their college-going familial capital, a term that "describes the rich knowledge, information, inspiration, and resources students of color gain from their families (nuclear, extended, and fictive kin)."[2] In fact, researchers have found that Black families offer critical forms of support for their youth's college aspirations and preparation, including through messaging, encouragement, educational opportunities, and material support.[3]

Michael: "You're just saying that and it just sounds like a dream"

I noted that each of the men recounted receiving messages from their families that were intended to encourage them to attend college. Their stories about these messages do not simply take a linear approach but also show how they analyzed these messages based on individual backgrounds, family dynamics, and their own experiences and aspirations.

Michael grew up in a household that included his mother and, at various times, his grandmother. The eldest of eight siblings, he lived and grew up in economically depressed neighborhoods that, to those outside these communities, were known for poverty, joblessness, crime, and gangs, and he described a range of challenges that he faced during his teenage years in navigating these environments. These neighborhoods are examples of what sociologist William Julius Wilson described as truly disadvantaged—they continue to be deprived by changes in the economy, are marked by racial discrimination in residence and employment, and ultimately create an "underclass."[4] Many of these factors coalesce into a neighborhood effect that can create grave challenges for the schooling experiences of Black and Latino youth.[5]

In describing his home neighborhood, Michael noted that it was "noisy, not outrageously, but in the amount of sounds that you'd hear. The noises you'd hear were sirens, voices, kids outside; you could even hear people on the main strip." And, he elaborated, "My favorite part about living there is making it out." Michael, along with a number of other young men in this study, identified "making it out" of their neighborhoods and communities or even simply living beyond the age of eighteen as significant milestones that they saw and interpreted as accomplishments and achievements. He shared that there were a number of things that he experienced and was witness to while traveling to and from school that, although he never engaged in any physical altercations, were challenges that impacted him emotionally, mentally, and psychosocially. Michael identified these experiences as things he would "have to go through leaving school and going home"; he further explained:

> Gangs! Gang violence and just violence in general. I've seen kids get jumped on; I've seen countless fights. Just kids who looked like they couldn't wait to get out of school so that they could go outside, take their coats off and fight. Students getting harassed. It was a time when I was on the bus stop and it was a guy at the bus stop by himself. (I saw him when I left school.) The next day we were in school talking about how he got jumped on.

These and other experiences weighed heavily on Michael's psyche and sense of self. In many ways, they left him hyperaware and hypersensitive about navigating these neighborhood contexts and at the same time created anxieties and conflicts about his plight, how his siblings might fare, and how to make it through these environments and not succumb to the challenges, temptations, and threats.

> It made me feel like there had to be somewhere else that I could end up and still be able to still feel like a child. When you're around all of that stuff, it makes you wonder about the surroundings; it makes you wonder even if you're going to the school in the right place. It actually makes you nervous. . . . It makes you nervous to get near a certain street because of the

> reputation that that street has. It made me feel like I *had* to go somewhere because of those things, it was a must!

Critical to Michael's experiences in the neighborhood was structural racism, which created a range of inequities that adversely impacted community members' lives. To this point, as he navigated his secondary school years, Michael's "dreaming" included beginning to translate his notion of "somewhere else" into getting out of his city and as a way to reduce his proximity to the neighborhood and the life challenges he had experienced thus far. In considering these realities, he also identified getting to college as a possibility, whereby he could leave the pressures and tensions of navigating the neighborhood behind him. In this environment, Michael was being psychologically and emotionally stressed.

Pressed into the psyche and sense of being of a number of these young men was the focus they needed to develop strategies to successfully navigate neighborhood perils, gang violence, interpersonal harassment, and concerns about their health and well-being. Michael's narrative and meaning making correspond with a number of discussions I had with Edwin, Chris, and Jamal about their experiences and thoughts and what we referred to as "making it through hysteria." During our conversations, we often referred to and called on hip-hop songs, poetry, or popular culture as all these are part of our cultural background, experiential knowledge, and even forms of communication. As a result, hip-hop and other kinds of music, movies, books, and other slices of both Black and popular culture were part of our ongoing conversations, check-ins, and text messages beyond interviews. Chris and I initially borrowed the phrase "make it through hysteria" from hip-hop artist Skyzoo's song of the same name on his 2012 album *A Dream Deferred*. Both the song and the album as a whole strongly resonated with Chris, mostly due to his studies about and attempts to understand Black communities; music was critical to our relationship as we often shared music and creative writing with each other and discussed and analyzed lyrics, songs, and albums such as Skyzoo's. For Michael, the song and many others resonated because of his own interests and engagement with hip-hop music. Additionally, he used writing and performing poetry as a way to make sense of and articulate his lifeworld, and he even performed at local venues, including several colleges.

It is important that hip-hop served as a source of knowledge and cultural sharing among myself and several of these young men. In our conversations, hip-hop songs, albums, and lyrics especially were used as reference points, connections, community, representations of ourselves and our lives, and even as language. From Joey Bada$$'s song "Devastated" to Kendrick Lamar's "DNA" and "Alright" to Chance the Rapper's "Angels," to name just a few, these songs spoke to us and allowed us to speak to each other in nuanced and insightful ways.[6] As "language," hip-hop allowed us to discuss experiences that were individual and collective; in a similar manner, it served as a tool of analysis that informed how we spoke about and referred to different experiences and events in our lives and how we made sense of these as well. For instance, in Skyzoo's song "Make It through Hysteria," the opening line, which riffs on Nas's song "Street Dreams," begins by noting the dire circumstances of his youth (growing up in or near public housing and the challenges this environment induces) and how these inform his aspirations (constantly dreaming of different opportunities and hoping for a different reality).[7] This line and several other lyrics in the song related to some of the experiences we discussed in our conversations, especially as these young men talked about the material conditions of the communities they lived in and navigated and how hope and aspirations, from themselves as well as from family and peers, helped strengthen their mindsets and resolve.

Given some of the conditions he faced, and also based on his parents' backgrounds, Michael struggled to detail any serious message from his parents about college. In fact, based on these factors he questioned the encouragement to attend college, at least initially, because he did not see the merits of college in his parents' lives. In recalling the messages that he received from home about going to college, Michael explained:

> From home, honestly none. Outside from the fact that my mom said I was going to go to college, but how is that enforced? For one, you [my mom] didn't go to college so that limits how much you can help me. Unless you go out and get some information before I embark on that process, then I'm basically doing this on my own. Between that and her knowing the importance of college, the importance of college was known, but it wasn't reinforced on why it was there.

Based on his narrative, while Michael heard messages about attending college from his mother, he struggled to perceive these messages as connecting to his future endeavors. Inherent in Michael's concerns were his own uncertainties about his educational plight and academic performance.

Moreover, he believed that his mother's personal inexperience with and lack of knowledge about college undermined the support she could offer him on his pathway. Thus, given his family's dynamics, and perceived limitations, they were unable to reinforce the message through their own experiences and accomplishments, so Michael felt that pursuing college was a venture he had to figure out on his own. These realities put even more emphasis on the importance and potential effect of these youth's peer groups, social networks, school culture and educational opportunities, and their relationships with school-based personnel.

Michael continued reflecting on the messages he received about attending college and added:

> It almost felt like a very hypocritical situation really. "You're going to college . . ." But you didn't go? For a kid, who doesn't even know how to experience that type of life, [who] had only seen some stuff on tv; and I didn't even know how I'm going to get there. I literally didn't know how to get there. You're just saying that and it just sounds like a dream. You're my mom and you're supposed to say that but there was no guidance on how to get there. . . . I could tell she wanted to help, so let me help you help me. And, I figured that this was something that was going to help our family, so let me try to help figure this out.

Several points from Michael's sense making are important. First, he expressed ambivalence and frustration in receiving his mother's encouragement to attend college. To him, her lack of college degree attainment meant that she was limited in the perspectives, insight, and information she could offer him. Second, Michael also expressed a lack of clarity regarding his own potential pathway to college; beyond a vision and hope, he needed critical direction on how to build and navigate his pathway to college. His attestation that "I didn't even know how I'm going to get there" suggests a clear lack of material knowledge of college requirements, college campuses, what colleges might have to offer, and how he could access higher education. Along the same lines, as he shared in different parts of his interviews, Michael was unsure why he should pursue higher education; he did not have family members whose lives he could examine to help him make sense of the potential benefits of having attended or graduated from college. Thus, Michael, like a number of other youth across various racial and class backgrounds, wanted and needed clear guidance on how to turn his educational desires of attending college into a reality, and he needed input on the tangible ways that attending and graduating from college could impact a person's life. It is important that even with this uncertainty and lack of guidance, Michael still believed that attending college could make a positive contribution to his family. A portion of this belief was situated in being the eldest among his siblings and, as a result, feeling a sense of responsibility to create college going as a new norm for them.

Even as he was unclear on how attending college would help his family materially, he operated on faith and hope that it would create change. "To be honest, I didn't, I didn't know how it would help my family. But, the way I was looking at it like, I can either continue the cycle that was already there or you step out and see if this college thing can be the thing that helps change the family." Michael was emphatic in crediting "the issues and the hardships" that his parents endured throughout his childhood—"I think their situations—their unhappiness personally"—as factors that contributed significantly to his educational urgency and his pursuit of attending college as a desire and dream even in the face of challenges, struggles, and uncertainties.

EDWIN: "I ALWAYS BEEN A SMART KID . . . SO I DIDN'T REALLY WORRY ABOUT MY ACADEMICS"

As Edwin contemplated his academic experiences during his secondary school years, he emphasized, with great clarity and certainty, "I always been a smart kid, even though I was doing my . . . making poor choices growing up, so I didn't really worry about my academics." Edwin shared that his major focus during his early secondary school years was on his athletic participation and performance. He discussed his educational mindset as, "Just do enough to get a 2.0 [grade point average] and really challenge my mind academically. Just tryna get through it day-by-day"; he also noted that he spent his first year "not applying myself as much as I needed to that year" and that it took "maybe six months to buy into the [academic] program" at Ellis Academy.

Edwin's second year at Ellis Academy was a turning point that informed and inspired his educational desires and urgency. Although he attended a college preparatory school, Edwin admitted to spending the bulk of his first year at the school using a "day-to-day" approach that was not focused on strong academic performance. He did reach a number of his athletic goals, such as being a significant contributor to both the football and basketball teams, as these were his two major sports. Additionally, Edwin was a key member of the track and field team during the spring, which was his first year ever participating in the sport. At the end of his first year, he had played three major sports, earned significant achievements in each, and as a result, he was acknowledged with one of the school's distinctions for athletic contributions.

Having previously participated in both football and basketball throughout his adolescence, Edwin approached his participation in these sports with a sense of expectancy: he knew he was talented in both and spent hours practicing and playing in his neighborhood, in community-based leagues and tournaments, and recreationally with his friends. His performance in track and field, however, was totally new. He earned a top-ten performance in three events and the team performed well also, as they secured a top-ten performance for outdoor track and field in the conference championships. These experiences with athletics informed his approach and goals for his second year. He explained, "I think track had a big influence on how my second year would play out. One thing that I learned was that if you don't trust your teammates, if you don't trust the system set in place, then things might not work out as planned—or hoped. But, if you can take care of your grades then it's no telling how good you can be."

Edwin's points about trust were related especially to his track and field experiences, as he participated on both the 400-meter and 1,600-meter relay teams. These events require trust among team members, especially in relation to important elements of their coordinated efforts, such as communication, baton exchanges, support, and believing in one another's ability and performance. What is more, trust related to academic performance was important as well, as he realized after witnessing some of his teammates be prevented from participating in several important track and field meets or be unable to finish competing through the end of the season because they did not earn a 2.0 grade point average during grade checks throughout the season, which they needed to remain academically eligible to participate. He learned from all these experiences, which also included "meeting new people who came in and started getting in tune with the [school's academic] program. My academics got better; [I] had a 3.5 [GPA] that year and got a couple of awards for my academics."

The academic performance and acknowledgments helped Edwin begin to see some of his own academic potential while his athletic accomplishments reinforced his athletic identity and helped him see how both were beneficial to his schooling experiences and life.

> By the end of my sophomore year, I really did better [academically] and bought into the [school] program. Tried to keep it separate from my academics and sports and social life. And I tried to use that as my motivation to keep going. . . . I got people around me that's rooting for me and they're there for me, as well as my social life. I just wanted to keep that going and try to be successful.

Even as he improved his academic performance, Edwin relied on sports to teach him what he considered to be valuable life lessons. He acknowledged that his primary motivation during secondary school was his athletic participation:

> Sports is what motivated me the most because there's a lot of things you can learn from it. . . . You can learn how to be trustworthy, you learn respect, discipline and be respectful. You have encouraging people, whether it be people supporting you or cheering you on. If you played any sports—football, track—it teaches people how to deal with adversity. I know everybody doesn't live a perfect life but with sports it has a lot of components of life. Also, I believe that sports helped me develop my spiritual growth. Being able to develop what you believe in and even doing things like team prayer.

All these young men attended a college preparatory school, and they all agreed that the school offered a forceful and singular message about their postsecondary school pathways: going to college. Even though he said he was motivated by athletics, Edwin also acknowledged that he began to accept and internalize the message from school personnel at Ellis Academy that students were college bound.

In recalling how teachers and staff members talked about going to college, Edwin stated that they offered an unwavering, overwhelming message about college going:

> **Edwin:** They brainwashed us! They brainwashed us from beginning to end. Before I even got to that school that was the message, you really didn't have a choice. That was the whole purpose of the school. That was the thing every day, we always said, "We are college bound." So every day, in some kinda way, it was brought up.
>
> **DB:** How did you feel about the college message—on an everyday basis?
>
> **Edwin:** Sometimes it got tiring to hear, every day, the same stuff over and over again. You know, you lose sight of stuff every time when you're kinda not there yet. I feel like my first couple of years [of high school] were long. You keep saying these things over and over again and you start thinking, "Is this ever gonna come? They must be playing now; when is this stuff going to be completed?" . . . We say we were college bound freshmen year, but some of us didn't last through their freshmen year. I saw a lot of people come and leave and some came back and a lot didn't make it to their senior year. I didn't want to lean on not making it because of me. You hear it over and over again; you get it drilled in your head every day and you start thinking about it, "I don't know, dawg! That year that I just had I don't know if I'm gon' make it?" It's like there's a question mark but you can't let there be a question mark, you just have to push through it.

While students appreciated the consistency of their school's message that they were "college bound," which was conveyed as early as their first year of high school, college was so far away for students like Edwin that it was difficult to see, internalize, or feel connected to the possibility. Still, though, Edwin attested that the major factors that contributed to his college aspirations included the school's message, his connections to and relationships with peers who had college plans, and his family and their college-going history.

> I guess one major factor is something that's been drilled in our heads since we were freshmen in high school. Every day

> we walk into the school we were drilled with "we are college bound." And, to continue on, my peers were a major factor. Seeing my friends getting accepted to a college of choice or receiving a scholarship boosted me more in wanting to go on to college. And, we can go back to me being the first person in my family going to college—and we can say that's most of the guys' cases. . . . But, my family influenced me as well.

Through constant and consistent messaging along with critical relationships, Edwin garnered social and cultural capital that helped strengthen his pathway to college. Researchers contend that relationships offer students a range of valuable support and encouragement on their pathways to college. For instance, peers can affect social behaviors and influence academic aspirations and achievement; along the same lines, school culture and family can aid in students' college aspirations and college-going decisions.[8] Additionally, these young Black men credited their families with encouraging and inspiring their aspirations, even when higher education was beyond their own experiences.

PAUL: "I DIDN'T EVEN KNOW HOW TO GET TO COLLEGE"

Prior to his secondary school years, Paul considered attending college as a remote potential reality, which was so far away that it was difficult for him to envision or understand how he could get there. During his adolescent years he and his two younger brothers lived with his great-aunt and great-uncle; although both were his guardians, his great-aunt was his primary caregiver and the one with whom he developed the closest relationship. While his guardians offered significant support for his schooling efforts, he recalled receiving no clear messages about college and, as a result, he did not believe pursuing higher education was attainable.

> First off, I always believed that college was a fairy tale, it didn't really exist. I thought it was a place that was only for white people. I remember seeing [the television show] *Saved by the Bell* and wanting to get a letterman jacket with different sports letters on it—and I wanted to have a girlfriend. I didn't think there was anything after high school. But at home, I didn't really get any messages about college. There

> were people who went to college but didn't finish and some that just stopped going.

Paul's lack of knowledge about college does not speak to his goals or aspirations but rather his lived reality. He was not necessarily familiar with representations of Black college going during his formative years and neither of his guardians earned high levels of formal education. Still, they offered support and messages that helped Paul develop and center his strivings for college. In reflecting on his great-aunt's support, he explained:

> Well she was supportive in my school efforts. First off, the highest education she ever received was a eighth-grade education; she wasn't book smart, but she always knew that whenever you put your best foot forward you could achieve. She always said put my best foot forward and stick to my faith [laughing in recollection]. Those were the words pretty much every time. I didn't make all A's all the time and she'd say, "Did you try your best?" I'd say "Yeah," and she'd say, "Well, okay, you should be happy."

The support Paul received from his great-aunt regarding school was consistent and empowering. Despite her own educational attainment, Paul still honored and appreciated her understanding of the world and her lessons regarding the importance of one's personal efforts. Messages from his great-aunt about school resonated with Paul especially strongly because he considered the sacrifices she and his great-uncle made in caring for him and his siblings as well as her ongoing and consistent support as significant investments in and encouragement toward his possibilities. Paul internalized these messages and continued to reconcile how he might actualize the gifts, knowledge, and wisdom that his great-aunt imparted in him.

Education, effort, and faith are the hallmarks of Paul's sense of self. Beginning in his secondary school years, Paul identified education as a pathway to his future. He learned valuable lessons from home regarding character and values and he also observed and internalized his great-aunt's personal efforts related to work and caring for the family. Paul admired his great-aunt and held her in the highest regard. As he put it:

> For me, what made my great-aunt my hero was the hard work, determination, how humble she always stayed. All traits of a hero in my opinion. She was very strong; she was my Wonder Woman. She had every trait of a super hero. Every time I tell people about my great-aunt, people would want to say, "I want to meet her, I want to meet her." If I say this to her [my great-aunt], she'd say, "I didn't do anything." She'd never take credit for it. That right there shows her attitude and it shows her character.

Given his great-aunt's presence in his life, Paul expressed a deep understanding that his personal efforts were not his alone but rather were representative of his family. Not only did he desire to heed his great-aunt's messages and teachings, he also began to shape his educational desires as a way to display gratitude for all that she offered. He noted, "She didn't know nothing about college. She just said, 'Do your best, don't make a fool of yourself [laughing in amusement as he recalled these conversations]; don't give yourself a bad reputation.'" Although his great-aunt could not speak specifically about college from experience, she had a clear understanding about character and how one's efforts, in some ways, were representative of one's character. Thus, her message to Paul that he not "make a fool" of himself also related to the effort she continuously coached and taught him about. Effort, then, for Paul encompassed both his attempts to secure his goals or complete various tasks and his determined focus in honoring and heeding his great-aunt's teachings.

Paul coupled his learning from home with Ellis Academy's college-going ethos to inform his pathway to college. As he reflected on his pathway, he acknowledged, "I didn't think I was going to college [laughing in recollection]; not me, un uh. I didn't even know how to get to college!" For Paul, neither the lack of formal guidance about how to get to college nor even the lack of specific encouragement to go to college deterred his aspirations. In fact, he chose Ellis exactly because the school was clear and resolute in sending its graduates to college.

> If I'm not mistaking, that's the only thing that they were preaching in high school [laughing in amusement at the singular message]! Every day, that's what they were talking about. [The principal] kept telling us that we couldn't be

> statistics and we had to stay focused and committed to our work. [The headmaster], he'd come in every blue moon, and he'd tell us that we're going to college and, "We're not trying to get you to college but through college." I always tell people that I always thought college was a fairy tale. You graduate high school and then you work [laughing at his own lack of knowledge]. But they talked to us about going to college and finishing college and you'd have more options. So, I believed in it and I just stuck it out.

Like several of his peers, the consistent message about college going from the Ellis Academy staff was critical for many students. For some students like Paul, this message helped him sharpen his educational aspirations as he developed a newfound belief that he would be a college goer, which was contrary to his thoughts and ideas about college prior to his secondary school years.

In addition to the ongoing messages and the academic work at Ellis Academy, Paul noted that attending a college preparatory school was what he needed to help inform and guide his pathway to college. "Man, what was it like? It was a blessing," he declared in reference to attending Ellis, whose culture and curriculum he believed also helped prepare him for college. During his secondary school years, Paul developed a number of significant relationships with school staff, whom he acknowledged for providing authentic care and tremendous support, both personally and academically. He noted, "All of my teachers were amazing. They never gave up on me, they were willing to hear my story, and they were really there for me."

The teachers' willingness to show up, be present, and offer encouragement and support for Paul's schooling efforts was empowering. He acknowledged his twelfth grade Spanish teacher, a Latina who had graduated college recently, as "truly amazing" because she "was willing to come to school early or stay late to help me"; and he told me that his math teacher during his eleventh grade year taught him a great deal about himself and that some of the feedback corresponded with messages from his home. He faced some trepidation as he was not secure in his mathematic knowledge and abilities. He acknowledged that his math teacher, a young Black woman who also recently had graduated college, "taught me to keep believing in myself. If you really want to do something, keep believing until you do it."

The combination of positive messages and encouragement with teachers' willingness to avail themselves before and after school to provide further instructional support fueled Paul's academic ambitions, engagement, and performance. That his teachers were always there—at the school in the morning, available during lunch, and staying on after school—left an indelible imprint on Paul's academic work and his efforts in attaining, and even raising, his goals. "I believe it was all the teachers. They didn't always say the word 'believe' but you put two and two together and you get the same thing. Ms. Johnson [the math teacher] said it and it stuck in my head; but it was every teacher and staff member."

Not only did school staff encourage students' college aspirations and self-beliefs, they also shared their own stories, connected students' lives and interests to college opportunities and experiences, and made college a relatable experience that students could desire.

> They always led by example. Every time we walked into a classroom we'd see a college banner hanging up. They always talked about the experiences you could have by going to college. The mission of Ellis Academy was going to college, not just going to college but graduating from college. They talked about college in a positive way; there was nothing negative about it. I already knew that I wanted a higher education and college was a part of that.

Overwhelmingly, Paul remained impressed and inspired by his teachers, "They always kept their words with me." He felt that the teachers and staff helped instill pride in his classmates and himself; they not only encouraged students to pursue their potential and possibilities, they also provided examples, shared their own stories, and added to students' own social and cultural capital. Much of this sharing included discussing strategies that students could employ during their college years, identifying various college resources they believed students should know about, identifying different types of colleges and the benefits they offered, and encouraging students to stay focused on their academic endeavors. A number of the young men credited their teachers, staff members, and mentors as cultural guides who proved critical in counseling them in their learning about how to get to college and some of the efforts needed to be successful once there.

Malik: "With college, I always knew I was going to go anyway"

Similar to his peers in this study, in my conversations with Malik, he discussed his years at Ellis Academy with great admiration and affection. Overwhelmingly, these young men focused on relationships as the pinnacle of their secondary school experiences; these relationships spanned their connections with teachers and staff (including coaches) and their peers.

As he reflected on his pathway to college, Malik credited his family for providing consistent support and messaging that encouraged him or, in his words, "pushed" him, to go to college. He noted, "Ever since, man, ever since I can remember my family has been trying to push me to college." Most significant in his family's messages was that they planted the seeds for college going, or at least college aspirations, very early in his life. Although his parents told him later, during his secondary school years, that striving for college was his own decision, Malik, who also paid close attention to his family's college-going and lived experiences, had internalized their early messages and was already planning to pursue college immediately following secondary school. We discussed his parents' contributions to his thoughts about higher education and he recalled:

> **Malik:** They played a big role. Ever since I can remember as a kid, they were telling me that they wanted me to go off to college. As I got older, they told me that I didn't really have to go. But, by the time my junior and senior year came around I had already made up my mind that I was going to go whether they wanted me to or not.
>
> **DB:** Why did they want you to go off to college?
>
> **Malik:** One, not a lot of people in my family had the opportunity to finish high school and then go on to college. My father has an associate's degree and he wanted me to kind of beat him, if you know what that means. My mother doesn't have a college degree just a high school diploma, so she wanted me to pursue my options.

These early experiences and conversations were important ways for Malik to learn even more about his family's educational history. These conversations served as powerful messages that college degree attainment would fulfill some of his parents' goals for him. Malik noted that his pathway was not one necessarily sparked by motivation or a pivotal moment; instead, his route to college was one cemented in knowing his capabilities and activating his educational desire.

> I don't know. . . . I don't really think there was an overall motivating thing, I just think I went to high school knowing that I was going to graduate; I knew I would graduate in four years because that was what you're supposed to do. There were times when I wasn't the best student, but having friends and teachers and mentors who cared about me helped put me on the right track. With college, I always knew I was going to go anyway.

Malik's discussion of his pathway to college is intriguing as it involved a number of different nuances. For instance, he was fully confident that he would be "successful" in high school, at a minimum, in terms of graduating in four years. Moreover, even though he claimed that he "always knew" he was going to college, his pathway was not always clear. In particular, his route to college was marked by his personal growth and development, coupled with shifts in his academic seriousness.

> **Malik:** My freshman year of high school, man I was just going through the motions. I can say that I was excited to be in high school because it was a new realm of freedom that I was responsible for. I was going through the motions. It was a nice time.
>
> **DB:** Why were you just going through the motions?
>
> **Malik:** I guess at that point in time I didn't feel like I needed to strive for anything. I had heard from my family and other people that you really need to start thinking about college junior and senior year [of high school]. So I figured freshman year I can just chill and focus on passing my classes.

DB: And what do you mean by going through the motions?

Malik: I was just going with the flow and just how things went. I mean, I swam and played football but on my part there wasn't a lot of decisions about doing things.

A two-sport student-athlete who competed in football and swimming, Malik was deemed academically ineligible for swimming during his second year because his grades fell below the minimum 2.0 GPA requirement. He recalled having a long talk with the track and field coach, which spanned across three days, about potentially joining the team. Since he had missed a significant portion of the swimming season and still wanted to compete athletically after increasing his academic performance, he thought that track and field, among available options in the spring, could contribute to his athletic development or at least satisfy his athletic desires. During these conversations, the track coach inquired about Malik's academic seriousness as compared with his athletic pursuits. The conversations, joining the track and field team, the relationships he developed and deepened with these new team members, and his determination all proved pivotal to his academic performance, educational aspirations, and personal development.

In analyzing his first two years of secondary school, Malik was clear that he "was missing some guidance" and declared that the relationship he developed with his track and field coach, whom he still considers one of his mentors, as well as his active engagement in several student activities and academic programs were prominent in guiding him through his last two years. These experiences and the guidance he received helped support his goals and development, "I got guidance and stuff just took off from there. I started being a better student and a better person." In specifically discerning the guidance he received, he explained:

> Because . . . I was just kind of walking around the school and doing things that I thought I should be doing. The last two years I had a better understanding of what I needed to be doing because the guidance I received definitely helped me with that. Also, it was time for me to start looking at colleges and think about where I was going to be next. So, I had to straighten up and get things in order.

Malik's declaration that he had to "straighten up and get things in order" meant that he needed to perform better academically and, similar to Edwin, buy into Ellis Academy's academic program to help strengthen his pathway to college. The summer between his eleventh and twelfth grade years, with his college counselor's support and encouragement, Malik participated in a writing program at a local college. He identified this as an important experience that provided him with practical skills he could use once in college: "Definitely had got some really good writing points while I was still in high school there. Honestly, when I first heard about it I wasn't too stoked about the program. . . . I think I just wanted to do something other than writing."

Malik's academic profile during his secondary school years revealed an upward trajectory of performance and engagements that helped him affirm his academic possibilities. His promise and potential were recognized by a number of his teachers and his mentors, which helped provide significant support for his efforts and aspirations. Malik entered high school "going through the motions" in his first year, but later, as he developed a clearer sense of direction, he was afforded the opportunity to enhance his skills and learning while spending time on a college campus leading into his twelfth grade year. Although he wasn't "too stoked" about the writing program, being on a college campus enhanced his aspirations and educational urgency. In making meaning from the writing program, he noted, "I would say that being on a college campus was by far the most significant experience I take away from that [program]. That is something that most people should experience." Further, this refocusing of his academic behaviors also informed his peer associations as well:

> I would say most of my friends in high school were like me; some were better than me academically. Yeah, I would say better—more hard work. All of us were on the same level at Ellis and that was to get to college and get out of whatever type of situation we was in during high school. So, for the most part, I tried to pick friends who were on the same level or higher.

As Malik's narrative shows, his pathway to college was initially informed by messages from family as well as his family's history. Although he experienced several academic struggles during his first two years of high school, his friendships, athletic participation, and the relationships he developed were critical in his growth, maturity, and development. What he identified as key to strengthening his pathway to college was improving his academic performance. As he did so, Malik also sought out educational opportunities that ultimately afforded him with chances to study on a college campus prior to twelfth grade. This experience, combined with the foundation he laid, helped illuminate the vast and diverse opportunities that lay ahead of him in pursuing college. Additionally, these experiences provided Malik with a deeper understanding and appreciation of his potential and possibilities.

Summary

For too many Black boys and young men, pursuing college is considered and construed as unimaginable—or even as a fairy tale—because it is incongruent with their lived realities or the resources they have or can access. For some Black boys and young men, they are unsure of how to get from where they are to college, whatever their backgrounds, aspirations, and performance may be. The seemingly "simple" lack of information about accessing college can be debilitating to their goals and aspirations; in fact, they can internalize this lack of knowledge as a personal failure or shortcoming, which can undermine their academic efforts and engagement. Additionally, or alternatively, this lack of knowledge and information can manifest in ways whereby some Black boys and young men fail to express strong desires to attend college. How do we make sense of Black boys and young men who want to and try to aspire to go to college and are encouraged to pursue higher education but are unsure of how to access college and also unclear on how college can contribute to their lives—or can make an immediate contribution to their family's lives?

Research shows that for some families of color, college aspirations can be confronted and undermined by various limitations, such as knowledge regarding accessing higher education institutions or even a mismatch in families' educational desires.[9] Likewise, especially as it relates to young Black men, and as the narratives in this chapter reveal, families can play a critical role in influencing their college-going processes. According to their narratives, these young men benefited from crucial messages, lessons, values, beliefs, and encouragement from their families, which served as motivation and support for their educational desires. However, it is important to recognize that understanding and receiving these messages was wrought with internal and external struggles. Internally, young men like Michael struggled to discern their family's message and encouragement that they should pursue higher education; externally, young men like Michael and Paul acknowledged that they were unsure how to make the idea of pursuing college a reality. Even as young men like Edwin and Malik felt secure in their abilities (such that they "always knew" they were smart) and educational goals (they also "always knew" they were going to go to college anyway), they still leaned on and benefited from their family's nurturing, support, and cultural logics.

That some of these young men felt empowered and inspired by their families, through their relationships, and by national events, such as the presidential election of Barack Obama, all reveal how their social and cultural capital mattered to how they thought about themselves. That is, these young men received and extracted both direct and indirect messages regarding their potential and possibilities from their families, schooling experiences, and current events. A number of these young men felt that various social institutions (e.g., popular media and criminal justice system) "don't give us a chance to be us," and the points they raise in this chapter helped affirm their capabilities, aptitude, and somebodiness. Their sense of self and cultural ethos were strengthened and supported by their communities, including Ellis Academy. As their narratives in this chapter reveal, these young men wrestled with, refined, scrutinized, and benefited from the messages they received about college, which ultimately were messages about they themselves. Each of these young men, in their own individualized ways, identified pursuing higher education as a way to support, contribute to, and honor their families—even when their parents and guardians did not possess deep firsthand knowledge themselves about college going.

What these young men offer is their sense of urgency in the decisions they make about their lives and their futures. The decision to pursue higher education, even with uncertainties and no clear or discernible path on how to get there, reveals these young men's educational desires and the value they place on the messages, encouragement, and support from their families. Important, too, as discussed by several young men, were their secondary schooling experiences. I take a close examination of their school-related experiences in the following chapter to understand how these youth believed that attending a college preparatory school mattered in their pathways to college.

Chapter 4

"Getting the preparation and knowledge about college"

Schooling and College-Going Support

> Man, it's a blessing; a blessing! Because people don't understand how much a school that's centered around getting you to college makes. I know kids who went to Arnold High and other schools and a lot of kids didn't go to college; a lot of kids didn't go to college. But Ellis Academy definitely made sure that they sent kids to college. That's one thing that I can say; it's a blessing.
>
> —Chauncey

Getting to College

In this chapter, I explore how the young men made meaning from their experiences in attending an all-boys, college preparatory secondary school. Most importantly, this chapter is intended to show how the young men's aspirations toward college and sense of self connected with their schooling experiences. In the main, although they alluded to school-based messages in the excerpts in the previous chapter, here I zoom in to examine the young men's reflections about their academic experiences, their interactions and relationships with teachers, and Ellis Academy's cultural ethos of students' college going. In other published work, I have written about how the young men in this study thought about attending an all-boys school that was designed specifically to cater to the needs of Black boys. For instance, these young men have noted how many school personnel promoted academic excellence and helped them build community with their Black male peers, discussed the critical importance of connecting with and learning from Black male teachers for their personal development, and explained how the school culture enhanced their sense of belonging and academic success. Each of these benefits was situated specifically within their secondary school experiences.[1]

While I write about the young men's secondary school experiences here, I do so as a way to understand their pathways to college and how school helped mold their college-going mindsets. In particular, I was interested in how they bridged their college aspirations and the messages they received about pursuing higher education, as discussed in the previous two chapters, with the school-related experiences they thought contributed to their interest in college going. In talking with these young men about their college preparedness, they often spoke about aspects of their secondary school that they believed helped get them ready for and better focused on college. According to Chauncey, who was quoted here, and as noted by Paul in the previous chapter, their opportunities to attend a college preparatory school dedicated to educating Black boys was "a blessing" precisely because the culture of the school focused on getting Black boys to college. Again, and related to findings from my other work, these young men discussed how attending Ellis Academy helped instill pride in them by focusing on their promise and potential and helping them move from a status of uncertainty when they entered secondary school ("I was just trying to make it") to being college bound. In Chauncey's case, he believed that some students could underappreciate the importance of an environment focused on college going and, as a way to provide some perspective, he identified the significant difference in culture across two of the secondary schools that he attended. Indeed, Chauncey made direct connections between school culture and students' college going.

As the young men continued developing or increasing their desires to pursue higher education, they also reflected on the information they received for getting to college and the preparation they garnered that they thought they needed to be successful once in college. To this point, in writing about schooling for Black boys, education scholar Jawanza Kunjufu contended, "School culture is the most important factor that determines whether students are successful academically or not."[2] Moreover, researchers note that a lack of rigorous academic preparation and readiness among first-generation college students can serve as significant barriers to accessing and succeeding in higher education.[3] The majority of the young men in this study spoke about significant academic-oriented experiences, some of which challenged them to raise their academic efforts and focus. Moreover, they identified lessons and relationships with teachers, their repertoire of skills, and their personal characteristics as factors that contributed to their preparation.

Jamal: "It was just a challenging experience"

As Jamal reflected on his pathway to college, he talked about some of the academic rigors of his secondary school experiences: "During my years at Ellis, I took sciences, geometry, US History, AP [Advanced Placement] literature, honors Spanish, trigonometry, and Algebra 2; I've taken chemistry, I've taken a music course. I took two AP English courses. . . . I've taken a lot of honors classes; well, I don't know if it's a lot. And I took calculus, if I didn't mention that. Oh, and physics. . . . Wow! That was like the hardest class I ever had!" I asked Jamal about his decisions to take Advanced Placement and honors courses, and he explained:

> Well, a lot of people were saying that AP classes would look really good on your college application—especially if you place out of a college course. I think you have to get a 4 or a 5 [on the AP Exam]. So, I figured why not take the chance to see if I can place out of a college course before I get there? I knew that college would be hard, so why not try to get out of one hard class so I wouldn't have to take it.

Even though Jamal performed well throughout his secondary school years, achieving over a 3.7 GPA each academic year, one of the messages that he clung to along the way was the need to build his academic portfolio for applying to college. In addition to his strong academic performance, he still wanted to ensure that he pursued the highest-level courses offered at Ellis Academy, which included taking two different AP English classes and a host of other honors classes. Aside from receiving messages about the potential benefits of taking these courses, Jamal also rationalized his decisions by ensuring that he challenged himself academically, trying to improve his academic profile, and exploring academic opportunities that could benefit him in college. It was because he "knew that college would be hard" that he welcomed and pursed academically rigorous courses.

Jamal noted that his AP English classes during his eleventh and twelfth grade years were both helpful and challenging. According to him, AP English "was really good because he [the teacher] challenged me to think outside the box. He had us watch *Hotel Rwanda* and we read a book, it was *Invisible Man* and we read *Things Fall Apart* and *Their Eyes Were Watching God* in AP Lit, but he got us to think about different things and helped improve my writing. My writing still needs work but at that time it was awful. They just kept pushing me." Jamal appreciated being pushed academically by the rigor of his courses and being asked to "think outside the box." Being pushed out of his comfort zone, both in the quality of his work and through the content of these classes, and being challenged academically in his course load, he believed that he was being prepared to matriculate to college. In summarizing his college preparatory experiences, he noted, "I mean, academically it was tough just because where I was as far as my grade levels for reading and math and science, but they helped us, in some ways, to get prepared for college—hence college prep. I thought they did a great job, they could've done better—but that's with every school, nothing's gon' be perfect. It was just a challenging experience."

Jamal combined these school-based academic experiences with participating in an ACT Test prep course and a separate three-week college summer program that provided him with a firsthand on-campus experience. This college program experience not only helped make his college going more tangible, it also helped sharpen ideas about his academic focus once in college, "You hear people say I want to be an engineer, or a Black Studies major, or a music major but you won't really know what it's like unless you're in that position." In recalling his summer college program experience, he recalled,

> I would say it's to help you gain experience on different things that are out there like different majors, different careers, and it'll help you decide if something is for you or not. . . . I had an experience of coming to a college [program] for like three weeks. You don't get the full college experience, but you get the feel of it. You get to see if this is for you and it can be fun. You learn what else is out there.

The opportunity for Jamal to gain firsthand experiences at a college was important because it helped expose him to various aspects of college life and allowed him to explore different opportunities as well. Additionally, this college immersion experience allowed him to learn more about himself and the types of students who would be his classmates or members of his college community.

> That was a different experience because it was the first time being around people that talked differently than I did. People sounded country, so I had to get used to that. We had Asians, Hispanics, Indians, it was just different. We didn't have any white people just because it was the Center for Diversity for STEM [Program]; it was just for minorities only. That was fun! You stay in a dorm for three weeks, take two classes, and it gave me a little bit of a feeling of what college would be like. I think that's the first time I got a glimpse of what this [college] could be, and it got me away from home.

The quality of Jamal's experience was revealed in what he shared with his school counselor and several friends, "I learned a lot about STEM and when I got back to school I shared my experiences with my friends, my college counselor, and my track coach." Given that he participated in this program the summer before his twelfth grade year, this experience helped Jamal envision himself in college, helped him learn about science, technology, engineering, and math (STEM) fields including majors that he was considering at the time, and provided him with an opportunity to learn with a diverse group of students of color.

Michael: "It got me even more focused on college"

Like Jamal in some ways, Michael also believed that he could benefit from taking higher-level courses during his eleventh and twelfth grade years. He believed that taking such courses could help him solidify and illuminate his college pathway. Although he had received strong messages from his mother about pursuing college, Michael declared that he "didn't even know how I'm going to get there" and felt that he lacked "guidance" on how to get to college. These concerns left him feeling somewhat anxious and stressed as he began his eleventh and twelfth grade years, and they also made him heavily reliant on the information and opportunities that Ellis Academy provided.

Academically, Michael struggled in his transition to high school and had to attend summer school after his ninth grade year to recover credit for a class he failed. During his tenth grade year, he performed better academically and earned a B– grade average through the year. Still, he had several instances throughout the year where his performance in different classes required him to attend after-school tutoring. At one point during both his tenth and eleventh grade years, his athletic participation was suspended because his in-class performance dipped below the academic eligibility standard. This academic performance also coincided with financial and relational struggles within his family, and he faced several personal challenges with his girlfriend as well. The combined effect of all of these experiences, both academic and person, led to significant frustrations, self-questioning, and stress, which undermined his academic performance.

As he reflected on and made sense of the courses he decided to take, he explained, "Junior and senior [years] I started to take some AP classes and that was important to me because it got me even more focused on college." In explaining how Advanced Placement and honors classes got him "even more focused," Michael declared, "It was just the level of work, the level of difficulty, the level of expectations. You could be the traditional class walking right in after an AP class and you can see that the work is different. What was on the board is being erased. . . . It challenged you mentally, so it was harder work and you had to push yourself harder." Part of several of the young men's decisions to take AP and honors courses was to be challenged academically, and at the same time, a byproduct of these decisions was the opportunity to strengthen their academic confidence.

Michael, who admitted to not liking science, explained that he wanted to build an academic profile that would be attractive to colleges and universities. As an example, in deciding to take AP Biology, he acknowledged his own rationalization, which included trepidation and academic strategizing, in the following way:

> **Michael:** It was . . . it was more so . . . I didn't necessarily want to, but it was one of those decisions that I knew would look good on my transcript, especially if I performed well in that class. I would definitely say that it was one of the classes that I needed.

> **DB:** What was your experience like in AP Bio?
>
> **Michael:** It was one of my most difficult classes because I didn't like science—I didn't like science! It interested me; certain aspects of science interests me, others drive me crazy. But I'm all about a challenge and that's why I was in that class. The fact that all three of my best friends are in that class, am I gon' be the only one not in that class? So, just looking at it in that way.

Initially in his discussion about course selections, Michael declared that taking higher level courses could strengthen his transcript and college application. However, beyond this clear strategy for appealing to colleges, Michael also noted that advanced biology was "one of the classes that I needed" because it aligned with his interests and he felt that he would be challenged academically. He also acknowledged how his decision to take this course was rooted in positive peer connections and peer social capital as well. Because his three best friends were in the class, he wanted to demonstrate that his academic standards were on par with theirs.

The peers of these young men had a significant influence on the activities in which they engaged and their academic efforts, as well as how they thought about themselves. In Michael's case, he wanted to share academic experiences with his closest peers as a way to keep their bonds intact and also to access critical support for his academic efforts. Moreover, he also believed he would benefit from being pushed academically, which he considered to be an essential component of his college preparation. "I had to be pushed if I wanted to be successful. If I wasn't pushed in high school, then I wouldn't be ready for college. I wouldn't be ready for the rigor, which is why I looked to be pushed so much."

Whereas students like Edwin felt that the daily messages and focus on getting to college were burdensome and far away during his early years at Ellis Academy, students like Chris (discussed in chapter 3) and Michael believed that the college preparatory school offered them a pathway to college. Michael explained:

> **Michael:** There were a lot of expectations and even if we felt like college wasn't the place for us the expectations was like, "We're going to college." So that kind of woke us up in determining where we were going. We started believing that we were college bound; you heard it every day and you

> start to believe it. We heard it every day. So that put me in a mindset that that [college] was where I was going. And it helped me believe that I was going to college and I could be successful.
>
> **DB:** How do you feel about attending a school where the expectation was going to college?
>
> **Michael:** That's the reason why I went! Coming from an environment where you don't hear about college besides someone saying, "You're going to school" or "You're going to college," but you didn't know how to get there. Then, you step into an environment [like Ellis Academy] and every person you come into contact with has a degree and many of them are working on another one. You don't see that every day; so, you put yourself in the mindset that you can accomplish these things too. I knew that at the end of the day, to be honest, if I wanted anything for myself *I had to do it!* Regardless of my mother and the things she said she wanted and even my dad; I had to do it.

As Michael makes clear, the school's college-going culture positively impacted students' self-efficacy and self-expectations. Through the messaging, course offerings, and support that he received, Michael was able to envision himself as a future college student. The relationships he built with teachers—a number of whom attended his athletic events, supported his nonschool activities, and several whom he spent time with outside school—put him in close proximity to learn from their experiences as well. Through these relationships, he paid close attention to his teachers' lives; as a result, his teachers' achieved statuses signaled to him his own possibilities and positioned them as potential contributors to his development and his own college going.

MALIK: "I'D SAY THE ASPECT OF ME BEING RESILIENT IN HIGH SCHOOL"

Although these young men had aspired to go to college, several also revealed that they had not been sure how to get there. As they made sense of how they got to college and the ways in which their school contributed, a few students focused less on academic preparation and potential academic-oriented lessons and instead focused more on their noncognitive abilities and their character. In discerning what he learned from his secondary school experiences that he thought would help him succeed in college, Malik explained:

> **Malik:** Having to work, having to be resilient . . . you know, I had to learn, my sophomore year, everything isn't going to be easy. Freshman year, I sorta cruised through there and my sophomore year I had to relearn how to do school—sports wise and on a personal level. So, I felt the lesson I learned was that work needs to be done for success to happen, it doesn't come easy.
>
> **DB:** In what ways did you learn resilience?
>
> **Malik:** Definitely learned resilience during my sophomore year when I failed science first semester. Pretty down about it and I should've done better; I feel like I didn't have the best instructor. The next semester I had a really great attitude for it. I had the second-best score in my class for it and I basically showed myself that I could do the work.

According to Malik, he learned valuable lessons about himself during his secondary school years. Most prominently, his academic setbacks revealed that he needed to improve his academic efforts and performance. It was in his struggles that he developed and refined his resilience, perseverance, and positive attitude.

In reflecting on his overall secondary school experiences, Malik acknowledged that it was "a little bit of ups and downs, but more ups." He was just "cruising" through his first year and a half based on a "turn it up" approach whereby he had decided to "get serious" about his academic experiences and strivings toward college in his eleventh and twelfth grade years. "I started off not bad but mediocre. In my sophomore year, I took a big down turn . . . it got worse then it got better. I couldn't finish the football season, I couldn't compete on the swimming team, and I failed a class. My GPA went down, it decreased." He explained that his secondary school experience improved after these challenges, "My GPA got better because I earned my first A in a class. I was personally doing well for myself in track and field. I had a newfound confidence in myself in sports and in academics."

These experiences connected with Malik's burgeoning educational urgency. In his attempts to prevail academically, he described developing a more concentrated effort and relying on some of the relationships he built. He noted:

> I would say I just started, one, I had to check my attitude. I had what people like to call a temper; I was in a classroom, a class where I had a teacher who definitely cared about the students but he'd push your buttons to test you. I knew that that could be the last straw for me or something like that. Two, I just wanted to! I had developed a relationship with someone at the school and I could check in and let them know how I was doing; I could receive advice and keep moving forward. Three, after I got home from practice, I didn't care how tired I was, I would do whatever homework I had. Before, I would wait 'til the morning, but I didn't any more.

Even as Malik changed some of his academic habits, such as timeliness and focus in completing homework assignments, he remained unaware of what he needed to do to prepare for college. He learned about various types of colleges (e.g., liberal arts colleges, research-intensive universities) and, in order to succeed in college, he thought it would take "great study habits, knowing how to manage your time. Choose classes and professors that will help you out with the work and work out for you instead of taking any class."

In reflecting on his preparation and planning for attending college, Malik began to learn more about various types of colleges. Through this process, he learned about the type of school where he believed he could be successful, "I really wanted to go to a small school, so any school that was above 5,000 students was out of the question for me. The selection process was easy; the higher ranked the school was it moved to the top of my list." In reflecting on this process, Malik recollected:

> I started thinking about college toward the end of my junior year. The colleges I had on my list at the end of my junior were very different from the ones that I had on my list my

> senior year and these were the ones that I ended up applying to. The summer before the beginning of my senior year, I focused on just learning how to persuade a college admissions office and learned how to talk about my best attributes.

He explained that the school counselors were pivotal in assisting him with the college application process and he also benefited from the guidance he received from his mentor. "I guess my mentor helped me out; he started me off on the right foot. Once I started my senior year, the college counseling office helped me out a lot and I just started applying [to colleges]." He described his mentor's guidance as pivotal in directing his efforts in identifying and applying to colleges.

> He . . . I guess he, first he gave me a list of colleges. I asked him about a list of colleges and he gave me a list. Luckily, the college I'm attending now was on the list. And, he helped me out with my personal statement. He had me start it early and I decided to write about how he helped me become a better student. He helped me out too because I wasn't really sure what to put down on my college applications.

The trust that grounded Malik's relationship with his mentor was evident in the college application process and is part of the reason why he declared that the guidance he received "helped me become a better student." It is significant that Malik initiated some of this guidance by asking his mentor for a list of potential colleges to consider, and he clearly benefited from his mentor's cultural capital as well as personal knowledge about and validation of Malik's interest and capabilities.

Chris: "It was a opportunity for me to go to college"

Chris shared that he spent "maybe between like twelve and sixteen" hours per week on his academic work outside the classroom during his secondary school years. For Chris, getting to college was pivotal in his belief that he could create greater personal and professional opportunities for himself. He noted that attending a college preparatory secondary school was important for his development and critical to improving his access to college.

> **Chris:** For me, it was a good experience just as far as getting the preparation and knowledge about college. Before then, I only knew what I saw on tv from watching sports. I had some uncles that went to college but I didn't know much. It was a good chance to learn about college and it was a opportunity for me to go to college. And, possibly make more money to help out my family.
>
> **DB:** What kinds of preparation and knowledge did you get about college?
>
> **Chris:** Ah man, one of the main things was just knowing more schools in general. I remember we had like the first day [of freshman year], I'm assuming other classes had to do this, but we had to write down all the colleges that we knew. I think I wrote down about twenty to forty and I only knew those schools mainly because of sports, but I didn't know anything about those schools. I didn't know what portion of the state they were in or anything like that. Also, having a college counselor who had worked in college admissions helped tremendously because he was able to give more of the behind the scenes things about admissions that I definitely wouldn't have found out.

As several of these young men mentioned, the school culture at Ellis Academy was centered on increasing students' access to higher education. As Chris noted, students were engaged in activities that helped them reflect on their own prior knowledge about college and provided information throughout their schooling years that helped expand their knowledge as well. Given that Chris identified attending Ellis Academy as an "opportunity for me to get to college," his academic practices, attention, and performance were geared toward performing well as a way to increase his college options.

As it was for Jamal, attending a summer college program was a critical experience for Chris's college-going maturation. Going into his second (tenth grade) year, and based on his high academic achievement in his first year, he was approached by his college counselor about participating in a weeklong summer college program at Georgetown University.

> The Georgetown [University] program specifically, probably the reason I wanted to go to it, I don't know how much they told me about it, it gave me a chance to travel and experience new things. I think it was like a week. It was interesting, it was a very diverse environment; it's what made me think about diversity in college in terms of this is how it would be. I met a lot of international students, so that piqued my interest. It was a good experience; it was very different. My neighborhood, my school, it didn't look like this. I met folks from Honduras, I met folks from Sri Lanka; my roommate was from Mizzou [Missouri]. I was slowly learning about these environments. Well, I didn't know about all of these countries. Learning about these people and these countries was really good. These folks were some academic beasts! Folks were my age sounding like they were seniors or in college already!

The firsthand experiences that Chris enjoyed during this immersion program inspired some of his academic efforts in the following year. In particular, his exposure to peers from various national and international backgrounds expanded his thinking regarding diversity in college and the potential types of academic environments that he could experience. Engaging with peers whom he thought were more educationally and intellectually mature motivated him and gave him a glimpse of his own potential as well.

In conjunction with programs and activities, Chris specifically identified his teachers as pivotal motivators, instructors, and guides for his schooling experiences and educational aspirations. He recalled that these individuals along with his mentor constantly provided academic and personal support that helped him raise his level of academic self-expectations.

> **Chris:** Overall, for the most part, I've had good relationships with most of my teachers and they tried to help me do better—or, perform to the best of my abilities. Like, "Hey, if you were present in school more often you can do much better." So, they just wanted me to do well and they wanted me to succeed. They tried to push me. In elementary [school], I never had that experience. I didn't have people pushing me

to do better and wanting me to succeed. So, it made me a better student and I wanted to succeed.

DB: How did your teachers pushing you make you want to succeed?

Chris: I think my teachers played a critical role in my development and success in high school—and in the future. The fact that they weren't pushing me to do all right in classes but to do well because I had the potential to go much further. That was something that was great for me, having a support system that I hadn't had before. It was great for me as a young Black male from the inner-city, I had so many obstacles out there and so many things could trip me up. It was just motivation for me to want to do well because other people cared about me and they put in their time and effort for me to do so.

Early in tenth grade, Chris missed some school while one of his parents faced some challenging health complications. He mentioned that he was saddened at times when considering what potential deteriorating health could mean for his family in general and himself personally. In trying to navigate and make sense of different potential outcomes, and in dealing with the emotional and psychological stress this experience induced, Chris missed a number of school days—typically one day a week—and, in several instances he arrived at school so late that he missed his first one or two classes. Given the quality of the relationships that he developed with his teachers, and because he was embedded in a caring schooling environment, Chris received critical support and nurturing from his teachers. He shared his experiences with a few teachers, and they allowed him to stay after school late to work on several assignments; he also met with teachers during his lunch period. These opportunities helped him stay afloat academically so that he did not fall behind; additionally, these relationships and the understanding he received from teachers also were pivotal, especially since he was dealing with some stressors and emotional strain based on family experiences and personal issues.

Even as he was learning to cope with these external challenges, which in some ways adversely affected his academic performance, Chris tried to keep some of his focus on his schooling efforts. The supportive relationships and environment that he was embedded in at school provided essential support; and because he was able to exceed a 3.0 GPA that semester, Chris believed he could attain educational success. The support he received throughout his secondary school years enhanced his academic motivations, strengthened his persistence, and emboldened his college aspirations. Chris specifically benefited from high-quality relationships with some of his teachers, and he noted their high expectations; being pushed and expected to perform better was consonant with his burgeoning academic identity.

In specifically referring to how he was pushed, Chris, who considered himself a "decent writer," learned values about the importance of consistently completing and submitting high-quality work through his interactions and relationships with his teachers. "Teachers helped me with writing. I remember a teacher, he probably shouldn't have used this language, but he pretty much told me that my paper was BS. He said it was garbage [laughing in agreement] and I knew that it was! He said I could do better and that was helpful because he believed that I could do better and he held me to a standard. So, I think those things helped me prepare." Ultimately, above and beyond his own aptitude and ability, Chris credited Ellis Academy's school culture and the relationships he had with school personnel with helping him maintain high self-expectations and in preparing him for college.

Chauncey: "The whole college bound thing, that's the goal"

As we discussed factors that contributed to his college going, Chauncey continued to center our conversation on Ellis Academy's school culture. He believed that the conversations at school and even the decorations within the school all contributed to keep students reminded that getting to college was a fundamental goal of the school. For instance, he recalled the banners that adorned classrooms, teacher and staff offices, and the hallways as visual representations of the students' possibilities for higher education.

> That was cool, too! That just shows you that college is right there. And if they were to do college banners based on the schools we went to that would be good, too. It subliminally put college right there so that you could see it, so that you didn't think it was far away. It was like you just have to put the work in and you could be at one of those schools. I liked having the banners up.

As Chauncey and several of the young men discussed, these college banners spoke to many of the students personally and connected with their educational and personal goals. In speaking about college banners in the school, Jamal described them as "a sign of motivation," while Julius remarked, "Those were pretty dope because when it came to colleges that you wanted to apply to you saw it. College was all around you; it was pretty cool seeing the college banners all around you." Along the same lines, Paul revealed that he was so motivated by the symbolic power the banners conveyed that he wanted to secure one for himself through college graduation as a representation of his achievements: "I want to have one of these banners in my house or home one day. In order to do that, I gotta go earn. I don't want one off-line [the internet], I gotta earn it. I want to get one and make my family proud."

Important in Chauncey's and Paul's statements was their point regarding the discipline and effort that students needed to engage to help make attending college a reality. Chauncey compared his experiences at both Arnold High and Ellis to make sense of Ellis Academy's academic reputation and what they offer students. He reflected:

> In some subjects it was pretty hard, but I wouldn't say it was as hard as Arnold [High] but I wouldn't say it was easy either. We had homework pretty much every day, maybe not in every class but always something to do. The teachers at Ellis were nice, they would help you out. You would get individual help from teachers and they really cared. They might be a little more lenient with the grades and helping to make sure that you got stuff in. But, at Arnold, they didn't care. It was like, "No, it's due today; if you don't turn it in then you get a zero." I had a whole bunch of zeroes.

Unlike his experiences at Arnold High, Chauncey identified teacher care as a critical component of his schooling experience at Ellis Academy. In being provided with "individual help" to assist with the academic expectations, Chauncey believed that teachers not only desired for students to do well but also helped prepare students for college. "We had a lot of AP classes and stuff; I know a lot of that prepared me for college. Like, in AP English, we were writing fifteen-page papers which really prepared me for college. And, the way they set up the classes is how college is."

Chauncey believed that the structure of the classes he took along with the assignments and workload helped orient students toward college expectations. He continued to refer to writing intensive classes that he took as significant in embodying college-going expectations, which provided him with insight on what he might need to do to prepare for and succeed in college. "The work, having to do your work [and] the workload. There was a lot of work and we had to get it done. Classes, they really challenged you, especially the writing classes with Ms. Scott [pseudonym; a middle-aged Black woman who served as an AP English teacher]; she really challenged you. Ms. Scott's class was more intense than some of the classes I've had here [in college]." This schooling environment, including the course offerings and the academic expectations, helped instill in students like Chauncey that their academic focus—such as study habits, managing course workload, completing complex assignments—was paramount for success. Beyond specific classes, he asserted that some of what students could focus on to help them prepare for and get to college was high-quality academic performance: "Really the study habits; you have to put your work first. The whole college bound thing, that's the goal, so the only way to get there is to perform well in the classroom."

Summary

This chapter focused on how the young men in this study made sense of attending a college preparatory secondary school. The goal was not to try to identify an exhaustive list of experiences that contributed to the young men's college going, but rather to pay attention to how they made sense of their school-related endeavors within the context of aspiring to go to college. Overwhelmingly, according to the young men, the stated mission of the school helped establish and center their expectations. The school's focus on sending Black boys to college aligned well with these young men's educational aspirations (as shown in Michael's statement, "That's the reason I went!"). There were a number of elements that helped spark and sustain these young men's aspirations and, at the same time, various facets of their secondary school experiences helped get or keep them on a pathway to college. Beyond the mission, the ongoing conversations with school staff and the representations of college within the school building helped keep college within students' purview even without explicit conversations. Additionally, regardless of students' backgrounds and early impressions about college, these representations were explicit statements about what students' academic focus should reveal: getting to college.

Being embedded in an environment that included rituals and routines that affirmed and declared that Black boys were "college bound" was empowering to each of these young men. Researchers identify that these types of environments are meaningful for helping Black boys and boys of color in enhancing their schooling experiences, helping them access college, and empowering their sense of belonging and resilience.[4] With the institutional mission and expectation communicated clearly, and in conjunction with their own college aspirations, these young men began to formulate, identify, and learn about how to make their college-going aspirations even more tangible. For some young men, like Michael and Jamal, this meant taking college-oriented and college-level courses, such as Advanced Placement. Even though they "knew" that college would be hard or that Advanced Placement and honors courses were rigorous academically, these young men identified these course types as desirable because they believed it would prepare them for college—both from a skillset perspective and in their content. These courses challenged the young men to think more deeply about course-related material, engage with more complex information and assignments, and demanded significant attention and focus.

Another facet of their school-related experiences that helped support (or even amplify) the young men's educational desires was their relationships and interactions with teachers, mentors, and institutional agents. Beyond some of these young men stating explicitly that they wanted to be pushed, their narratives also reveal that teachers helped empower students through their teaching, support, and expectations. That their teachers held high academic expectations and continuously pushed these young men is noteworthy for several reasons. For one thing, these expectations were embedded in trusting and caring relationships. At least in retrospect, the young men identified these pushes either as a desire or as a need. For some young men, being pushed academically contributed to their college-going mindset: college courses would be difficult, and probably more difficult than secondary school classes, and they must be prepared mentally for such demands. Moreover, being pushed academically, whether by course content, teachers' expectations, or both, contributed to these young men's academic confidence, self-efficacy, and sense of self.

Their ability to navigate these demands successfully could be banked as material experience and also could be called upon as firsthand knowledge during their college years.

Finally, each of the young men believed they were a "better student" because of these challenging academic experiences, through their relationships with peers and teachers or mentors, and because of the guidance and support they received—even when they faced setbacks and challenges. They scripted resilience into their sense of self in being able to respond to their academic challenges; they saw, learned, and reaffirmed their "potential to be somebody" because of the investments that teachers poured into them; and they took all these lessons and experiences with them into their college years. Researchers continue to note the benefits of rigorous academic preparation during the secondary school years as critical preparation for college.[5] For instance, education scholar Pedro Noguera asserted that too many Black boys "are excluded from rigorous classes and prevented from accessing educational opportunities that might otherwise support and encourage them."[6]

In addition to coursework, some of which was rigorous, some young men participated in a variety of college summer programs. Regardless of the subject matter, program design, or length of the program, all the young men declared that the overarching and most significant benefits they garnered from these experiences was exposure to college. The young men noted that gaining exposure to college institutions, similar to the HBCU college tour that Chauncey participated in (discussed in chapter 2), helped them envision themselves as students in college. These experiences provided them with firsthand knowledge that helped them see that they could perform at a college level, demystify college and college life, learn more about major areas of study, and build community with other young people. Also important was the fact that participating in these programs could allow students to self-assess their academic engagement and effort and discern how it might align with their program-based experiences.

Collectively, the schooling environment, messaging, and support, the academic opportunities, and their peer relationships helped them develop, build, and expand their college-going mindsets. For these young men, a college-going mindset must be anchored in a school culture that includes: (a) exposure to critical information about college, incorporating specific information about institutional types so that students can learn about higher education options and also being informed about completing the application process and demystifying the financial aid process as well;

(b) academic coursework that revealed and aligned students' secondary school experiences with what they might experience in college; and (c) educational opportunities beyond their school, such as opportunities to participate in college immersion programs and garner firsthand experiences on college campuses. In the next chapters, I turn my attention to these young men's higher education experiences.

PART II

COLLEGIATE EXPERIENCES

Chapter 5

"I knew I was gon' struggle"

Stories and Expectations of College Struggles

> Second semester [of my first year], I was taking four classes and I failed half of them. It was the first time I had failed classes of any kind. I was upset. These classes were taught by the same professor and I felt like I was being targeted. It was nothing I could do, so I had to take the classes again. I took them and I got B's the next time around and it just showed my resilience. Freshman year, academics weren't where they were supposed to be and it really showed me how much harder I needed to work.
>
> —Malik

In sharp contrast to research labeling young Black males as ambivalent toward education and lacking drive or determination, the students in this study weaved their resilience and aspirations into their educational narratives and sense of self. Given the challenges that Black youth, including the young men in this study, face in navigating their secondary school years, the need to be resilient in the face of and in response to obstacles can be imperative for reaching their educational goals. In this chapter, I explore these young men's potential and promise through some of the challenges they anticipated and experienced during their transition and college experiences. Important here is their first-generation college status and their knowledge of college, which can impact the forms of capital at students' disposal to assist them in building networks and navigating college.[1]

In sharing his early college experiences, Malik acknowledged that he struggled academically in his first year. Specifically, he failed half the classes he attempted in his second semester, and these academic shortcomings were new experiences that created self-doubts and anxieties regarding his educational goals. In the face of these struggles, though, Malik, like the other young men in this study, continued to pursue his possibilities and sense of self. Their personhood and character both were challenged. The young men learned valuable lessons in these struggles and revealed parts of their interiorities in making sense of their experiences. This sense of awareness speaks to these young men's self-authoring ways of knowing, particularly in becoming authors of their lives and their internal foundations.[2] For Malik, the ability to respond positively to academic struggles was reminiscent of his secondary school experiences. Thus, he scripted resilience in his self-narrative ("it just showed my resilience") and, at the same time, he viewed these struggles as a direct lesson regarding the attention and increased academic effort needed to accomplish some of his educational goals.

Malik's narrative helps identify and frame some of the academic challenges these young men experienced during their transition to college and the early college years. In particular, they viewed struggles as connected to their burgeoning sense of self. Some of the young men transitioned to college anticipating that they would struggle academically. Some of this struggle was connected to their performances during their secondary school years. While each had accomplished a great deal academically, they each relayed experiences they had had that undermined their academic confidence. In addition, they each discussed a number of ways in which they harbored anxieties during their transition and early college years. Some of the young men discussed relying on messages from their families, teachers, and community that helped them strategize and prepare for college. Others noted that the institutions they attended demanded increased focus and efforts for their academic performances. Across the range of their experiences, these young men showed themselves to be deeply reflective of and proactive toward becoming themselves.

Stories and Expectations of Struggle

In the sections that follow, I share parts of these men's lives and narratives that reveal stories and expectations of struggle. For some these struggles were anticipated, while for others the struggles were new. In both cases, their struggles required action and (re)strategizing regarding their academic focus and efforts. These young men extracted two critical lessons from their experiences. The first lesson was that struggle does not define who they are. While their family histories were dynamic and complex and their socioeconomic backgrounds may have posed some limitations, neither of these factors could limit their educational pursuits automatically. The second lesson that these young men's narratives reveal is that failure is not final. Throughout this chapter, I share parts of these young men's stories that include feeling lost and isolated on campus, experiencing anxieties because of the academic rigor at their respective college or chosen area of study, and dealing with and responding to poor academic performances. It is significant that these young men's narratives also reveal that they are in the process of actualizing their promise and potential.

Michael: "I knew I was gon' struggle"

For some young men, like Michael and Malik, academic "struggles" were identified as part of their educational journeys—from secondary school to college. In part, some of this identification was through their own secondary school experiences, personal and academic challenges that they faced, and, to a degree, the concerns they held as they entered college. In talking with Michael about his educational journey, and his college years particularly, his first-year experiences proved to be full of tensions that included excitement and stress, challenges and triumphs, and self-questioning and a burgeoning sense of agency.

> **Michael:** My first year in college was fun. It was fun because I cried, I laughed, I fell, I succeeded, I learned, I've forgotten; it was the total package. I can't say it was just one emotion; it was a bunch of people, a whole bunch of experiences. It was what it was supposed to be and that's why I can say it was fun. I struggled my first year but I learned; my sophomore year was way better.
>
> **DB:** Talk to me about crying, what made you cry?
>
> **Michael:** I was homesick. But at the same time, I just missed being where I'm from. It wasn't like, "Oh, I miss my momma." I missed what my home city had to offer; I missed things that

> weren't there [on or near campus and] that I wasn't home. All that made me homesick. I started missing all those things—such as my favorite restaurants. The fact that it wasn't a dope breakfast spot in my college's city, I'm a little salty right now.
>
> **DB:** How did you get over being homesick?
>
> **Michael:** Just deal with it, just one of those suck-it-up type things. 'Cuz I didn't want to go home. I liked being able to talk about different things that mattered and I liked learning about new things. I wasn't gonna get that at home; well, I didn't think I would. Plus, being at home would just put me right back in challenging situations that I wasn't tryna be in.
>
> **DB:** Talk about failing.
>
> **Michael:** Grades weren't what they should've been. You talk about social failure, I had a girlfriend when I left home. Me leaving, that obviously put a strain on that relationship. Me not going to school with my best friends, that made it difficult too. I knew we wasn't gon' be the best friends that talk every day [during our college years], but I really missed being with them when I got to college. That's something that I wish I could change and I wish I could have. Just those relationships, you tell those brothers that you love them.

The relationships that Michael enjoyed and relied on during his secondary school years, especially with those whom he considered as his best friends, provided him with ongoing and consistent support—academically, personally, relationally, and socially. These "brothers" helped sharpen his academic focus and sense of purpose, they joined together in scholastic sports, and they often spent time together after school and on weekends. During their second year of high school, these friends banded together and adopted the moniker of "the four brothers." This was an affirmation that signified the importance of their relationship and it was a statement of commitment to each other as well. Thus, his use of the word "brothers" speaks to the depth and value of their relationships, relates to the ways in which they depended and counted on one another, and also relates to how sticking together helped them navigate a range of neighborhood challenges to pursue their educational goals. For each of the young men in this study, their male peer relationships during their secondary school years enhanced both their sense of mattering and their sense of self.[3]

Michael's discussion of being homesick reveals a number of ways in which he felt a void and gap in his transition to college as well as his relationships and proximity to family and friends. This relational distance also was exacerbated by his physical distance from his hometown and the temporary separation from fond memories and meaningful places. His homesickness was amplified by his early college experiences, especially those that led to his emotions and expressiveness ("I cried") and academic struggles (grades). Additionally, his response to just "suck it up" also speaks to his growing sense of independence and is harbored in his assertion that he "didn't want to go home." A critical component of Michael's laughing, learning, and succeeding during his first year was the shared experiences he garnered in the community he had developed.

Beyond a general conversation, we also specifically discussed his academic and social experiences during his first year of college. In reflecting on his first-year academic experiences, Michael recollected:

> I knew I was gon' struggle, which made that fall a little bit graceful. I knew it was gon' be some things that I just really wasn't prepared for. My first class, Monday morning, was Comparative Politics. See, what was I doing in that class? [laugh] I got an A in that class though. We didn't have any readings over the summer and the first thing this dude [the professor] does is roll into class like we had class yesterday. I was that lost! Luckily, I had one of my teammates in class with me. She said, "Boy, you look lost!" If it wasn't for that, she was a junior and she sensed that, that helped. Me, I wasn't panicking; I was just like, "I'mma sit back and take notes and see what everybody else was saying." I knew I was gon' fail; that's a different 3.0 right there. Not to take away from high school, that's different.

It is interesting that Michael both sensed and anticipated academic struggles in his transition to college. He questioned his decision about taking a political science course as his first class on Monday mornings. Some of his challenges were self-induced, such as course selection and class schedule. Even though Michael "knew [he] was gon' struggle," he disclosed that he "wasn't panicking" but at the same time he had decided to "sit back and take notes and see what everybody else was saying" and doing in class. At least in one of his classes, Comparative Politics, Michael lacked a solid understanding of the professor's teaching and expectations, and his confusion and lack of clarity were evident to those around him, including one friend who was his classmate and teammate.

Michael's social experiences in transitioning to his college were informed primarily by the college's culture and racial demographics. In speaking about his social experiences and social networks, and given the predominantly white campus culture at the college he attended, he considered his experiences through the lens of attending a college with a very different institutional and cultural context than what he was familiar with previously. Michael explained:

> If I went to an HBCU, it would probably be difficult because there is no minority. At Adams College [pseudonym], Black was a minority. So if you see a Black face, you count the Black faces you see because you can identify. You looking for them and they're looking for you; so, we were just there, we were latching onto each other. We were close because we closely identified with each other. We all identified with each other closely because we were from similar backgrounds. So, socially, it was easy for me to find friends and I ran track so that helped. Socially, at the college campus, I was able to flourish. That's that open-minded freedom; I can create this identity for myself.

According to Michael, his first-year social experiences were marked by the small number of Black students on campus and the ways in which many of these students sometimes felt racially or culturally isolated. Black students accounted for about nine percent of the overall student population. His statement that many Black students "count the Black faces you see because you can identify" affirms the desire that some students feel in developing and being connected to a community of people with whom they shared racial identity, which suggested common experiences or desires. For some Black students, and students of color more broadly, attending predominantly white institutions can challenge their sense of belonging, and they often have to rely on each other to help stave off feelings of isolation and loneliness.[4] Michael benefited from his ability to develop relationships through his athletic participation and he felt he was "able to flourish" socially given the ease that he was able to connect with others and navigate social life on campus, at least initially. Still, even though he expressed enjoying comfort in some aspects of the social arena on campus, which may have buffered some of the sense of isolation he experienced, these social experiences did not diminish or make up for his academic struggles, challenges, and self-doubts.

Malik: "It was a lot for me to learn"

A number of the young men in this study also discussed various ways in which they experienced struggles during college, especially in their transition to college and their early college years. For several young men, including Michael, some of these struggles were related to the predominantly white campus climate and their attempts to navigate these campuses as white spaces. For young men like Malik and Edwin, their concerns most prominently focused on their perceptions of their abilities to succeed academically given the academic reputations of the schools that they attended.

My interviews with Malik began the summer prior to his transition to college. During this time, he focused on enjoying his summer by ensuring that he spent time with family and friends and he also gave time to making some final preparations before leaving for college, which was about three hours away. Tilton College (a pseudonym), the small, private liberal arts college that he was preparing to attend, was located in a small rural city in a neighboring state; Tilton is renowned for its academic instruction, is ranked in the top fifty of national liberal arts colleges, and is also ranked nationally for student experiences (e.g., best classroom experience).

Malik was impressed with the school and what he believed it had to offer students based on his college visit, conversations with students and staff there, and discussions with his mentor and college counselor.

> I loved my visit! I got a tour of the campus, met with football and swimming coaches. I met with some students and attended a class. It was a two-hour class and I liked it. Felt like it was just like my senior year British Lit class; I felt like I didn't need to adapt that much because it was discussion-based and I really liked that aspect of class. I feel like I know the campus already. The campus is great and the community is great.

In considering the differences that he anticipated between his secondary school years and what he might experience in college, Malik noted that it would be "very different . . . there will be no one telling me that you have to do this or that. I know for sure that academics will be more rigorous. It'll be a new life away from home." He also benefited from conversations with several Tilton alumni who affirmed the academic rigors that he would face and they encouraged him as well. "Just from, you know, word of mouth, what I heard and what I'd been told. Everybody was telling me that college was a lot harder [and] you'll get homesick. They told me that I had to buckle down [academically] and don't hang my head. I talked to a lot of alumni who are from a similar area as me and they told me that it would be hard but that I could make it." These early conversations with alumni helped Malik develop and expand his social and cultural capital. Being connected with alumni provided Malik with opportunities to learn from peers who had navigated the college successfully and could speak from their firsthand experiences. They offered him suggestions and guidance on what to expect at the college. In conversations with students in the upper classes, he learned that "the school gets kind of depressing in November and December because of all of the work." While he appreciated the guidance and information he also acknowledged, "I just don't want that to happen to me."

At the beginning of his college career, Malik shared concerns of a number of young men in this study related to their academic performances, social status, and fit into the college culture. He shared, "I was sorta concerned about my abilities to succeed; I was concerned about my social status. I knew I wasn't going to go to an HBCU, I knew I was going to go to a college that was predominantly white. So, I just had to kind of think about how I was gon' fit in. So, it was academics and social." Malik's concerns about his academic performance and social status both are important to note. Academically, he harbored concerns about his ability to perform well even before he got to college, which primarily was based on his self-acknowledged need to improve his study and writing skills as well as his need to adjust to the academic rigor quickly. He noted that he was "fifty-fifty" in his college preparation and foresaw "maybe learning how to study" as one of the obstacles he thought he might encounter in his transition to college. He went on and acknowledged, "I wasn't sure . . . I didn't know what I would need help with. When I got here I needed a little help with just about everything. I think it would be difficult with the college I went to; it was writing intensive."

Michael's discussions of his struggles in his first year of college and his transition, were echoed by Malik and several other young men. Given the student demographics and cultural environment of his college, Malik spent time considering how he would fit into and establish a sense of belonging within the predominantly white campus culture. In managing his concerns, especially with regard to connecting with some of his college peers, he noted, "The social one [concern] withered away pretty soon. I played two fall sports and that gave me some friendships right there." Although he was able to navigate some of his concerns about his social status during his transition to college through his athletic participation, Malik's academic concerns required much more time, effort, adjustment, and learning. "First year of college to me was a struggle. I say it was a struggle because it was a lot for me to learn and a lot for me to catch up on. It was great for me in a sense because there were a lot of resources on campus. I joined the Berry Institute for Black World Studies here on campus. But, for academics, I kinda struggled." Part of Malik's learning was becoming more aware of and using available resources on campus that were targeted to Black students. Similar to how he benefited socially through athletic participation, his engagement in the Berry Institute for Black World Studies [a pseudonym] helped him develop a community on campus. The Berry Institute offers cocurricular, cultural, and social programs from a broad perspective of Black experiences—including historic, contemporary, local and global—throughout Africa and the Diaspora. The Berry Institute served as a critical resource on campus where students identified it as a type of "homeplace" and even acknowledged it as an important site for Black placemaking.[5] For Malik, this community was important in holistic ways as his engagement helped smooth some of his transition experiences, helped him access and learn more about campus resources, and assisted him in developing relationships with peers and key institutional agents who provided support as well. He noted, "The academic thing came through time, just learning how to be a student, at Tilton specifically. Learning that edge and the ability to do things that I thought I'd never do just sort of comes with time."

Malik's anticipated challenges were realized as he engaged in coursework and academic life on campus. Most notably, in discussing his first year of college, he specifically highlighted "struggles" as the main component of his experiences. One specific area of challenge and potential growth for Malik was his performances in his written work. He learned of his need to develop his writing skills at the onset of his transition to college. He specifically identified writing assignments as the primary source of his academic challenges during his early college experiences.

> They were absolutely tough. . . . Actually [laughs in astonishment], my first year was my only year that I actually turned my paper in on time just because I was afraid to fail. I'd say that those papers I did my freshman year were probably the worst papers I've ever done! [laughs at himself] I opened up some papers from my freshman year and I was like, "What was going on? Did I even read?" [laughs and shakes his side-to-side in disbelief]. So I knew that it was going to be a process to this thing.

Based on his overall academic performance, in some regards, Malik's academic struggles lasted throughout each semester and throughout his college years. These early college experiences were times that the young men continuously (re)negotiated and established their academic approach, strategies, and behaviors. In some ways, because he was "afraid to fail" Malik's academic performances may have been impacted negatively by his concerns, which created some stressors and tensions in his academic efforts. Some of these performances, including writing some of his "worst papers" and wondering if he "even read," also relate to the self-questions that he harbored in his early years and that lingered throughout his college years.

Important in the young men's development was learning through their experiences. This learning was pertinent to their personal development, academic performances, and their sense of becoming. For students like Malik, being stretched academically took time to get adjusted to and provided him with opportunities to learn "how to be a college student." This acknowledgment proved to be a critical learning opportunity as it was a revelation that informed his help-seeking behaviors and academic focus. This was expressed best in his explanation about learning how to be a college student.

> Just, uh, just learning what it takes to succeed. Even if it means getting all Cs, I needed to learn what Tilton students needed to do to pass the classes that are here. One thing that I learned that is different from going to a state school,

> you really don't get large papers at those schools like you get at Tilton. It's no reason to be upset; so I sorta gave up my opportunity to be a social butterfly [laughs in amusement] and instead worked on my ability to express things in a written form. I think it worked out for the best.

Malik discussed his learning not simply through content, but even more specifically through his experiences and the knowledge he gained from his trials and efforts. It is significant that he did not place pressure on himself with regard to trying to achieve a specific grade point average, which can have drawbacks; instead, he recalibrated his aspirations by placing a focus squarely on learning more about himself so that he could accomplish his goals. By reframing his focus and accepting that the academic rigor at his college meant making sacrifices in his social life, Malik put greater emphasis on learning how to be successful in college and strengthening his writing skills given his chosen social sciences major and the liberal arts focus of his college.

EDWIN: "AM I SMART ENOUGH?"

In conjunction with the struggles these young men anticipated that college might present, students such as Edwin talked about internal dilemmas, which are based on individuals' "beliefs about their own cognitive, academic, or personality-based attributes."[6] These young men identified college as an opportunity to help them reach some of their educational goals even as they developed their educational aspirations.

Edwin and I talked about a range of topics related to his college experiences. During the early parts of our interviews about his college experiences, we discussed his transition to college and his academic and social experiences on campus during his early years. Throughout Edwin's school years, he tried to reconcile his results on various standardized tests with his own self-perceptions and thoughts about himself. Overall, because he did not perform as well as he wanted to or thought he could, he expressed frustration and developed some anxieties about these tests. During one of our conversations we talked about his ACT score. In the following excerpt, Edwin explains at length how his performance on the ACT impacted his academic self-perceptions and his beliefs about being able to attend a four-year college.

> Statistics shows, when it comes down to Edwin Johnson that he's not quite good at taking standardized tests. I figured it out a long time ago. You know, in eighth grade you take the State Assessment Test; I didn't score high enough. But, our scores didn't come back in time but they had to go back to the previous scores and I had like a 68 percent and you needed to be at a 70 percent. In high school, we had a test and I know I bombed that! It was just a test to see where your reading level for English was. We constantly had these tests. If it's a test that I can study for, I'm good; if it's like these state tests I'm not good. If you say there's no wrong answer but you're getting judged on these tests, then how do you make sense of that? I felt okay taking it [the ACT].
>
> First time I had a 15 on the practice tests and that was without studying. I said, "Okay, if I do a little studying and maybe I can get a 18 or something like that." So, I studied a little, went to bed early and did everything I was supposed to do. I got the first test back and I got a 15. I was like, "Man, that's not good!" The thing about those tests is that they don't tell you where you didn't do well on. [The second time I took it], I'm cramming and I didn't do well again. So, then I was like it's the environment. So, I figured let me change the environment and I can do better. But, it didn't work out like that either so I was stuck with the 15 score. And, at the conclusion, I was like, "I'm not fit for this type of test; some things you're not good at and I'm not good at standardized tests." People were like, "Just take it again" and I said, "I took it three times." I guess it's gon' be 99.9 percent of people going to college. Every time somebody say something about ACT scores I used to be so ashamed.

Given these challenging experiences that Edwin endured related to standardized test taking, he developed some self-doubts about his academic ability and how he thought he might be able to compete with college students. Prior to attending college, he revealed:

> My thoughts about college, I was ready to the point to where it became second nature to me being by myself and on my own. That wasn't the scary part; I was doing that already. It

> was more of a "Am I able to compete?" at the same level as these kids that I don't know or know where they're from? It became an image thing with who did I want to portray; did I want to portray this Black male kid from the hood or did I want to try to fit in?

For Edwin, considerations about whether he could compete with other students academically weighed on his psyche as he transitioned to college and tried to figure out how and where he might belong on campus. These questions led to some initial struggles during his transition to college as he worked to acclimate himself to the campus's social milieu and academic demands.

Edwin shared with me his self-appraisal throughout our conversations. In particular, he mentioned that he was concerned about his academic preparation for college:

> One concern, am I smart enough? You know, I barely just got by in high school—at least from my standpoint. I don't believe that I was fully academically prepared for what college had to offer. And, it was kinda frustrating to where I didn't technically know what college I was gon' go to and it became unrealistic to me every time I thought about it. But me being fully academically prepared for college, I didn't think I was ready for it.

Considering young Black men's self-appraisals is important because they provide critical insight on how they think about themselves and their capabilities. Edwin's self-doubts were a combination of factors and experiences. Not only did his performance on standardized tests shake his academic confidence, he also was concerned about his ability to compete with his peers and about the college selection process. All these thoughts, accompanied by significant financial concerns and worries about being supported by his family, coalesced into Edwin's stated frustration and his acknowledgment that he was not fully academically prepared for college.

During his first year in college, Edwin tried to buffer himself from these academic concerns by shifting his approach to his academic work as well his academic success strategies. "I just tried to do well, you know, do the best I knew how. Tried to retain information better than I did in high school. I wrote stuff down, tried to do as many notes as I could and taking advantage of the student resource center and tutoring and stuff like that to allow me to put myself in the best position to pass my classes and stuff like that." The first significant change in Edwin's approach from high school to college was his mindset. Whereas he primarily focused on his athletic identity and performances during his secondary school years, once in college he gave even greater priority to performing well academically and meeting the academic demands of his college. He explained that his first-year experience made for "probably the most memorable year," primarily because "that was the year of me finding my own way to survive on a more mature level." After failing one of his classes in his first semester, he was placed on academic probation.

> It sucked! I was on the watch list to where I actually lost my, I was gon' lose my academic scholarship if I didn't make a change or a choice that I wanted to get better. When you on a scholarship most people don't think about that, that you have to perform in the classroom at a high level. I didn't really think about it. I had to retake some classes. I took a twelve-credit load and I got nine credits that semester, so that sucked knowing that eventually I know I'm gon' have to make up those classes. I was trying to cheat the system; I was barely going to class and I wasn't doing everything I needed in my classes. So, the probation was a reflection of the work that I was doing that semester.

Edwin took full accountability of his academic performance and noted that both the grades he received and his probation status were both earned.

He responded to this early setback by refocusing his academic effort and acknowledged, "It was just that I already knew I was smart in certain classes that I knew I shoulda been passing in." The next semester Edwin earned a 3.5 GPA. He credited his academic turnaround to a more detail-oriented approach and sharper focus. "For example, one class I failed I got an A in the next semester. So I was like, 'How come I didn't do this the first semester and I didn't have to waste my time?' I knew it was gon' be some challenging classes at my college. I just made a few adjustments, made some changes with my daily planning." Due to his strong academic performances in his second semester, Edwin was inspired to continue his academic strategies and maintain his academic focus into his second year of college. His first year triggered some of the academic and family concerns that he held prior to attending and once in college he had to learn how to navigate, manage, and overcome these concerns. What helped, primarily, was a shift in his mindset and effort for his academic work, developing relationships with peers and college personnel who provided important support, and getting a job on campus to help alleviate some of his financial anxieties.

Jamal: "I thought I was well prepared"

Jamal was a high-achieving student during his secondary school years, which was accentuated by earning Dean's List acknowledgments across multiple years, numerous academic awards, and over twenty-five college acceptances. Jamal was motivated by "knowing that I had the potential to be something" or, what Paul Johnson has described as somebodiness—a "sense of worth, purpose, and community."[7] As part of his experiences and accomplishments, he also noted "I surprised some people in high school and I surprised myself sometimes too." I restate these points here because they are important to how Jamal thought about himself and his possibilities as he transitioned to college and they also relate to why he applied to thirty colleges.

In discussing the college application process, he explained, "At first, I wanted to go to a historically Black college or university. I got accepted to a lot of them or a good deal of them. I actually chose one, which is Morehouse in Atlanta." Similar to what Chauncey expressed, one of Jamal's primary concerns as he prepared for college was how he would afford tuition and other expenses. Knowing that his family did not have the financial resources to afford high tuition costs, Jamal acknowledged that he strongly considered taking a year off before attending college and gave some consideration to joining the military as a way to pursue his higher education goals. "I mean I wanted to go to college because of all that I experienced in high school. But, I really didn't know how I was gon' pay for it so I was thinking, 'Why not go into the military?' "

Jamal's thoughts about which college to attend changed when he was accepted to what he considered his "dream school." This acceptance also induced a second primary concern, his academic preparation and his ability to succeed academically. He stated, "This university was my dream school but I didn't know if I could make it. But I talked to my track coach and my college counselor and they helped me figure out what was best for me." Jamal received strong encouragement from his track coach and college counselor, both of whom he viewed as otherfathers.[8] Besides his family, he relied on these two Black men for critical guidance and support throughout his secondary school experiences and through his postsecondary years as well. He relied on this community to help him discern opportunities and choices in his life; thus, his point that these individuals helped him decide "what was best" for him reflects the trust in their relationship and the prominence of these relationships in his life. This support enhanced Jamal's sense of self and his somebodiness, it also helped strengthened his academic and personal confidence that he could accomplish his educational goals.

In our conversations about his preparation for college, we initially discussed messages that he received about navigating college and trying to accomplish his goals. In our exchange below, Jamal shared one of the messages he received from his mother:

> **Jamal:** Just, when I get to college, don't try to change myself because I'm in a different environment. And, it'll be hard to try to fit in with a lot of people, especially financially. Also, academically, don't try to change myself either, just push forward and I'll be all right.
>
> **DB:** What did your mother mean by don't change yourself?
>
> **Jamal:** I feel like, that she made an excellent point because I see a lot of people here trying to be like people that they're not. I see a lot of African Americans from the suburbs and they're trying to act like they're from the inner-city and they look like fools. And, my mom was right, I shouldn't have to change myself to try to fit in for nothing.

Jamal engaged in a number of conversations with his mother about navigating college; some of these conversations centered on his sense of self. On further reflection, he interpreted a number of these conversations as lessons that he could learn from and apply during his college years. These types of conversations with his mother provided Jamal with critical insights that he believed could help him stay true to himself and stay focused on his goals during his college years. He valued this insight and drew significant inspiration from his mother's own efforts. Jamal's mother returned to college during his secondary school years and as a returning student with valuable knowledge from her life experiences, which included raising Jamal and his two brothers with the help of her own mother, she examined education from a very practical standpoint. She understood college to be an important opportunity for social mobility and, at the same time, she shared with Jamal that it was only one season of his life. That is, pursuing postsecondary educational opportunities should not turn Jamal away from himself or his community, and he should not burden himself with trying to fit in if these efforts mandated losing parts of himself.

Another aspect of our conversations was discussing academic preparation for college and the efforts that Jamal thought he needed in order to accomplish his educational goals.

> **Jamal:** That's kind of difficult question. . . . Um, right off the bat I knew it would be hard so I figured it would take a lot of work and dedication. A lot of people [my secondary school teachers] would stress use your resources and go to office hours. So, right then, I just knew that that was what it would take to succeed and get through college.
>
> **DB:** Why did you think college would be hard?
>
> **Jamal:** Just growing up in the predicament that I grew up in. Like, once I got to Ellis Academy, I thought it was going to prepare me for college and I saw the classes that I needed to take but we didn't have some of them. So, I just knew that it would be hard.

In making meaning from his own academic efforts related to his preparation for college, Jamal interpreted his high academic performance as being prepared. He explained: "I thought I was well prepared because I was doing real well for the past three years. I didn't do as well my sophomore year as I did my junior and senior year. I did well because I still had a 3.7 [GPA], so I felt prepared. There was a time when I didn't feel prepared because of my scores on the ACT."

Jamal's academic concerns for succeeding in college was threefold. First, he shared knowing that college "would be hard" even before he arrived and he used this knowledge to inform him of the transitional strategies that he might engage once he arrived on campus. A crucial component of his preparation was receiving valuable insight and coaching from his teachers about the importance of accessing institutional resources. He learned from his secondary school teachers the importance of finding and using resources, such as interacting with faculty, to assist in transitioning and garnering success in college. Researchers note that interactions and relationships with faculty can provide Black males with valuable forms of social and cultural capital in college and can strengthen their belongingness and persistence as well.[9]

Second, Jamal believed that his background could present a challenge to being successful in college. Much of this concern, though, was specific to the academic culture and campus climate of his chosen institution. As one of the top public research universities in the United States, the institution attracts a great number of academically high-achieving students both nationally and internationally. Jamal was concerned about competing academically with other students who had been schooled in elite private secondary schools or some of the premier public schools across their respective locales. One of the "disadvantages" that education scholar Anthony Jack highlights in his work on Black and Latino students navigating selective colleges and universities is the cultural knowledge of accessing resources and information along with interacting with faculty. Jack contended that students from low socioeconomic backgrounds who attended traditional public secondary schools often were "doubly disadvantaged" by their class status and due to attending underserved secondary schools.[10] And, third, Jamal hung on to some anxieties regarding his preparedness for college because of his performance on the ACT test. "When I went into the ACT testing room, I was like, 'I'm gonna destroy this exam so I can get into a really, really good college and get scholarships.' But, then when I got the scores back it was depressing because I didn't feel that smart."

Thus, a significant portion of Jamal's transition to college was reconciling his anxieties from his secondary school years with developing the mental fortitude and mindset necessary for performing well academically at a postsecondary institution renowned for its academic rigor. Even though he harbored concerns about his academic preparation because of the lack of specific course offerings at Ellis Academy, and because of his initial ACT score (he later scored higher after retaking the test), Jamal had developed cogent ideas about being successful in college. On the one hand, he identified noncognitive factors such as working hard and being dedicated to his studies as essential to his academic efforts. It is significant that these noncognitive factors were centered squarely within Jamal's own agency and locus of control; also, they were not relative to a specific college major or dependent upon a particular course schedule. Jamal entered college with the mindset that he approached his academic work during his secondary school years: practice and dedicated, structured time spent on task will improve performances.

Another dimension of Jamal's transition to college was navigating the social milieu. Even though he thought he would fit in socially, he still expressed concern about the racial dynamics of his chosen college and reaffirmed his anxieties about his ability to perform well academically.

> I figured since I was going to the Mid-Atlantic [region] for college, I figured that I would experience racism. . . . I thought that might impact trying to make friends. I figured that the school I was going to people would be conceited and high maintenance, so I just had to get through that. I also had the fear of not being smart enough to be at the school and once we get there we'll see how it plays out.

Jamal's academic and social concerns were actualized during his first year of college. His academic struggles shook his confidence and this was exacerbated by his early social experiences. "First year of college was a big struggle. Before going to college, I thought I was prepared but it was a huge smack in the face. STEM classes was the first time I had ever taken anything like this before. I got my first few F's on assignments, so I went to talk to my professors and they worked with me. They saw that I was trying and I started to do better." Jamal, like several other young men in this study, expressed experiencing mental and psychological anguish based on his academic performances. He summarized these early college experiences as, "Stressful . . . kinda depressing just because I wasn't doing too well academically. . . . I just felt like I didn't belong. I didn't know why I was here anymore."

Summary

The young men in this study pursued college with great enthusiasm and expectations. As mentioned in previous chapters, part of their educational desires included ways that they believed that obtaining a higher education degree could matter in their lives and contribute to their families. As first-generation college students, their narratives reveal that even aspiring to college was wrought with a number of uncertainties and concerns. As part of their college selection process, to go with what might be considered as anticipated concerns (e.g., academic preparation and finances), especially given their first-generation status, these young men tried to identify a college where they believed they could thrive. Edwin, Malik, and Michael all matriculated to highly selective, small liberal arts colleges, while Jamal attended a large, research-intensive public institution that is renowned for its undergraduate programs. That each of these schools have a highly regarded academic reputation could have contributed to some of the concerns that these young men harbored. They were concerned about the academic rigors of their respective institutions, while they appreciated the newfound independence that college offered them they also understood this independence as responsibility, and they each were concerned about fitting in to the college atmosphere.

The young men were able to alleviate much of their social concerns through their involvement on campus or active participation in athletics programs. Their athletic participation provided them exposure to peers who also included returning students who had personal knowledge about navigating the institution. Athletics helped ease their social transition to college. Academically, though, they realized quickly in their experiences that they had a lot to learn about meeting the academic demands of their respective institutions. Each of these young men struggled, harbored self-doubts, questioned some of the decisions they made and behaviors they engaged, and learned through experience that, as Malik noted at the beginning of this chapter, their academic struggles "really showed [them] how much harder [they] needed to work." Their early academic experiences, whether they knew they would struggle like Michael or thought they were prepared as attested by Jamal, challenged these young men academically, socially, and personally. That young men like Malik felt like they had to "give up my opportunity to be a social butterfly" was part of the adjustments they believed they needed to make so that they could develop coping and success strategies to meet their academic and educational goals.

These young men's early college struggles spanned the gamut of academic and social terrain. They experienced conflicts and tensions in their college's social domains given the predominantly and historically white institutional context, which included being racially marginalized on campus. Their academic struggles stemmed from their lack of familiarity with the academic pace and rigor of college, including a variety of classes and faculty expectations, which produced a rollercoaster of emotions and triggered internal dilemmas. These internal dilemmas made them feel lonely and isolated; the internal dilemmas also included a range of self-doubts, such as: "Am I smart enough?," "Did I even read?," and "Am I able to compete?" These internal dilemmas shook their academic confidence and sense of self, they led to some distressing emotional and psychological experiences, and they undermined these young men's sense of belonging—academically and socially. Jamal's attestation is summative of the young men's experiences discussed in this chapter as he noted that his early struggles were "kinda depressing just because I wasn't doing too well academically." Part of what they acknowledged needing to learn was "how to be a student," which included sharpening their academic approach, learning more about and accessing resources on campus, and shifting their mindset.

Chapter 6

"I never wanted to give up, but . . ."

Navigating and Coping with Challenging Experiences

> Yeah, I doubted myself but I just had to keep on going and keep on believing in myself. As long as I did that, I knew I would be all right.
>
> —Paul

This chapter continues my exploration of these young men's transition to college and early college experiences. Whereas chapter 5 focused explicitly on the ways in which they anticipated and tried to negotiate struggles in transitioning, this chapter takes a broader perspective of some of the adjustments and strategies they developed and depended on. The perspectives that the young men in this chapter discuss are all related to their sense of self and self-beliefs. As Paul states clearly in the statement that opens this chapter, the doubts that he harbored about his intellectual and academic abilities were tempered by his self-efficacy. Because these young men believed in themselves, they believed, at least initially, that they would perform well enough academically to earn their degrees. However, this was complicated by a range of differing personal interests—ranging from an academic focus to social standing and athletic pursuits.

Based on their early college experiences, which are described throughout this chapter, the young men also provide insight about their meaning making and how they continued to adjust to the culture, climate, and demands of their respective colleges. These insights are critical to understanding their sense of self, goals, maturation, and expectations. Through narrating each of their experiences, they also share their interiorities and efforts to accomplish their goals. Paul's attestation that he "just had to keep on going" speaks to these young men's sense of resolve, resilience, and perseverance.

Chris: "The correlations between race and class . . . made it difficult for me"

Other students' first year of college paralleled both Michael and Malik's experiences and, at the same time, were unique as well. The point here is not to compare the young men in their first-year experiences, as there are clear nuances in their backgrounds, expectations, support systems, institutional types, and actions. Instead, my point here is to offer an in-depth view of the young men's lives and experiences. Exploring how these young men narrate their first year and transition experiences sheds light on some of their efforts, decisions, and responses and adjustment strategies relating to college life.

Chris noted that his first year of college was tough all around. It was difficult to attend school far away from home, it was tough acclimating to the campus culture and climate at his college, and it was difficult adjusting to the academic rigors there. Individually, each of these issues contributes to students' transition to college; collectively, these first-year experiences were challenging, and they challenged Chris in unfamiliar ways. In seeing and going through these experiences, he noted that his time management skills were critical to how he balanced college life and were informative to his decision to center his focus on his academic endeavors in his first semester. "My first year of college was interesting. My first semester was all right; I had 3.5 [GPA] my first semester and I made the Dean's List. It was tough adjusting with time management; that was the hardest thing, just managing time. It was difficult too with the work, the reading and the writing. The first semester was tough but I had to do what I had to do."

Chris's academic performance during his first semester was personally inspiring and rewarding. In an attempt to respond to the rigor of his college, he used isolationist strategies during his transition so that he could give greater attention to his academic endeavors. In this approach, students like Chris remove themselves from many social activities on campus, which has the potential to undermine their engagement in and integration into campus life, thereby making them miss out on important support resources. In his approach, Chris made three critical decisions that he believed were important to his early academic efforts and successes. First, he decided on a study schedule that included spending time on Friday nights and the weekends in the library studying and completing his academic work. Second, he decided to begin working on assignments as soon as he received them; to be specific, he believed that working on them in parts could help him make progress and avoid feeling overwhelmed. And, third, he connected with several classmates, some of whom formed study groups. When asked what he meant by "I had to do what I had to do," he explained, "I had to be focused that first semester because I wanted to have a good semester."

Chris and I had multiple conversations throughout his first year in college. Our conversations focused on his transition to college, his social and academic experiences, and his adjustments. In talking about his in-class academic experiences, he explained:

> I think, for the most part, my classes my first semester in college were pretty good. My two favorite courses were my Anthro class, which focused on gender and sexuality, and my African American Studies class. My Anthro class was interesting because it introduced me to different ways of thinking and social constructions of reality, or gender and sexuality. It just made me think differently about them, how gender and sexuality operate in society. Like, assuming that you're a male automatically means that you don't have to exhibit any emotion because it means that you're acting like a female. So, learning those constructions were really helpful. My African American Literature class allowed me to learn about many writers, scholars, and activists that I hadn't heard of before. If I had heard of them before it helped me think about them in different ways. Like, I had never heard of Frederick Douglass's Fourth of July Speech. But in hearing it, made me really reject and not celebrate that holiday.

Chris discussed his in-class learning and exposure to various literatures, people, history, and culture with great enthusiasm. This learning stood out to him because it challenged his ways of knowing in a manner that helped him grow and expand his knowledge base. For instance, his discussion of learning in his anthropology course is aligned with how he felt challenged in his secondary school years—both intellectually and also in his positionality. Chris was receptive to these new concepts and learning he was taught and identified both courses as his favorites. Being introduced "to different ways of thinking" helped Chris learn to "think differently" about his social world. Fundamentally, learning about social constructions of gender and sexuality "were really helpful" in teaching him to challenge his assumptions, privileges, and hidden biases; this learning also challenged his previously held ideologies about gender norms, roles, and performances (such as males exhibiting or not exhibiting emotion). Similarly, his experiences in his African American Studies class also encouraged him to "think differently" about himself, his history, and his communities through the perspectives of the "many writers, scholars, and activists" that he was exposed to in his studies and learning.

Still, even as he appreciated these learning opportunities and performed well enough to earn Dean's List, Chris still described his first semester as tough.

> **DB:** What made the first semester tough?
>
> **Chris:** Being in a new environment, the space that I had thought would be more diverse was really predominantly white. And, what I thought was middle- to upper-class students, well it actually is pretty much middle- to upper-class for the most part [laughs in surprise at his near misstatement]. But it was predominantly white, and it was people of a higher class. It was just a whole other way, or this is how I thought about it at the time, it was just another way for people to engage and it seemed like they weren't interested in people who came from my kinda background.

Here, Chris identified the campus climate and culture of his institution as especially tough, which ultimately added to some of the struggles he experienced during his transition. The predominantly white campus ethos was a significant shift from his all-Black secondary school context. This environment was totally different from what he was accustomed to and did not resonate with any of his precollege experiences. As he continued, Chris further discussed how socioeconomic class at this highly regarded institution contributed to his transition struggles; he added:

> It was tough academically adjusting to the rigors of work. But, I think it was more so, it was more so the other aspect of that. The aspect of noticing the differences between race and class or the correlations between race and class that made it difficult for me. Another thing that was tough was my learning. Just because someone else is Black doesn't mean that we share the same experience. Like, most of the Black students on campus come from a different class. Coming into college I thought that would be the group of people that I would connect with more, at the time, but I really couldn't connect with them because of class differences.

Chris's narrative and experiences point to the need for and benefits of educators engaging an intersectional perspective and understanding about how race, gender and class impact Black males' college experiences. Also, this perspective and analysis can provide insight on college, peers, and community. Chris specifically noted the difficulty he experienced in relating to some of his peers due to "the differences between race and class or the correlation between race and class." Realizing that many of his Black peers had a different (and higher) class background helped Chris see the intraracial diversity among the group and contributed to him feeling a bit isolated.

Chris acknowledged that a critical aspect of his first-year experience was getting connected to a support system that was geared specifically to focus on and support students from low socioeconomic backgrounds. Being engaged within this support system allowed him an opportunity to connect with students who shared his class background; besides that, these connections helped enhance Chris's sense of belonging on campus. In sharing how he got connected with this support system, he noted:

> I think it was more so through my classes and maybe, yeah it was more so through class or just me speaking to people I had seen or maybe had not had an interaction with before. It was mainly through people I had classes with. Like, one of my friends is from [my hometown] as well; I hadn't really seen her but I had class with her. But it made me feel more comfortable in knowing that I had people who I could connect with in some way.

Chris's connections with a support system occurred in multiple phases. As he shared, during his first semester, his engagement in class and interacting with various individuals helped him develop associations with his classmates. Based on his narrative, his transition to college was marked by feeling isolated because his background was very different than the mainly white, apparently upper-middle-class, students at the institution. In our discussion, he noted material markers that can be used to distinguish people in the middle class, such as the types of cars, clothes, and material items students had access to and possessed. Likewise, he noted students' social activities, which included frequenting local upscale stores and restaurants and traveling for weekend trips together as examples of markers that distinguished the realities of his limited material possessions and social access.

In addition to developing relationships with classmates, during his second semester Chris also began participating in a program for first-generation students and families. The program offered support and helped students think about their educational futures.

> My second semester, I got connected with a support system specifically designed for students from low-income backgrounds. Not just a support system but also pursuing education after finishing college. Second semester was more rocky as far as my grades. I think I may have gotten a bit too confident and forgotten that I was still new to college. I didn't give some stuff the same attention and put in the same work as I had in the first semester. I had a 2.8 [GPA] for my second semester. So, I had some imbalance with regards to academics.

The program, which attempts to help students adjust to college by offering a number of opportunities and resources that range from academic support to social activities, helped Chris establish a sense of fitting in and belonging on campus. Even though being engaged in the program provided him with more resources, Chris acknowledged that he didn't approach his academic work with the same focus as he did during his first semester. Chris's early successes in his academic performance and his approach to the second semester led to "some imbalance with regards to academics," primarily because he had "gotten a bit too confident."

Paul: "I got on my knees and asked God for strength"

The young men I interviewed entered college from diverse backgrounds and with a wide range of concerns, expectations, and hopes. Paul was an honor roll student every semester of his secondary school years and attained a number of accolades and experiences along the way. His high achievement provided him with tangible benefits that mattered significantly to his educational experiences and informed his educational aspirations as well. He participated in college preparatory and exploration programs during his first two years and in a college immersion program at prestigious institutions during his final two years. These experiences, coupled with his high academic achievement, earned him honors of distinction, such as "Student of the Week" multiple times, "Student of the Year" honors, and an "Academic Excellence" award.

Paul decided to attend a private liberal arts college that focused on undergraduate education. In reflecting on his college decision, he noted, "Well, I got accepted to a lot of prestigious colleges but it came down to my great-aunt's health ultimately, my great-aunt's health and financial aid. I had to go where the money's at." Also, Paul felt very supported by the college during the application and recruitment process. In particular, he noted that he felt welcomed and valued even before he was an official student of the college:

> [They were] so open to hearing my story and helping me out and I really appreciated that. It felt like I was at home. Everybody was so friendly. . . . I don't know, [this college] was just for me. The money was there, the people were nice, and they supported me. And, it was different; I was tired of being around only Black people all my life. In the workforce, it's not going to be that way. I didn't want to miss out on the big picture of working in a diverse area. I always knew I wanted to have something different.

As Paul attests, his earliest experiences signified that he would be a valued member of the college community, which was comforting and helped him foresee his college success. The college's location within the regional area of his home was beneficial so that he was not too far away from his family. At the same time, the academic reputation of the institution combined with the institutional financial assistance offered, the support he received, the overwhelming positive interactions he experienced, and the fact that he wanted to be nested in a community whose racial demographics were very different than those of his home community and secondary school helped make Paul feel that the college "was just for me." An important component of Paul's college decision-making process was considering his future self and his engagement in the workforce. He believed that being in a predominantly white environment that included people from diverse backgrounds, including those from international backgrounds, would provide him with insights about many professional workplaces within the United States and life beyond his community.

Although Paul had established a sense of comfort through his interactions and communications during the recruitment stages, this comfort was complicated during the summer prior to attending. As part of his matriculation process, he needed to complete several transition components, which included communicating via email and completing academic-related assignments. Even though he felt confident in his academic preparation given his high achievement, he immediately felt challenged and concerned by his experiences. He explained:

> [laugh!] I don't know, I didn't know what the heck I was doing. You know, I was trying my best to get on my school email. I was trying to do my summer assignment but I didn't have access to my school email. I was like, "Oh my God, I'm starting off bad already!" I couldn't go to the library because it was lot of gang activity [in my neighborhood]. I tried to explain this to my advisor. I don't know man, I was lost; I was just lost. I didn't get a good grade on it, but I got it done. I know that I was lost.

The difficulties Paul endured in trying to complete his summer assignment led him to feeling "lost" and confused about how to make sense of his challenges and communicate them effectively. His attempts to tell his advisor about the vulnerabilities he faced and the precariousness of accessing his local library were not as effective as he had hoped. Although he did not earn a "good grade" on the assignment, he was satisfied that he "got it done." Still, though, this early experienced increased his anxiety about being successful academically in college mostly because he knew and understood the difficulties of rebounding when one is "starting off bad already."

It is significant that Paul had activated a number of lessons and efforts during his early college years that he developed during his secondary school years. Primarily, this included his belief and commitment in always turning in his work and being willing to spend whatever amount of time he believed he needed to in order to complete assignments and try to increase his academic understanding.

> **Paul:** I always got my work done [laughs in affirmation]. I never struggled with doing the homework; I was the student who always got his homework in. I wasn't the smartest, but I knew I wouldn't let anybody outwork me. That's what I took with me to college. I didn't miss any of my assignments. The least I could do was a C average; it's not great but I can still get my degree. I thought I could do better, so I wasn't too worried.
>
> **DB:** Where did your work mentality and that approach come from?
>
> **Paul:** My great-aunt [laugh]. My great-aunt man; she's a workaholic! From her waking up at five o'clock, preparing a breakfast for us, working every day, paying the bills, and making sure we had dinner on the table when we got home. So, I get it from my great-aunt.

Paul credited his great-aunt, who, along with his great-uncle, was his primary caregiver and guardian. Not only did he cherish these relationships, he also learned valuable lessons, skills, and characteristics as well. He took these lessons to college and activated this learning and approach during his college years. He internalized his great-aunt's work ethic and made that part of his own approach. Thus, his point about using his work ethic and effort to accomplish his goals helped alleviate concerns about his ability to attain his educational goals. In fact, he put more emphasis and focus on minimally performing at a level that would help him earn his baccalaureate degree rather than being overwhelmed about trying to earn Dean's List or garner academic honors from the onset of his early college years.

A serious setback that Paul experienced was in completing a paper that was a major assignment for his college studies. This assignment was part of the second-year curriculum, which students needed to complete in order to qualify and transition to higher-level courses. This experience left Paul doubting his ability to succeed and jeopardized his matriculation. He initially submitted a paper that did not use proper citation guidelines and, as a result, the professor identified his writing as plagiarism and notified him that his infraction jeopardized his opportunity to pass the course successfully. A failing grade on this assignment would mean that he either, in the best-case scenario, would have to petition to take the course again or, in the worst-case scenario, have to leave the college and transfer to a different institution. This academic experience created serious self-doubts and stress for Paul. In trying to make sense of his mistake he relied on his faith for understanding and endurance. In reflecting on how he doubted himself, he shared:

> Ohhhh, YES! There was a time when I got that letter. Is this professor really gon' give me this opportunity to prove myself? I remember I plagiarized in college; I didn't do it intentionally. I used a different format; you were supposed to use APA but I think I used Chicago [style]. In high school, I was taught that you couldn't copy word for word. Once I explained myself to my professor she kinda understood where I was coming from. I didn't really do it on purpose. She realized what I was saying, so she gave me an opportunity. Thank God she wasn't racist—she was white. I asked, "Please give me another chance? I'll write another five pages."

Paul's statement about his professor's racial ideology revealed a major concern about how he might be treated because of his infraction. Given that he attended a historically white institution, where Black students accounted for only about 5.5 percent of the student population, he surmised that his intentions in completing the assignment would be dismissed if the instructor held racially disparaging views or stereotypical assumptions about Black people. As he continued, he discussed how his spiritual faith played an important role in helping him persevere through challenging college experiences: "Any time I did doubt myself, I got on my knees and asked God for strength. [God] won't really put anything on me that I couldn't handle—[writing] forty-five pages [for this one paper], psychology courses, learning new programs like SPSS, or something like that. I knew this girl who was a psychology major and she helped me out. God was putting people in place to help me out." Similar to the statement used in the beginning of this chapter ("Yeah, I doubted myself but I just had to keep on going and keep on believing in myself. As long as I did that, I knew I would be all right"), Paul's faith played a critical role in helping him persevere, seize opportunities, maintain a positive outlook, and pursue his educational desires.

These experiences, including both the trials and triumphs, helped Paul learn a great deal about himself including his character and capabilities. In reflecting about his self-learning, he specifically acknowledged his resilience and educational urgency:

> I'm like the most resilient person at that college [laugh]. Just because I've been through so much. I was on academic probation my freshman year because, like I said, I was hanging out with the wrong people. I went from not even being close to being on the Dean's List to being just one or two points away. That says a lot about my character and that I can accomplish anything if I put my mind to it.

Paul's attestation about his resilience was intriguing. Initially, he centered his sense of resilience on the trials and tribulations of his college journey. Being placed on academic probation his first year of college tested his mental and academic resolve and forced him to reconsider his friend groups, his social engagements, and a number of his activities and behaviors. Through critical self-reflection, he asserted that his academic performance reflected the limited energies and time he committed to his studies, "mainly because I did not prepare myself." These early experiences were essential because during these years, as Paul admitted, he "learned a lot like what to do, what not to do, who my friends were, who I could call friends." He believed that some of his "friends" did not have his best interest in mind and allowed him to engage in behaviors and actions, such as staying up all night playing video games and pool, that seriously undermined his academic focus. Paul's ability to recover from these early setbacks and challenges helped him realize his own capabilities. He engaged in proactive philosophies, which entails making extra efforts to search for and secure additional resources, information, and support; for instance, he consistently went to his professors' office hours as a result of learning "that you gotta ask for help." Additionally, he connected with different individuals to form study groups and began going to the library to study immediately following his classes. Each of these actions reveal his intentionality in focusing his mind and efforts on succeeding in college.

Although he praised himself for his sense of resilience, Paul also made direct connections for his ability to recover and persevere in college to his spiritual faith and the holistic support he received from family, friends, and his community. "First thing first, was definitely God. God definitely played a big role of keeping me going, keeping me healthy, and keeping my mind clear. God played a big role in that! My great-aunt never stopped believing in me, never stopped loving me as a person . . . my pastor of my church, too."

Julius: "I never wanted to give up, but . . ."

Like Paul and several of the other young men, Julius achieved at a high level academically throughout his secondary school years and was engaged in a number of athletic and extracurricular activities as well. He identified college as an important step in accomplishing some of his life's goals and changing the family's trajectory. Even though he had clear goals and educational desires, he still entered college concerned about his ability to be successful academically. In considering his concerns, he acknowledged the most pressing to be "if I was gon' make it! Yeah, if I was gon' make it; I don't know. I knew in high school I always had the bros [his closet male friends], Ms. Anderson [a staff member at Ellis Academy], and my track coach. I was going away [to college] by myself. So, it was different."

Julius's concerns about his ability to succeed in college receded almost immediately during his transition, as he quickly connected with the Black student community on campus. He joined several student organizations upon his arrival and got involved with his college's NAACP chapter. Julius also achieved solid academic performances during his first two years as well. Although he had to contend with "being alone sometimes and learning that not everybody [are] your friends," he described his transition as "smooth" because he "went from being Mr. Popular in high school to being Mr. Popular in college. It was the same thing; I knew everybody in high school and I knew everybody in college." Julius's social integration on campus provided him with a wide cast of peers to connect with and add to his social network. He paired his heavy involvement in the social life of campus with a clear academic focus:

> I was a firm believer of Monday through Friday I'm gon' put in work; you weren't gon' see me Monday through Friday if it didn't involve work. But come Saturday and Sunday I was gon' kick it, especially because of how much work I put in for four and a half days. And it worked. I got "Newcomer Student of the Year" from the Black campus community. So I was rewarded for my work.

Julius credited a relentless academic work ethic for his high academic performance. He earned a 3.6 grade point average during his first year on campus, which he believed was because "I worked hard! I was spending countless hours in the library." He used study time to read and prepare for his courses and complete his assignments, adding, "I work on some papers, I did some organizing." Julius felt that he earned the acknowledgments he received because he "put in massive amounts of work. And, it paid off."

During his first two years of college, Julius revealed his academic excellence and social intelligence. He established meaningful connections with students across a variety of organizations and backgrounds, he garnered social and academic accolades from his peers, he earned a prestigious internship during the summer, and a number of faculty members seemed to think highly of him. Additionally, he was elected and chosen by his peers for several leadership roles on campus, represented a couple of student groups beyond the campus, and was viewed by a number of his peers as a campus leader. Early in his third year of college, however, Julius made a series of what he called "poor choices" that led to him being dismissed from school. He was devasted and in disbelief.

As he scrambled to make sense of his dismissal, Julius reached out to a small group of individuals for both personal and financial help. In addition, he activated his educational desires by seeking out other colleges to attend. He applied and was accepted to several colleges that were in close proximity to his first college. Leaving his campus was difficult because of the relationships he had developed and because of his strong academic and social performances. "It was . . . I guess difficult at first, initially. Because I was always doing really well there, really, really good and I had to go. It was difficult! But it made me more determined . . . to get back and finish out." Although he had to leave, he expressed his determination and commitment to return to Region State University (a pseudonym) and "finish out" his bachelor's degree. After applying to several different schools, he identified two specific reasons that he decided to attend a school in close proximity. "The number one reason I didn't go to [the other public institution] was because my most important relationships were here and I didn't want to leave those. And, two, I wanted to come back and finish at Region State, and defy the odds."

By defying the odds, Julius meant "just the whole [idea of] me graduating from Region State; getting back to the school again and finishing because you can come back and not finish." Even given the difficulty of having to leave Region State and dealing with the frustration and shame of his dismissal, Julius was determined to complete his degree at what he considered to be his "home" institution. Among a variety of possibilities, he surmised that it would be "easy" to complete his degree at a different institution because he could avoid Region State, which in many ways also functioned as the "scene" of his transgressions. He recounted spending hours contemplating his decisions, options, and possibilities. He had spent time in the social arenas at nearby schools, had built a number of significant relationships, and easily could see himself as a student at any one of them—and completing his degree there. Yet his desire to complete his college degree at Region State where he started was a central focus.

> **DB:** What made leaving Region State difficult for you?
>
> **Julius:** Because in theory it was home. It was like . . . I been there since my freshman year, I was like [a] poster boy. Doing very well; at one point I had the highest GPA for African American males on campus. I won Newcomer Student of the Year; I had all kinda accolades. I was getting ready to get nominated for Mr. Region State University. It was like, "Up, can't come back!" So, it was like losing all of that.
>
> **DB:** What was that experience like for you? In some ways it's . . .
>
> **Julius:** I low key went through a depression for a minute 'cuz . . . I couldn't be on campus and things like that. All my friends was at Region State; everything! Everything in this town revolves around Region State [laughs in frustration]. I

> think the hardest time period when I was at Pierce [College] was that first homecoming because I had just crossed [in my fraternity]. My whole line was there, people was wondering where I was at; they were blowing up my phone. I was just looking at my phone like, "Yeah, I'll catch y'all on the flipside."
>
> **DB:** So, talk to me about being down and a bit depressed.
>
> **Julius:** I never wanted to give up, but . . . I think my esteem of self was high initially and I just knew at that point, I knew I was gon' be a powerful Black man; I just knew it. I think I acted like it too [laughs in acknowledgment]. Then all of that happened, I think I got humbled. As quick as you got it, you can lose it all. I think for the very first time in my life I felt like an average dude, or a below average guy. My whole life I've always been above average, in everything, and for the first time in my life I felt average. I felt not exceptional. I felt like I wasn't making progress; I've never not made progress—even if it's slow progress. For the first time in my life I felt like I wasn't making progress and I felt like things could only get worse.

Julius's considerations for "defying the odds" involved a tug-of-war of between his emotional state and psychosocial well-being and his desires to return to Region State and complete his degree. The restrictions that he faced in not being able to engage with friends or the community he built at Region State was deflating. His experiences of what he referred to as a short-term depression had him on the brink of considering giving up on his educational goals and aspirations, at least temporarily.

As a way to cope with the transition from Region State and all the emotional taxation that he experienced, Julius insulated himself from others, actively avoided a number of interactions with peers, and engaged in activities of personal interest such as running, lifting weights, and developing a music collection. He also increased his engagement in social scenes at two other local colleges. He acknowledged that he wanted latitude to choose the social scenes that he participated in yet at the same time he did not want to be isolated. Julius noted, "I just traveled to other schools and learned about the people there; I guess to make me feel like a college student again." In addition, beyond a very small group of individuals whom he believed he could count on without reservation, he revealed that he rarely talked to anyone about what he experienced during the time. "Very, very few people. I didn't really talk to anybody about it. There's people who knew like if I needed help with a particular thing but I didn't talk to anybody about it. I wasn't meeting the expectation and I wanted to meet the expectation and I was gon' fix it." On the one hand, Julius's self-focus was an attempt to insulate himself from the potential barrage of questions about the actions and decisions that led to his dismissal. Battling with feelings of not being exceptional and feeling that he was not making progress weighed heavily on his psyche, emotions, and spirit. On the other hand, Julius looked at himself as the ultimate solution. While he relied on a very small group of friends and family as recourse to help him navigate some of his educational and financial needs, such as selecting and enrolling in a new college, he still held himself accountable for accomplishing his goals, meeting his own self-expectations, and ultimately reconciling and achieving his educational desires.

CHAUNCEY: "YOU TALK ABOUT HEARTBREAK AND DEVASTATION!"

Given the range of experiences that he garnered during his secondary school years, combined with his educational desires, Chauncey had a breakthrough experience regarding college when he participated in a spring break program during his eleventh grade year that took students on a tour of various Historically Black Colleges and Universities (HBCUs). He identified this trip, even years later, as transformative for his academic performance during high school and important for his college aspirations, "It was my first time away from home for real, I was on the campus with these other Black kids, and it showed me that that could be me."

In specifically reflecting on his college tour experiences, we discussed various colleges that students visited during the tour and how Chauncey made meanings from touring multiple campuses and being in a collective setting among his peers. He made clear the impact of the trip by identifying it as a "game changer" in how he thought about and aspired to go to college. He recalled: "I remember going on the college tour and the school helped us with that—[a classmate] went too. That was a game changer; that was the first time I saw a college campus. These kids look just like me, they can't be that much smarter than me. And then, being away from home I was like, 'I can do this.' I didn't even want to go back home." The experience of being on a college campus was critical for providing Chauncey with an opportunity for firsthand exposure to college as well as allowing him the chance to envision himself both away from home and as being a college student. Besides gaining familiarity various college types, such as HBCUs and liberal arts colleges, college tour participants also were able to see and interact with students on campus. According to Chauncey, this exposure to colleges and interacting with Black students, at the HBCUs in particular, helped contribute to his college knowledge as a first-generation college student. Specifically, the experience helped demystify what being on a college campus felt like and allowed him to visualize his own college going. His point that "these kids look just like me" reveals how he associated his proximity to same-race peers who were college students as a reflection of his own possibility and, furthermore, he used the college visits to envision himself as just as capable as the current college students.[1]

In gaining these firsthand experiences, Chauncey expressed his self-efficacy in believing that he could be in college and be successful, which was articulated in his statement, "I can do this." From this experience, he learned, "basically, that college isn't what I thought at first. I thought college would be extra hard; I hadn't seen that many Black faces but we went to HBCUs and that really helped." Chauncey appreciated the opportunities that the college tour provided and had an interaction that made a lasting impression.

> I remember the last stop and we came across some white people. They were like, "Which basketball team do you play for? Or what choir is this?" We were like, "Nah, that's not us!" It's funny though because they did exactly what you would expect because it was all [Black] guys. We told them we were on a college tour and what was best about it was that it was a 3.0 [minimum GPA] tour. So, we had to flex on them a little bit.

In sharing this experience, Chauncey relays how, for the white individuals whom they shared this interaction with, the sight of young Black men together was relegated to some athletic engagement or music-related activity. Knowing that they had earned their opportunity to participate in the college tour based primarily on their academic performance provided these young Black men with a way to both refute such claims and resist stereotypical views of them. Interesting in this experience is Chauncey's appreciation of his academic accomplishments; the college tour participants had earned this opportunity through their academic performance. Although he still maintained high athletic goals and intentions, participating in the college tour was based solely on students' academic profiles and, as a result, these young Black men were students who performed above average academically—that some were athletes as well showed that they were well rounded.

Based on these formative experiences, along with encouragement and support from his family, Chauncey explained that he decided to attend an HBCU even though it would be a considerable distance from his home. As for many of his peers, finances were critically important to making college attendance feasible. Chauncey considered how his college choice would impact his family, both financially and collectively. He noted the following about his parents: "They was big on not paying for nothing. I was like, 'Don't worry about it; I'll go to wherever [college] give me the most money.'" He truly enjoyed his experiences during the tour and felt a sense of comfort in being on the HBCU campuses. Given these considerations, Chauncey decided to attend Banneker University (a pseudonym), an HBCU in the southern region of the United States. Chauncey believed this to be a solid choice since he visited the school during the tour and the choice was what he considered a financially wise decision that was rooted in his family's financial realities and affordability. He noted, "They gave me the best financial aid package even above state schools. It was the farthest school too but I was like, 'You gotta grow up someday.'" Additionally, in attending Banneker University, he believed he could continue his athletic participation by pursuing his basketball dreams.

Banneker University seemed to be a place that Chauncey could thrive, especially given that he could continue his sports participation. Though he was interested in HBCUs from the college tour, attending Banneker felt like a culturally engaging environment that would position him toward and support his success.

> I end up going to Banneker by chance; they end up giving me the most money. When I got to Banneker, it felt like home. We young, we Black, we can do it [accomplish our educational goals]; it was empowerment. We said it at Ellis Academy every morning. That's how I felt at Banneker. You

> got kids from Cali [California], they smart as hell; you got kids from New York, they were smart as hell. Every HBCU has that. So, at a HBCU, I felt like home; even though I haven't gone to a PWI [predominantly white institution], it felt like home. The confidence they build up in you; it felt like family.

In transitioning to Banneker University, Chauncey felt a sense of empowerment through the institutional culture and climate along with the connections he made with peers and classmates. In noting that getting acclimated to college felt like he was at "home," Chauncey connected the early affirmations he experienced at Banneker to those at Ellis Academy. Overwhelmingly, he felt that the college environment was welcoming and supportive; equally strongly, he felt that he could accomplish his educational goals because he was embedded in an environment centered on enhancing students' sense of self.

As part of his transition, Chauncey decided to participate in fall training for returning and aspiring members of the basketball team. The training was an opportunity for individuals to get acclimated to the physical conditioning expectations of the coaching staff and at the same time served as a way for aspiring team members to get "noticed" as well. Chauncey's efforts during physical conditioning helped earn him a spot on the team's preseason roster. His first-year basketball experiences were complex and difficult. First, he noted a schism on the team because some teammates were unhappy about who had made the team and who had not. He acknowledged that making the team "was the dream that I wanted the longest," but his teammates "felt like I took one of their friend's spots. He was out of shape and got cut. We didn't have the chemistry." Ultimately, in reflecting, he recognized, "It wasn't the experience that I wanted."

Second, although he didn't recognize it at the time, the rift that Chauncey experienced on the team slowly developed into a chasm between himself and several other young Black men on campus. "As far as social life, on campus, it was great. Those guys got put off the team and they were upset. I should've just nipped it in the bud then. Whatever woulda happened then would've been better than later." Still, even as he began to make sense of what was transpiring, he did not see the larger picture of the turmoil that brewed. He was unsatisfied on the basketball team because "I didn't get as much PT [playing time] that I wanted" and at the same time he was working to maintain a romantic relationship with his girlfriend, who lived in his home city. Interestingly, he noted that his relationship kept him focused both academically and socially and a change in the basketball coaching staff led him to believe that the following basketball season and school year could be a better experience for him.

> I was in a long-distance relationship, so that kept me focused. I was on Skype or on the phone talking to my girl because I missed her. That was different because most of the freshmen boys were out there trying to talk to the girls [on campus]. Spring semester, I did track and we won conference; I got a ring for that. Not playing basketball kinda put a drain on me, just not being able to do something that you wanted to do. Once that coach got fired, I was ready to try out for the next year.

Beyond these experiences, Chauncey also expressed interest in fraternity life on campus. Although he did not pledge, he attended a number of functions hosted by Greek (fraternity) life, made new acquaintances and friends, and reveled in his social status on campus, which was elevated because he was a member of the basketball team. He felt he was "noticed" by peers and attracted attention across campus even though, to his own admission, he "didn't get as much" playing time as he wanted. He performed well academically, received commendations from faculty and administrators, and "was just trying to build a resume" of engagement and quality performance for himself. The efforts and accomplishments were erased quickly following several negative interactions that ultimately led to a physical altercation between himself and the same individuals involved in the rift concerning the basketball team. "My name was mentioned, even though I wasn't Greek. So, I was on behavior probation; I don't even know how that works. I already had created a nice file on myself. . . . Got into a brawl. I finally confronted someone who was a bully. I didn't say it that way at the time. I didn't want to tell my mom."

Chauncey thought he could resolve the tensions between himself and several Black college men on campus by himself. In some ways, he felt antagonized by several of these students throughout his early college experiences. Although he developed multiple friend groups on campus, with one being a collective from his home city, he didn't realize the factions that existed on campus and the antagonisms that developed precisely because of his participation in and connection to such social groups. A number of male students who were from the local area where Banneker was located seemingly developed a disdain for several young men who were from his hometown, including Chauncey.

Several weeks into the spring semester, mostly following the physical altercation he was engaged in, he received a notice that read, "You must be off the premises." He was devasted and stunned at the notice; he tried in earnest to appeal the decision, talked with several faculty members with whom he had developed a positive rapport, and tried to advocate for himself. None of these efforts yielded any change in the ruling. He found himself in a state of limbo with what he believed to be very limited choices. "I was just hanging out for like a month and my parents didn't know it at that time. I couldn't go home because I had so many people counting on me."

In some ways, this experience was all too similar to what had transpired at Arnold High and at the same time rather different. In receiving the notice that he must leave Banneker's premises, Chauncey offered:

> Man, whew!! You talk about heartbreak and devastation! At the time, my face was on the school website; one time for basketball and one time in a suit and tie for Collegiate 100. I was doing big things for the school, so I never saw it coming. I had a few things on my record . . . that all added up. They told me I had to leave and they denied my appeal. "You are no longer a member of the school." I was twenty [years old]. All I knew was school at the time; that was my whole key to success. They take that away, what can you do? I couldn't tell my parents that. I ducked and dodged the question for like a month.

For the second time in his life, in different but similar circumstances—being in a physical altercation—Chauncey's schooling was disrupted. He had to make sense of the experiences at the same time that he tried to discern how he could reconcile education as a "key" to his success. First, he actively avoided informing his parents about the notification and, because he was "hanging out" on Banneker's campus, he was cited for trespassing. The entire experience was devastating, "It was heartbreaking;

I felt like a loser. Even though it's not all my fault." Even as he clung to his innocence regarding the altercation, Chauncey still acknowledged that he was wrong for being on campus: "Technically, it was trespassing."

Given that gang affiliations and gun violence increased his motivations for "getting out" of his home city and "getting away" to college, he did not want to return because "people were [still] getting shot, I couldn't go back." Even though neither his parents nor siblings initially knew the full details of his experiences, or the reasons for his dismissal, he eventually had to call his parents to tell them that he was no longer enrolled in Banneker and to help him move off campus. "My siblings were worried. I messed up! I think I shut off my social media then as well." Even with the whirlwind of events, the mental and emotional strain he endured through the experiences, and ultimately having to leave a school that "felt like home," Chauncey was comforted in being with his family.

> They were happy to be there. I was looking at my siblings. [My next younger brother] Lance knew. I looked at my Pops in the eyes, he was upset. My mom was upset. That was one of the biggest Ls [losses]! I was wondering, "How did I get there?" Not only did I lose, I couldn't take myself anywhere; they had to come get me. I felt like a kid again. It was humbling, you know.

With the aid of his family, Chauncey left the college and the state; he simply wanted to "get away" and create some physical distance between himself and the school location. Through three and a half semesters of college, Chauncey experienced both triumphs and trials. His triumphs included his personal life (e.g., maintaining a long-distance romantic relationship during his first year in college), athletic achievements (e.g., making the basketball team and winning a conference championship on the track and field team), and educational accomplishments (e.g., being inducted into a prestigious student organization). His trials included each of his triumphs: ending his relationship with his girlfriend, being dissatisfied with his basketball team experiences, being placed on behavioral probation, and being dismissed from the university and later being cited for trespassing. In trying to make sense of these dichotomous experiences, Chauncey was left with a number of self-questions, with the most prominent being, "How did I get here?" The notion of "here" relates to a position where his family had to pick him up from college midway through the semester and drive him to his grandparent's house in a neighboring state. He was left wondering both what could have been and what he might do next, especially since he declared adamantly that he "couldn't go home because I had so many people counting on me."

Summary

In this chapter, the young men discussed their experiences and challenges in transitioning to college as well as dealing with significant setbacks in their college endeavors. Chris and Paul both had challenging transitions as they tried to adjust to the academic rigor at their respective institutions while Julius entered college concerned about his ability to succeed academically. As it relates to academic challenges, these included trying to decipher how to negotiate their efforts to address the academic demands they experienced regarding coursework, course loads, and various assignments. That young men like Paul "didn't know what the heck [they] was doing" was revealed in the decisions that he made—and didn't make—such as not prioritizing his academic work, not preparing for assignments and exams, and what he called "hanging with the wrong people."

In trying to adjust to the academic rigor, each of the young men engaged a different strategy during their transition. Chauncey, Julius, and Chris each prioritized their academic responsibilities as they considered that doing well early on academically could help them establish a solid foundation for college success. For instance, Julius and Chris both placed a great emphasis on spending hours in the library, focusing on completing their course assignments, and preparing for upcoming classes and course work. Additionally, their stated "fear of failure" served as a powerful internal motivator for their early academic focus. Each of these young men experienced rewards for their academic performance, which included securing high grade point averages, receiving accolades from their peers, and being invited to and joining highly regarded student organizations.

Despite the challenges they faced and the ways they tried to confront their own academic concerns, the young men also reveled in the academic opportunities that were afforded to them. Even as they felt challenged in some of their writing assignments, the young men expressed appreciation for the exposure to critical knowledge of their social worlds.

For instance, the learning that Chris experienced through his anthropology and African American Literature courses provided him with a sense of empowerment and ideas about how to navigate his institution. Similarly, Paul identified a number of academic endeavors that peaked his interests and that provided him with salient learning experiences. And, Chauncey was able to join Collegiate 100, which allowed him to expand his social network on campus and provided him with access to critical mentoring and guidance.

Beyond their academic experiences, each of the young men had to learn to cope with, manage, and respond to the social milieu on campus as well. This was a bit different for each young man. Chris faced significant struggles in trying to adjust to the intersecting racial and class ethos on his campus while Julius and Chauncey experienced hardships that disrupted their status in college. They both experienced what Chauncey referred to as "heartbreak and devastation" in being dismissed from their colleges, especially given that each young man felt that their respective colleges felt like "home" and because they had performed well academically and socially since their start. Their dismissals also induced a sense of desperation regarding their educational journeys, displaced them from their social networks and significant relationships among peers and staff, which had proved vital in their early college years, and created anxieties, stress, and even psychological anguish. Chauncey's burgeoning question "How did I get here?" resonates with each of these young men's experiences, as discussed in this chapter and the previous chapter, and reaffirms the critical stakes at play in these young Black men's educational journeys and how they continued to make sense of, activate, and pursue their educational desires.

Chapter 7

"I didn't have no Plan B"

Staying Focused on Collegiate Goals

> I would say, uh, [I had an] intermediate supporting cast that would never let me fail. And a lot of it is knowing what I'm coming back to; that's the reason why I went [to college]. I knew what I was coming back to because nothing has changed. I knew when I was coming back I was prepared in a way with a different mindset and a different outcome. There was really no point to return unless I finished college.
>
> —Edwin

Making It through College

This chapter focuses on the efforts the young men employed in responding to some of the struggles and challenges they faced and takes a detailed look at how they tried to negotiate and navigate their college campuses. I explore the strategies the men developed and refined throughout their college years and reflect on some of their highlights and challenging experiences as well. Along those lines, the young men's narratives provide insight into their agency and sense of self along with the lessons they learned and relied on along the way. For all of the young men in this study, keeping their college strivings in perspective was a critical component of their strategies for perseverance and their educational urgency. Primarily, this is reflected in how they focused on their pathways to college and the benefits they believed they could accrue through completing college.

As Edwin reveals in the opening quote of this chapter, and in conjunction with the chapter title, the backgrounds of these young men continued to fuel and inspire their educational urgency throughout their college years. In trying to make sense of their possible pathways, young men such as Edwin believed that completing college was the only readily available and viable option. Regardless of their family backgrounds and histories, and precisely because of their family backgrounds, histories, and investments, these young men identified college completion as an intertwined personal, familial, and communal responsibility and achievement. Though some of these young men stumbled and faltered and had a variety of missteps during their college years, they constructed completing college as a way to change their lives and, for some, even to create a new trend or standard for their families. These young men's educational urgency is most evident in the ways that they embodied their desire and need to complete college. That is, earning their college degrees was paramount to how they thought about themselves, how they wanted to be seen by others, and how they hoped their siblings, friends, and associates might see their own possibilities.

In exploring how the young men tried to make it through college, I discuss some of the factors they identified as critical to their success, such as peer relationships, access to opportunities and resources, the role of their communities and institutional agents, and their mindset and determination. In addition, I focus on the men's discussions of the support they needed, desired, and received.

Edwin: "Just knowing that I didn't have too many options"

One of the greatest challenges Edwin had to endure in completing college began even before he stepped foot on a college campus. As he described it, "I wasn't sure how far I was gon' make it; I wasn't sure if I was college material. We said it for four years throughout high school, but in the back of my mind it was always, 'There's some barriers that I'm thinking about in the back of my mind.' In high school, it wasn't more believable." At his college preparatory secondary school, he was embedded in an environment where students pronounced affirmations about their intentions of college going, and attending the school also helped make college more accessible for him and many of his peers. However, he still battled self-doubts and various internal dilemmas, during both his secondary and postsecondary years, because of his standardized test scores, because of his mediocre academic experiences during his middle school years, and because he never felt he was able to give his full attention to his academic endeavors. His statement that he "wasn't sure if I was college material" speaks powerfully to how his early educational experiences still manifested during his college years. Mostly because of his performance on the ACT test (as discussed in chapter 5), a major internal dilemma that he harbored was the question, "Am I smart enough?" Moreover, Edwin's perspective of being "college material" was connected to his thoughts regarding his ability to compete with other students in college and successfully matriculate to graduation.

As he reflected on his early college years, even as he held on to these self-doubts about his potential to be successful in college, Edwin learned valuable lessons about strategies he could adopt and deploy to navigate his institution.

> I just learned that, academically, there's resources around to help you succeed. There's people on campus that's willing to help you, you know, get over that academic slump that you may have—everyone has it. Get through some classes, there's some professionals there that helped you get through it, but that's only if you say something. I had to learn how to ask for help, which was a big thing for me because I didn't want to be the only one asking for help. But, I learned that this was how people were getting [good] grades because they were asking for help and going to talk with professors. If I was struggling in a class and they know that I'm trying and I'm constantly coming to them and trying to get better, they would see that I'm putting in an effort. . . . From then on, I paid attention to everything coming up and if it was ever assigned I'd get on and do it. I had to learn quickly.

Two critical points that Edwin shared about thriving in college involved asking for help and accessing his resources. He learned these strategies through his own experiences and also by observing and learning from what his classmates did. As it relates to research regarding navigating college, Edwin learned to develop, expand, and activate his cultural capital. Scholars note that cultural capital, which refers to an individual's accumulation of cultural knowledge, skills, and abilities, can play a pivotal role in how Black male students transition to college, navigate some of the unwritten rules of higher education, and enhance their college experiences.[1] Furthermore, developing meaningful, positive relationships with faculty and staff can increase college satisfaction and sense of belonging for Black male students; in particular, these relationships help position college personnel in close proximity to students to help guide and support their efforts, especially for those students who do not possess cultural knowledge about the benefits of such interactions.[2]

Learning that there were professionals on campus whose role it was to assist students with their academic endeavors helped relieve some of the pressures and insecurities that Edwin initially harbored in his early college years. As opposed to feeling singled out as deficient because he was unclear or needed help, which placed him at a disadvantage because he was not accessing available resources, he later realized that asking for help was what assisted a number of his classmates perform better academically. This understanding helped Edwin envision how he could accomplish some of his college goals and helped him learn that he did not have to have all of the answers either to information presented to him or in completing assignments. He also learned that talking with professors was valued highly at his institution as this provided professors with opportunities to learn more about students and become aware of students' academic efforts. At the same time, these interactions also can provide students with greater insight about faculty expectations and details regarding assignments.

Edwin explained to me that his fourth year of college was quite stressful for several reasons. On the one hand, about a month into the semester, Edwin ended up dropping two classes that he learned he didn't need to take and picking up two new classes, one of which was an independent research study; missing the first four weeks of the new classes was stressful. He was confident that he could do the work; he initially felt stressed because he received erroneous information about the courses he needed to take and because changing classes required that he reorient himself to a different schedule without having much time to develop a strategy to negotiate this change. Edwin explained, "It was a time management type of experience because I knew that if I didn't have nothing to do I had to do something on this paper [for my independent study]." He continued: "It was really difficult from the time that I had to do it and the work I had to do in my other classes, what was most important to me was doing this work for this class that I had lost credits for. It taught me time management, discipline, and reflect on why you getting it done. If you don't get it done then you don't graduate."

On the other hand, during his fourth year Edwin's family endured a number of challenges that included housing insecurity and interpersonal stress; also, his romantic relationship with his girlfriend at the time demanded great attention. Edwin tried to prioritize where he would place his focus and settled on his academic work. He also had a financial balance due to his college that needed to be paid so that he would not face any restrictions on campus or lose privileges, such as accessing needed library materials. Edwin struggled to keep all these things in balance, and each one impacted his ability to focus academically. In trying to resolve some of his financial struggles during his fourth year, Edwin explained:

> I was more comfortable on campus with being an upperclassman. I really didn't focus on a lot of stuff that was happening back home, which helped me grow a little bit. It helped me be more active on campus and within the community as well. Also, I was struggling on the financial part as to how I was gon' pay for my senior year. I balanced that to where I could uphold until May. I believe, on a daily basis, I was thinking about that kinda stuff and it kinda like discouraged me a little bit. I also was going through some relationship-type problems, which was a ongoing thing throughout the year. So, that played a role in why I was getting stressed out. I wasn't sleeping like I should and I started slacking in some classes, but it got better towards the end of the year.

These collective experiences forced Edwin to make critical decisions about where and how to focus his attention and energy during his last year of college. As he discussed how he even managed to make it to his final year of college, given the challenges and self-doubts he experienced and faced along the way, he pointed to his educational urgency and his support.

As we talked about his college experiences, he explained that his educational focus was grounded in what he believed to be a severely limited number of alternative opportunities, which ultimately informed his mindset and efforts that helped him make it through college.

> Just knowing that I didn't have too many options. Just one option was to graduate because it wasn't nothing for me at home. It wasn't like I was homesick; I was never homesick. I lived on an everyday situation that it happens that I didn't want to go back to it. When I did go back to it, it was like everything was reversing in time. I had people who were believing in me and helping me through this process and I can't let them down. It became a need base, which was something that I wanted to happen. It felt like I had a lot on my shoulders but if I didn't have it then I probably would've been at home somewhere. I think the main thing for me was that I couldn't fail; I think for me failure is one of those things that I fear. So, I see a lot of people failing themselves first before they give it a try. So, I try to give it my best and push through whatever happens. I feel that everything happens for a reason and you just have to go through it and see where it takes you. There's no doubt about it that you're placed here on earth for a reason. If you don't allow yourself to apply yourself then you'll never figure out what you're made of.

For Edwin, returning home without his college degree had no appeal, primarily because it would not change the material conditions of his life or his family's life and he wanted to expand his potential employment opportunities. First, being at college reduced some of his worries about his family's challenges at home. Second, he also used his home challenges as external motivation to continue in his college strivings. In the same way, his support group was essential to his efforts and focus. He believed that obtaining his college degree would affirm the support he received and the people who supported him along the way. Similar to a number of his peers, Edwin viewed his college success as centered in his community and identified a fear of failure as a significant motivator for his academic and personal efforts as well.

PAUL: "WHY DID I COME SO FAR?"

Similar to his peers, Paul learned through firsthand experiences that adjusting to college life and accomplishing some of his academic goals required that he refocus his energy and efforts. In addition to relying on his family, friends, and church to support his college endeavors, Paul engaged in proactive strategies and philosophies to ensure that his academic performance met his own standards for success. Inclusive of the major paper that he wrote, as discussed in the previous chapter, Paul learned a great deal about himself as he reoriented himself toward academic excellence, which he had accrued during his secondary school years.

Early in his college years, Paul shared that he had given so much focus to the social activities at his college that he did not prioritize his academic work. He had classes about subjects that he had not studied previously and his academic performance included earning an "F" on a major exam. In discussing that experience, he offered a healthy and insightful observation:

> I got that F mainly because I did not prepare myself. I only studied for two hours, went to a lot of parties, talked to girls. Yeah, you reap what you sow. It was not fun, but, you know what, it was a hard pill to swallow and I got better. I told myself that I didn't want to experience the same feeling that I'm feeling right now. But, the main reason why I got that F was because I did not study and I did not prepare myself. I thought I could do it; I didn't prepare, I didn't go to office hours. I didn't even know what office hours meant! [laughs in disbelief] I didn't take the time to know what they actually mean. So, yeah, it was a life lesson and I learned from it.

According to Paul, his academic performance reflected the lack of time and dedication he gave to preparing for his exam. In the aftermath, he initially engaged in self-talk to help clarify how he made sense of his experiences. Through self-talk, along with conversations with his mentors and a few peers, he began to identify ways to turn around his performance, such as learning about and tapping into institutional resources. "Oh, I learned that you gotta ask for help, first off, you can't party all night long—like eight hours—and think you'll pass. You gotta study longer than two hours and try to pass biology. It's much easier if you get a study group; a study group makes it a lot easier if you study in a group." Some of the setbacks that Paul experienced were not necessarily failures; instead, he saw them as experiences he could learn from, as life lessons, and as ways to improve his academic performance and college experiences: "It was a life lesson just because, you know, it shaped or changed my life around. I knew not to make that same mistake twice. How else can I put it? When I think about life lesson, it changed my life around. I knew I can't be playing pool all my life; I was just doing silly stuff—silly, silly stuff."

Paul credited his early college struggles to a lack of focus and not using his resources. He talked about some of his mistakes, "Studying, hanging out with the wrong people who I thought were the right people to hang out with but they really wasn't. What else? Studying . . . also just not using my resources, not using the writing center, the math resource center, not using office hours the way I should use them." He identified these experiences as "eye opening" and he was determined to make significant changes to his studying as well as his academic and social activities.

> I got sidetracked [laughs in amazement]. After I . . . I just had to get my act together. Yeah man [laughs in astonishment], yeah, that was just a wakeup call. I knew if I didn't change some things I wouldn't be at that college too long. I was thinking about . . . I was fucking up, excuse my language; I was fucking up! I remember checking [on some of my high school peers] and it was like, "He got kicked out, he got kicked out [of college]" and I got a letter later that day and it said, "You are on academic probation."

Paul felt warned by some of his peers' premature college departures and acknowledged that some of his actions, such as partying too much or too long and hanging out with "the wrong people" made him distracted and less focused on his academic endeavors. His point that he needed to change so that he could stay at his college resonated even more given his peers' experiences. Additionally, Paul's self-assessment needed to be blunt, transparent, and accurate. Thus, because he knew and articulated that he was "fucking up," he realized his poor performance and lack of focus were part of a "wakeup call" that required him to "get my act together."

After some self-reflection, Paul responded to these "mistakes" by immediately developing proactive philosophies and prioritizing his academic work and efforts.

> I woke up at 6:30 that next morning, I was like, "I gotta make a list!" I gotta go to office hours, I gotta do make up. I just started posting up in the library. I did not leave the

> library and not leaving until like 2 o'clock in the morning. I remember waking up at seven in the morning, going to bio [class] at 8 [o'clock] and feeling like I was high. I went from bio to lab and then straight to the library. I was playing catch up. Luckily I was able to get my grades up. . . . I remember thinking, "Never again!" [laughs in amazement] I almost lost my life working that hard. It was a life lesson—a life lesson learned indeed.

The challenges and mistakes that Paul experienced were translated as life lessons primarily because of the tremendous efforts he needed to engage and call upon to get his grades up and get himself off of academic probation. Playing catch-up taxed him academically, physically, emotionally, and spiritually. Paul felt assured that centering his academic work would allow him to perform well academically, especially when considering the support he received from his advisor and faculty members.

Another strategy that Paul used through his college years was staying focused on his goal, "Just thinking about like, you know, why am I here? Asking myself, 'Why did I come so far? You know, you've been in worse positions,' so I always told myself that. If I had to write a twenty-page paper, I'd think about stuff like that." After overcoming a number of academic setbacks, Paul felt that he was primed for educational success. He used his experiences, both the trials and triumphs, to steady his educational focus and to fortify his academic efforts. "After overcoming that my sophomore year, I was like, there's nothing that can stop me—I'm unstoppable. There's nothing this college can throw at me that I can't do after completing me. So, that's what kept me going [laughs in affirmation]."

Paul credited a strong support group for helping to sustain him during his college years and making it through college. This support group provided him with personal and academic support and cared about his sense of well-being. He credited a number of his peers, his mentors, and a cadre of his teachers and staff at Ellis Academy for always checking on him, inquiring about how he was doing, and providing ongoing support. In the same fashion, he explained:

> I have a lot of people who support me and care about me. One of my mentors, he's like a father to me now. A lot of friends at the college, they never stopped believing in me. With all of that happening, I was bound for success and I

> was meant to be successful. And I believe that if anybody has a strong supporting cast, how can that person be a failure? If you have a strong supporting cast and the resources, you really can't fail as an individual.

In considering the breadth of his college experiences, Paul's question to himself, "Why did I come so far?" served to remind him of his journey and helped fuel his internal motivations and future efforts. He thought about his home neighborhood and the challenges he endured traveling to and from his secondary school; he considered the prayers and support he received from his great-aunt during his journey and the ways in which he was cared for by family and friends; he also thought about his faith, the importance of believing in himself, and his somebodiness. Because he had come so far, because of the struggles and challenges that he overcame, and because of the consistent support he received along the way, Paul not only believed that he was resilient; his assertion, "I was bound for success and I was meant to be successful" was a testament of his faith as well.

CHAUNCEY: "KNOWING THAT I DIDN'T HAVE NO PLAN B"

As discussed in the previous chapter, Chauncey's departure from Banneker University was both heartbreaking and devastating. He spent the remaining part of his semester with relatives, where he stayed through the early summer, and within weeks he found a job at a local retailer. His departure uprooted his sense of self and left him unsure of his educational future. Staying with his relatives allowed him time to isolate himself from a potential frenzy of questions from other family members and friends and provided time to reflect on his college experiences. Most importantly, he wanted to get his mind right about his future college decisions.

We spent some time discussing what types of options Chauncey felt that he had regarding college and how he thought about those potential options. For instance, he explained that his dismissal from Banneker was for one academic year and I wondered if he had given any thought to returning to the school. He remarked, "Ah, to go back there? I think they changed it to a semester; that was over the summer and I could come back in the fall. I just wanted to wash my hands. Dr. Taylor was gone and she was like a mother figure. I still keep in touch with her today." Part of Chauncey's decision making for potentially returning to

Banneker was considering the types of support he had in place. Dr. Taylor, a well-liked Black woman faculty member who poured her expectation and guidance into her students, had provided him with critical support during his years at Banneker, and he felt her departure was significant. Additionally, he acknowledged that he wanted to separate himself from the school and move on from the negative experiences he had encountered.

Sitting out of school and not being around his friends or closest family members left Chauncey physically and emotionally isolated. He talked at length about his experiences during this time and discussed how he translated and transformed isolation from a period of despair to one where he was more centered and focused on what he needed to do for himself. He reflected:

> Man! I'm not sure how other people deal with it, but I actually like it—I can't lie. It's scary because you can miss out; once you isolate yourself you can miss out on events, miss out on family. When I come out [of isolation], I'm hitting every mark. It's like when Rocky [Balboa in the *Rocky* movies] went to the mountains to train. That's how the isolation works; I'm in that tunnel vision, and I'm just focused on me. I come out so much better, every time. I mean, it's selfish to some people, but I really like it.

Going into isolation served multiple purposes for some of the young men. As mentioned, isolation allowed some to separate themselves from social engagements and interactions that potentially could focus on some of their negative or challenging experiences. At the same time, as Chauncey discusses, although he missed out on events and spending time with family, being in isolation allows him to focus on himself and sharpen his vision about what he wants to do, decisions he can make, and processes he can follow to accomplish his goals.

Chauncey was determined to recover from his dismissal from Banneker. During the summer, he applied to a different HBCU that he learned about from his younger brother, who had received some information about the school. He recalled, "My little brother went on a college tour and brought a flyer home. My mom told me to apply to Wells State University [a pseudonym] because they don't have out-of-state tuition. So, I did it. They were calling me over the summer and I just went on down there."

After starting at Wells State, Chauncey sharpened his academic focus and felt a sense of urgency in accomplishing his educational goals. He had experienced setbacks, trials, and disruptions in his collegiate journey. He was clear and determined not to repeat the same or any similar mistakes. But this approach was not simply about himself. As we talked about his experiences at Wells State, pursuing graduation, and staying focused, he made clear that his educational efforts and accomplishments included his family and his community. He did not want to return home without his college degree, especially because he felt he had "so many people counting on me." Attending college with his younger brother also sparked his competitive drive in different ways as he was determined that, because he was the oldest of his siblings, he should be the one who graduated first from college and set the standard for his siblings.

In considering some of his successes at Wells State, such as making the Dean's List and helping to establish a Collegiate 100 program on campus,[3] he reflected, "Really just . . . I don't know . . . I think the fact that I haven't been in the social life. I've really been to myself; I've been quiet. It really hasn't changed my grades. I'm really starting to feel a more sense of urgency because I'm about to graduate. I'm just trying to focus on life after graduation." Based on his previous experiences and some of the challenges he faced, Chauncey decided on an isolationist strategy in transitioning to his new school as he wanted to limit his social activities on campus. At Banneker, he found himself trying to leverage his athletic participation to enhance his social status, both in conscious and unconscious ways. On the one hand, he realized that being on the basketball team helped him stand out on campus, while on the other hand there were individuals who wanted to elevate their social status and importance on campus through affiliations and friendships with student-athletes, which was not as appealing. Also, as a student-athlete, he learned that many of his actions, especially his infractions, were scrutinized heavily and in a least a few instances were viewed through a microscopic lens.

At Wells State, he took a much different approach. He was much more aware about the social atmosphere of college and how "wanting to be the man" on campus could be loaded with unforeseen challenges and undesired consequences. Additionally, he did not desire the spotlight—at least not for social activities. If he was going to be known at Wells State, it would be because of his academic focus and academic accomplishments. Rather than looking for and pursuing attention, Chauncey was content with having a low profile, staying focused on his academic endeavors, and providing support to his brother. His social relationships were critical to this mental shift and academic focus. "The people I surrounded myself with, whether it be advisor, parents, friends, just the positive vibes, I want to be around people that are on the same things I'm on. I didn't have time to mess around just to mess around. So, just making sure my circle was right."

In addition to these adjustment strategies, Chauncey shared that graduating from college was his most urgent and pressing goal. He described his motivation and focus in clear and concise ways. "Knowing that I didn't have no Plan B. It was either make it or go home—and I wasn't going back home. I don't really have no Plan B; I go back home and be restricted . . . and play keep up with the Joneses or I could just stay in school."

Malik: "I just have to do it; I have to succeed"

As he transitioned and tried to adapt to the academic rigors of his college, Malik made adjustments, tested different strategies, attempted to learn from his past experiences, and tried to employ his learning in his newest or upcoming experiences. We met during a snowy winter afternoon right at the end of finals week during his seventh semester in school. We talked for nearly an hour before we even ordered lunch, following up on some points we noted and shared via text conversations and talking about college football and the beginning of the college basketball season. After eating, we shifted our conversation to the interview we scheduled and I began that discussion by asking Malik to reflect on the fall semester he had just completed.

> Honestly there's a lot to say about it. Coming into it, I thought it was going to be the hardest semester, the hardest semester of my life; it turned out to be the smoothest. I forced six classes on myself, I see the light at the end of the tunnel. I had to write two research papers during the semester, which didn't work out for me, honestly. I would never suggest to anybody to take six classes! Senior year, though, I've done a lot and this is a time to reflect on things I've learned, what different type of things will mean to me. I've sorta come to the realization that everything is not what it seems, everything doesn't turn out the way you want it to but you have to keep working on it. Things will come as long as you keep the faith.

I was intrigued by some of Malik's decisions and experiences, such as "forcing" six classes on himself, what it was like to write two research papers in one semester, and the reasons he felt that some of his efforts "didn't work out" for him. And, given that he was thinking about the time that we sat down to interview as "a time to reflect on things he learned," I also wondered what he thought about taking six classes in one semester, for the third time in his college career.

Some of Malik's early college academic struggles continued throughout his college years, which ultimately resulted in his decision to take an overload of courses several semesters. Given that he had just completed the fall semester, I thought that his recollection would be strong regarding the various experiences he had throughout the semester. I followed up my broad question about the semester by focusing on the number of courses he took.

> **DB:** What was it like taking six classes?
>
> **Malik:** This actually isn't my first time taking it. After the first time I told myself I'd never do it again! [laughing in disbelief] But, what it's like, in my perspective, it's a lot of work. It felt like grad school. I was in the library at least four hours a day—probably should've been in there longer. It's hard, nobody likes it. I do feel like this is that final test. I just have to do it; I have to succeed. It's only moving forward.
>
> **DB:** Why did you decide to take six classes?
>
> **Malik:** I had just got done with the summer semester, I took three classes, I had 10 courses to go [until I was done]. Honestly, it was [in considering] how my spring semester was going to shape up to be. I'm not going to take the even number of classes in the spring semester, so I wanted to take more in the fall. I've had five or more semesters where I've taken at least four classes. So, I wanted to make it easier on me, so I can do more reflection and think about my future. It's hard to do that when you take a lot of classes; it's no time for thinking, it's time for work.
>
> **DB:** You've taken six classes in a semester twice or three times now?

> **Malik:** Each semester it has not worked out. I don't know, I still have that . . . I don't know, has it worked out or not, I don't know? Altogether, not all at once, I've failed at least a semester and a half of classes. A lot of people say I'll take that ninth semester and I just feel like, why not, why not go for it [try to finish in eight semesters]? I don't want to fail any class.

A critical element in Malik's decision to take an overload of classes during the fall of his seventh semester was his attempt to reduce the number of courses he had to take in the spring, which he hoped to be his final semester of college. As opposed to taking five courses each semester, because he didn't want to "take the even number of classes in the spring semester" as he would have had in the fall, and because he wanted more time in the spring to "do more reflection and think about [his] future" after college, it seems that Malik was concerned about his mental and emotional capacity, knowing that he needed to think about and plan toward his future beyond college. He took this approach because he had previous experience with taking six courses in a semester, so he knew the workload would be "hard" and that there would be "no time for thinking."

Also important is Malik's acknowledgment of consistent academic struggles. Even though he did not get all the success he had desired in taking an overload of classes (he noted that "each semester it has not worked out"), he was focused and committed on graduating in four years. While some of his peers took an additional semester (or more) to complete their baccalaureate degree, Malik considered the financial costs of such a decision, which was funding that he did not have, and even with his previous experiences did not shy away from pursuing this goal ("Why not go for it?").

Similar to his peers in this study, Malik carried his struggles and challenges with him through each of his semesters in college and, at the same time, stayed focused on his goal of college graduation—on his own terms. He took courses during the summer in each of his first three years, an approach he chose given his lack of success in passing several courses and because he wanted to stay on the path to graduate college in four years. In thinking about his potential final semester of college, he explained:

> I think this is just, like I said before, this is that time where I absolutely have no margin for error if I want to graduate

> on time. I see it coming. This is another semester for me to do more reflecting on things I've learned and I can't say I know everything that I'm doing here already. . . . This is the wrap-up semester to get everything done, tie everything down. I'm not looking to do all that spectacular, my GPA is not the best, but I'll be able to say I graduated in four years. The average college student graduates in six years. It obviously plays heavy in future opportunities, but I'm happy I'll have the opportunity to graduate.

Malik felt some slight pressure that he placed on himself in committing to trying to graduate in four years. Knowing that he "absolutely ha[d] no margin for error" meant that he had to accomplish something that he had not before: successfully pass six courses in one semester. He helped balance some of the pressure that was inherent in such a course load, which he knew from experience, by trying to keep his effort in perspective. His point that "I'm not looking to do all that spectacular" grade-wise was a reality he felt he had to accept because he knew that taking six courses demanded a great deal of attention, effort, time, and focus.

I asked Malik about what he learned through some of his reflections during his college years and he noted that his greatest learning was not centered on a particular course, his program of study, or even specific readings but rather on self-discovery and self-exploration.

> **Malik:** I always continue to reflect upon how much I have grown myself in these last three and a half semesters. And things I can definitely say about myself is I've learned to be a lot more cautious about things I'm doing, being more thoughtful about things I'm doing, and learned to think before I act. The readings I've done, everything I had to work for in school, is starting to sink in. Everything that I've learned I think is going to mold me into the type of person I want to become.
>
> **DB:** What are some things you had to work for?
>
> **Malik:** Just having this opportunity to graduate in four years. I know a lot of people here at this college graduate in five years. . . . I've been lucky enough to fight hard enough to

> graduate on time. That, I think, is a sign of strength. I didn't back down. Even if I do fail I can tell people I didn't because I never backed down.

More than simply resilience, Malik's self-discovery helped him see and appreciate his drive and determination. These were characteristics and personal attributes that he believed to be some of his greatest strengths. Regardless of the struggles he endured during his college years, regardless of some of his academic setbacks, such that he "failed at least a semester and a half of classes," regardless of some of the racism he faced on campus, such as being racially stereotyped, profiled, and harassed on a number of occasions, that Malik kept pursuing his goals speaks greatly to his educational urgency. Indeed, Malik's educational urgency was most evident in his refusal to allow his background, lived experiences, and academic missteps to dissuade his goals; in fact, as he attested, his educational urgency is a strength.

As we continued in our conversation, Malik identified personal growth as the hallmark of his educational journey. Although he felt a bit naive during his secondary school years, he felt that he had accomplished a great deal and learned throughout the process.

> Freshman year in high school you know you're not the smartest guy in the world, but you know you're naive about some things. After graduating high school I kinda felt that way. I was doing things that I told myself in high school that I would never do, like twenty-five-pagers. Do crazy amount of research where you're up two days straight because it's so exciting. Definitely proving myself wrong and learning that I'm capable of things that I didn't even know I was.

A critical element in Malik's growth and maturation was his willingness and drive to try things that were beyond his comfort zone, from overcoming his shyness about speaking in class and engaging classmates in academic debates about historical and current events to engaging in the cultural life of his college through the Berry Institute for Black World Studies by organizing programming and events and spending countless hours improving his academic and intellectual acumen (such as hours in the library reading and rereading, practicing and improving his writing skills, and conducting research).

In looking forward to and considering his upcoming college graduation, even though Malik struggled to make it to his final semester of college, he centered his family in his sense making. For Malik, his upcoming college graduation was about uplifting his family and community.

> Being one of the first in my family to go [to college] means a lot and being one of the first to go and graduate is really special to me. I can start a new trend especially because I have family who are really proud and they can't wait to get here and celebrate. I'm at the point where it's not even about me anymore, it's not just trying to improve my life but trying to contribute to the larger cause.

Summary

For each of these young men, as shown in the narratives throughout this book, their college years were wrought with challenges, obstacles, trials, and tribulations. They all shared a similar goal: graduate from college. However, how they pursued that goal and made sense of their experiences was centered in the messages, support, and lessons they accrued along the way. As the young men discussed their college experiences and the efforts they engaged to make it through graduation, they specifically looked back to their pathways to college as motivation. Additionally, the efforts and strategies that they called on and deployed exhibited their educational urgency as well. Even as the young men recounted some of their struggles, challenges, and that they experienced in their college years, they also accomplished a great deal. Some of these accomplishments included resisting and rejecting deficit-based views about them as young Black men, bouncing back from academic setbacks and struggles, developing and sustaining significant relationships and friendships, and engaging in various activities and organizations on campus.

As part of the strategies that helped them persevere through college, the young men engaged with institutional resources to assist their efforts. In this regard, the young men's development and deployment of cultural capital proved prominent. Students such as Edwin learned from classmates the importance of accessing institutional resources and asking for help, while students such as Paul and Chauncey reoriented their academic efforts by prioritizing studying and preparation. Learning to ask for help and using campus resources became proactive philosophies that helped them reframe their lack of clarity or struggles not as needs that they harbored alone, but rather as part of the learning process and success strategies for a number of students. Along the same lines, interacting and developing meaningful relationships with faculty was important in their efforts to achieve success as well. These relationships helped them both academically and personally and it also helped enhance their sense of belonging.

Importantly, as the main title of this chapter bears clear, the fact that each of these young men felt that there was "no Plan B" and that they "didn't have too many options" outside completing college speaks powerfully about how they scripted their educational urgency, resilience, and goals into their college endeavors—from their transitions in college, through their struggles, and in the reorientations and refocus that they developed along the way. Each of the young men credited the encouragement, love, and affirmation they received from their friends (including girlfriends), family, and community as playing critical roles in supporting their resolve and keeping them focused on completing college. Because these young men believed that there was "really no point to return [home] unless I finished college," because they believed they "had so many people counting on" them, and because they had "come so far," they declared that completing college was the only "plan" that they wanted to give attention to and concentrate on. Additionally, these expressions all coalesced into their thoughts, focus, and consciousness that their successes and accomplishments were centered in their families and communities, as Malik offered, their efforts and desires to succeed were "not even about me anymore."

Chapter 8

"I'm creating my own story"

Young Black Men Enacting and Embodying Agency

> Just stay motivated. Just educate myself on being Black and being powerful; just looking up my roots and knowing who I am. Learning how to be yourself. When you look at the stereotypes and statistics that are given to you it gets to you sometimes. If you don't stay powerful then you won't be powerful, not in this environment.
>
> —Julius

Like the previous chapter, this chapter offers narratives from four young men as they discuss their efforts to make it through college. Unlike in the previous chapter, though, the discussion here also focuses on how these young men frame their college pursuits, efforts, and accomplishments. Primarily, I wanted to investigate how they made sense of their college experiences and educational journeys. Each of the young men offered critical perspectives about their endeavors and also provided deep insights about how they thought about themselves.

According to all the young men in this study, and as discussed by Julius in the opening quote, many of their schooling and lived experiences were translated into opportunities to learn a great deal more about themselves and their possibilities. For almost all the young men, being a Black male on their college campuses was rife with anti-Black racism that essentially made their experiences much more difficult. Julius shared experiencing Black misandry and expressed frustration and disdain for the ongoing racism, "Because it's like, we come all this way and we still have these subtle instances of racism." He noted that as a Black male, "just everything you do is under a microscope; you're looked at differently and you're judged." The feeling of being "under a microscope" deepened throughout his college years to the extent that he discussed them almost as an everyday phenomenon.

In response to the full range of their experiences, some of which challenged them personally, some of which challenged their academic selves, and some of which challenged their sense of self, the young men identified learning and knowing "who I am" and "how to be yourself" as young Black men as paramount to their sense of self, self-empowerment, and their efforts to persevere. In taking such an approach, and especially in knowing "the stereotypes and statistics that are given" to and about Black boys and young men, as Julius attested here and others discussed elsewhere (e.g., like Chris in chapter 1), these young men focused on creating their own stories and becoming who they are through their experiences.

Julius: "Just my fear of failure; I am so afraid to fail"

I sat on the couch in Julius's apartment, which was located right near the center of campus, during the winter break as he had just completed his final assignments and exams for the fall semester. We talked for a couple hours as we checked in on each other, discussed some events that occurred recently, we chatted about the college football season, and we discussed R&B and neo-soul music, particularly some of his recent acquisitions and his burgeoning collection, before we turned our attention to formal interviewing. Our earlier conversation had clued me in to several critical points that I wanted to talk with Julius about during our interview, the most pressing of which was transitioning back to Region State and looking ahead at his final semester of college. This was his fifth year in college, and he was determined to finish with a strong academic performance. As discussed in chapter 6, his college years did not go as smoothly as he had expected or desired; I admired and appreciated Julius's deep reflection as we talked about some of his challenging experiences concerning his sense of self, coping strategies, and goals.

In looking back at his year at Pierce College, Julius expressed frustration with the academic standards at the school: "Like, I was so above and beyond everything they expected from a student, which makes you really question some things because the school is like 95 percent Black. Coming from Region State, I was exceeding everything because I was operating from that standard." Julius engaged in a number of social activities and organizations at Pierce College, which allowed him to continue to sharpen and develop his leadership skills and pursue his interests. Most importantly, though, he remained quite focused on performing well academically so that he could make a case for trying to return to Region State, which required that he reapply to the school. He chose Pierce College because the course offerings aligned with those at Region State and, more importantly for Julius, the way in which he thought his selection might look to himself and others.

> Because I had to transfer from Region State and I had full intention in coming back. I knew the two colleges that offer classes along the same line and those are Johnson and Pierce. Johnson gives you classes that are along the same lines but Pierce gives you a schedule that is similar to Region State. Johnson is technically better but I didn't want to go to a community college. In retrospect, that would've been the way better option.

I asked Julius why attending the community college was not appealing to him and he shared that in addition to a community college not meshing well with his sense of self, it also failed to meet his academic standards. "I guess ego; going from Region State *University* to a community college sounded like more of a downgrade and going to Pierce *College* sounded better—but it was actually more of a downgrade."

In our conversation, I also asked Julius to make sense of his college years and help me see how he understood his college experiences. In reflecting, he began with the incidents that led to his dismissal from Region State and the lessons he took away from these experiences, and followed by discussing how he rationalized his desires to return to Region State to pursue his college degree:

> I reflect on it and man! Just a very dumb decision by me. Man, decisions! But, I reflect on it. . . . In theory, as far as my financial debt, it would've made more sense for me to transfer to another school. And I would've graduated last year. I could've started my career and stuff. However, me

> not coming back to Region State I would've always felt like I quit if I didn't come back; like, things got too hard and I had to run. So, the only way for me to correct that was to come back to Region State and finish where I started. Even though things aren't pretty now but it humbled me—a lot. Is there a word more powerful than humbled? It humbled me a lot and taught me valuable lessons, but it made me better.

In his statement, it seems that experiencing and learning humility was the most powerful assessment that Julius derived from his dismissal from Region State. He elaborated on being humbled and feeling like he was better because of the challenges that he experienced:

> I feel like I'm better because of those things. I'm more understanding and accepting of like, things happen. Sometimes you can't fix it, you just have to move forward. That's what I learned; that's what I learned. Resilience is what got me through, 'cuz, boy, if I told you how many times I could've quit! There were plenty of times. But it's not in me to quit—or leave Region State. So, if the opportunity happened again, where I had to leave Region State and transfer to another school, I would do the same thing again. This is where it all started, this is where it all began, I just need to finish up.

Similar to a number of his peers, Julius expressed one component of his educational urgency in the fact that he was fully intent on finishing college. While changing schools easily could have put him on a different educational pathway, which could have interrupted or further delayed the completion of his goals, he remained steadfast in his focus. In fact, as shown in a number of his reflections, he internalized his struggles and challenges and asserted that they added to his educational drive and determination.

Additionally, these experiences also allowed him to script resilience into his sense of self. His resilience and educational urgency included several critical steps. First, his educational desires were disrupted by his dismissal. Enrolling in school in the next semester was his first step toward getting back on track to rectify his missteps. Second, and simultaneously, he fixated himself on returning to Region State, which impacted the institutions where he considered transferring in the interim. He potentially could have transferred to a school farther away or even out of state, but he felt the proximity would keep his return to Region State fresh in his mind and in his view. Third, he recentered his academic focus once he enrolled at Pierce College. Although he had withdrawn from many of the social activities at Region State and thought in retrospect that Johnson Community College probably would have been a better choice, he used a formula that helped him garner success early in his college years: he refocused his study habits, similar to his "all business" focus on his academic responsibilities and assignments Monday through Friday, and he became involved on campus. This involvement and some of his leadership activities complemented his academic studiousness—even though he did not feel challenged academically at Pierce College. And, finally, Julius rationalized that if he could bounce back and return to Region State, then he would not falter again in his steps toward completing his college degree.

In addition to shifting his mindset ("Honestly, my biggest lesson was humbleness and letting my pride go"), he also placed his most recent challenges within the context of his early life experiences:

> Just my fear of failure. I am *so* afraid to fail. I grew up with just a hard life—and life is still hard—but life was so hard and I just don't want to go back. I just don't, not by any means. So, I'm at the point where I'm like trying to have that same motivation but that same motivation doesn't work at this point. Now I'm at the point where I want to be happy and I want to like what I do.

Collectively, these experiences were translated as "failures" and Julius simply refused to fail—or give up. He figured that he had come too far and there were too many goals that he wanted to accomplish in adulthood that not completing college was not an option—and could make some goals more difficult to reach. Additionally, he also cited his support system, which included a number of his Black male peers, his mentors, and some Ellis Academy personnel, with helping him remain resolute in pursuing his educational goals. Thus, even when he experienced frustrations and potentially lacked some internal motivation, he used an approach that was centered in his community so that his accomplishments and even his perseverance were not just about him but rather were collective in nature.

CHRIS: "I DIDN'T JUST COME HERE JUST TO COME TO SCHOOL"

As Chris and I talked during the summer prior to the start of his final year of college, he offered great clarity in discerning many of his college experiences, from his decisions to attend college, understanding his academic focus once he transitioned, and how he tried to identify and activate support during his college years. We talked about his educational experiences in detail and Chris offered a number of lengthy, insightful, and reflective responses. As an example, he talked about his college experiences in the following way:

> You know, college was ups and downs. I don't know what I really expected college to be like really. No, I do. I expected it to be enjoyable because I had been working towards it for so long and I got outside my community. As I got closer to it, I thought about being in an all-white space and middle to upper income environment. It was a really tough environment to get used to. So, those were some of the challenges that I had early on. But, at the same time, I had a small group of friends, including my girlfriend who helped me get through college. I think that would've made things that much more difficult if I didn't have that support and some positive moments within my experiences.

Chris's reflections here include a number of critical points. First, placing his college experiences within his expectations for college reveals that he continuously thought about his experiences beyond our conversations. Placing his experiences in a context that included his expectations contributed to how he tried to make sense of his educational journey. Second, the context of his college ("I thought being in an all-white space and middle to upper income environment") impacted how he thought about himself, how he thought about the navigational skills he needed to succeed at his institution, and how he thought that the intersections of his race and class background mattered during his college years. And, third, at a minimum, his support group was important in helping make his experiences less difficult.

I wanted to take time to unpack some of Chris's experiences, especially since he offered that his college years were "ups and downs." In considering some of his college highlights, his "ups," that he had shared:

"My very first semester I had a 3.6 GPA, which I was really proud of. I knew I was coming in with a disadvantage. Not having the same resources as many of the students that I would be in class with. I was proud because that wasn't really my goal; I was thinking, 'Hopefully I'll get a 3.0.' I worked hard for that; I spent a lot of time in the library." Based on his academic performance his first semester of college, Chris took deep satisfaction in what he was able to accomplish within the classroom. This was important because he believed that getting off to a great start academically could help smooth his transition to college and establish a solid foundation from which to build on throughout his college years.

In addition to this early academic accomplishment, he also cited his romantic relationship as a significant highlight as well. "My relationship with my girlfriend was a highlight too. She was one of my best friends in college and relationships make the college experience more enjoyable." For Chris, the importance of relationships also was revealed in his engagement on campus and in the local community. "Lastly, my participation in a campus student organization, called Males of Color Leadership Association. The goal of the program was to help increase the alarmingly low graduation percentage of Black and Latino males in the city. Being able to interact with others, including younger students, and I hoped that many others would have the opportunities that I did—or whatever they wanted to do, really."

Recall that Chris had primarily relied on an isolationist strategy during his first year of college so that he could focus on his academic endeavors. Throughout his college years, Chris continued to garner experiences that increased his sense of belonging on campus and enhanced a sense of personal satisfaction. The Males of Color Leadership Association program provided both benefits for Chris. He reveled in opportunities to connect with like-minded people on campus and appreciated that he could provide leadership, direction, and support to fellow male peers as well as local male youth of color. And, also important for Chris related to these experiences was for Black and Latino boys and young men to be able to pursue their own interests and be provided with opportunities that could enhance their experiences, their sense of self, and how they thought about their possibilities.

Not only did Chris identify some of his highlights, we also discussed some of the challenges he faced as well. Initially, he pointed to the academic rigors of college and, in several of our conversations, he put some of his academic challenges within the context of the academic rigor of the institution. Still, though, it was the racialized campus climate of the historically white institution he attended that presented social and personal challenges for Chris. In recalling some of the challenges he faced, he explained: "Academics, of course, were a bit of a challenge. But, I'd say the challenges for me were mostly social. Dealing with race on campus, being a Black man on campus. Just noting the different experiences I had on campus, like being profiled. Being around students who didn't really care about me or people like me—being Black and lower income. It's just tough being around those folks." Throughout his college years, Chris shared a number of negative experiences that highlighted the deficits that he faced because of his raced-gendered Black male identities. He recalled being racially profiled in both academic and social spaces on campus by faculty and staff; he experienced denigrations and stereotypes in the messages and communication he received through his work-study job on campus and during his participation in other university-affiliated activities; and he and several other Black male students were detained and questioned by the university police in several different instances on campus during his college years. All these experiences weighed heavily on his psyche, sense of belonging on campus, and sense of satisfaction with his college.

In regard to academic experiences, even though he performed well academically each year, Chris still shared that the academic rigor of his school created some academic struggles, which increased each year. Additionally, he noted that some of his academic challenges included time and self-management. Chris stated that as the intensity of assignments and rigor of coursework continued to increase each semester, he realized that his time commitment had to increase as well. "On an academic level, the rigor increasing over time it was really just time management or the time that I was putting into my studies. The time that I was putting into it was very different than when I started college."

Similar to the other young men in this study, Chris credited the support he received from various individuals, from friends and peers to several professors and his mentors, as contributing significantly to helping him make it through college. These individuals provided personal, academic, and socioemotional support; he credited one of his mentors with proofreading papers and helping him learn how to improve his analytic writing skills and he credited two professors with providing him with research opportunities and personal support that helped sustain his confidence and expand his skillset as well. "Just the amount of support I had. I had support from people on campus like professors that I built relationships with, who had faith in me. I had support off campus, during the summer, seeing college as a goal for after; that was the point going in, like, 'Hey, this has to lead to something.' There was a reason I came here, I didn't just come here just to come to school." Chris was not satisfied in merely saying he attended college. For him, along with his parents, family, and friends, the goal always was to complete his college degree. In some ways, he believed completing college could serve as inspiration for others who come from similar backgrounds and, at the same time, he viewed completing college as a responsibility that he owed to his community. "You know, as I mentioned, just my sense of identity. Being a Black male from a first-generation, low-income background, I realized how significant my position was in being a student at such an elite institution. I felt like my graduating and performing well mattered for another Black male or Black person. Showing people, 'Hey, I came from this background and made it through and you can too.'"

Jamal: "One thing that you can't take is their education"

As Jamal and I talked about his college experiences, he mentioned his academic challenges on several occasions. A significant part of these challenges was adjusting to the academic rigor of the university he attended and deciding on his course of study. Initially, Jamal pursued a STEM major, which he had been interested in during his precollege years. He experienced some academic struggles and frustrations in pursuing STEM, mostly due to what he perceived as the college's system of intentionally weeding out students. He noted that there were times when his professors declined to assist students in understanding course-related materials, several professors often declined to meet with him and his peers and instead told them to meet with the teaching assistants, and he experienced a number of scenarios in which some of his classmates adopted a cut-throat approach and continuously excluded Black and Latinx students from study groups.

In reflecting on his academic experiences, he noted that his academic performance improved with each year. In his first year, he earned a 2.2 GPA and struggled in his mathematics courses; in his second year, he had a better sense of what to expect, made several adjustments, and earned just over a 2.9 GPA for the year. In considering his academic experiences from his first two years, he explained: "It's a struggle. . . . It's been a struggle since the day I started. But now that I'm in my third year, I've kinda adjusted to it in ways that I didn't know my freshman year. Every year I've gotten better academically and I've been in study groups and learned how to work through some things. I can ask questions and stuff like that." Whereas he was excluded from almost all the study groups during his first semester in college, which added to his feelings of isolation and frustration, Jamal used his agency and began to develop his own study groups and in at least one instance joined a group with a good friend. He acknowledged, "A few of them were because of me and another one was because of somebody else. They would ask if I wanted to join and I would say, 'Yeah, of course!' because I didn't do too well on the first test and I wanted to do better; I wanted to keep it up."

The shift in Jamal's academic experiences and performance helped alleviate some of his initial academic frustrations, and he pointed to his determination and resolve as characteristics that helped him persevere through challenging experiences. During his first two years of college, he learned about his perseverance and resolve to push through difficulties. He acknowledged what he had learned:

> That I'm not a quitter, that although it's very challenging I still work hard to prove to myself that I belong here and I can do this. Yeah, it goes back to high school when you talked about being college bound and graduating from college every day. When you say it every day you don't think nothing of it until you leave that environment. I had to think of something that would inspire me and it helped me stay until graduation.

The concept of proving to oneself can serve as a powerful internal motivator and connects well with Jamal's family values for education and his educational urgency. Additionally, Jamal also relied on the cultural ethos that he developed during his secondary school years as both a reminder about his goals and as motivation to continue pursuing his college graduation. This was another form of self-talk that some of the young men engaged in to help center their attention and focus. For Jamal, reflecting back on his secondary school experiences also provided him with a context to put his college experiences and aspirations in perspective.

Another shift that Jamal made in trying to reach his academic goals was refining his study habits. Not including weekends, which varied from week to week, he said he spent about fifteen hours a week doing course-related work outside the classroom. Although he mostly studied in his room during his early college years, he also changed his approach in attempts to secure greater academic success. "Well before I used to study in my room because I hated the library because it was always packed. But I learned that I had to get out my room because there were too many distractions. I had my roommate and then there was the tv; you can cut the tv off but it's there. So now I study at the library or different cafes like Starbucks." The change in settings helped Jamal focus more on his work and reduced the possible distractions that might tempt him to turn his attention away from his studies. He created PowerPoint slides to study and prepare, he was persistent in creating notecards so that he could identify and review critical information for each unit, and he routinely completed practice problems, sample questions, and chapter review questions. He credited his high school Spanish teacher with introducing him to these strategies, and he called on them again during his college years. They helped him practice retaining information and pushed him to assess his own knowledge about course material well ahead of tests and exams.

Along with navigating the academic rigor and work of college, Jamal also had to contend with the social and cultural atmosphere of campus life. Given the ways in which whiteness was centered at his historically white institution, he declared, "Being a Black male is difficult at this school." He shared that he often felt invisible on campus and that many people, white counterparts along with some faculty and staff, simply did not care for him—or many other Black students. In describing the racial atmosphere on campus, he observed:

> I wouldn't say that it's very segregated but there are some parts on campus that Black students aren't welcome. Where frat houses are, Blacks are not really invited there and where some of the bars are they're not really invited either. Some professors, they don't really care about Black students. I mean, this is a racist state in general, some parts are worse than others, so you can expect that anywhere you go. I mean, I've experienced racism a couple times while I was here.

In describing the college campus, although Jamal did not want to label the campus as "very segregated," he still noted that anti-Blackness was apparent in Greek life, some of the local establishments in the community, and even on the campus itself. Here, I distinguish between Greek life and the campus because the fraternity houses at his college, similar to many institutions, were privately owned houses that did not have to cater to university policies.

As it relates to his personal experiences with racism, Jamal recounted incidents that occurred beginning his first semester in college and continued throughout his college years. These experiences ranged from racist comments and racial epithets used against him and several other Black male peers to racialized stereotypes from a few faculty and staff members and being racially profiled on and off campus. Jamal's statement that his school was located in what he considered "a racist state in general" meant that "you can expect that [racism] anywhere you go" in the state. One of his main precollege concerns in attending school in the Mid-Atlantic region was "being in a school that is predominantly white and being in a class that's dominated by that race is frightening because you don't know how they're going to act." In response to his personal experiences with racism, he shared that he did not want to give reason or cause for his opportunities to be limited and he understood that his completing college was not simply about him but for his family as well, "I didn't react because if I had reacted I would've jeopardized what I have here. I've seen it, I've heard about it, so it can be racism like every day."

Additionally, Jamal changed his major at the beginning of his third year from STEM to sports management. His academic struggles and loss of enthusiasm for STEM precipitated the change. We discussed his thoughts about what he might consider changing if he could do college over again; he shared:

> I guess like, besides the school I went to, it would be knowing what major I wanted to do off the bat instead of doing what my mother wanted me to do. I knew I liked athletics and I like helping people achieve their goals. So, I could've put that together and did kinesiology or athletic training; I could've still did sport management or put it together. It would've involved sports and being active; that would be the one thing I would change.

Jamal's response alluded to his desire to follow his own ambitions and interests as opposed to pursuing a major that his mother identified. Partly, he was speaking through the frustrations of his academic experiences in

STEM, and it seems that he also held on to a desire to help and work with people through athletics that developed during his college years. His response and some of our conversation suggested a bit of a conflict he experienced in trying to appease his mother while diminishing or delaying the pursuit of his own interests. Additionally, I asked Jamal if he would choose the same institution again and, after some thought, he responded that he definitely would change institutions.

> That's a hard question. . . . [long pause] Honestly, nah, I wouldn't! We're always told that the world we live in is white, so why not go to school where the majority of the culture and figure out what it's like on your own in this type of environment instead of just being around the same people that you grew up with or the people who are your same skin color or stuff like that. I think that if I had went to an HBCU I would've performed better academically, I would not have experienced the type of racism I experienced here, and I would've had a better college experience.

According to a number of the young men in this study, given the racial battles and Black misandry they experienced on campus, they wondered and held on to some lingering thoughts about what their college experiences would have been like in a Black-centered college environment. With the exception of Chauncey, they speculated that attending an HBCU would have been less of a racialized culture shock and would have placed them in an environment where anti-Black racism in both academic and social spaces was not a predominant component of their college experiences.

Even though he had a number of challenges, including academic struggles and dealing with anti-Black racism on and around campus, Jamal accomplished a great deal during his college years. He counted many of his personal relationships and his ability to turn around his academic performance as significant achievements during college. Also, he participated in college athletics, worked with student-athletes on campus, and tutored local Black boys in support of their academic and athletic aspirations. He credited his support system with helping him accomplish many of his goals and complete college.

> **Jamal:** Besides the Ellis Academy support system and my friends at Ellis, I would say some of the faculty here. I had a

couple friends and my girlfriend helped me a lot—and, just knowing that when I was younger, when people would ask me to do something I would say, "I can do that, I can do that." My grandmother used to say I could go to college and just thinking about why she did it, helped to contribute to everything else too.

DB: Why your grandmother did what?

Jamal: 'Cuz with her, there were no if, ands, or buts about it [going to college]. I could go and if I didn't like it, I could leave. But with her, she didn't play; and, it's just hard to make it with just a high school degree [in society]. Just to have that [college] degree, and being a Black male, opens up a lot of doors and I can do whatever I'm interested in. You can take things from people, but the one thing that you can't take is their education. Yeah, that's the one thing that you can't take.

Jamal identified his friend group, which overwhelming included Black male peers, and his relationship with his girlfriend as critical factors that helped him persevere in college. It was important that he also called on messaging and lessons from his mother, an uncle, his grandmother, and his mentors as vital sources of motivation and support for his college strivings. He held on to his grandmother's message closely and translated it as another way for him to value his own educational accomplishments and his sense of self. As Jamal thought about his educational journey and the range of his lived experiences, he felt that he was worth all the investments he made to his personal and educational endeavors. "It's all going to pay off soon because I'm going to have two degrees in six years; that's just amazing because I didn't want to get my master's and I kinda didn't want to get my bachelor's. Now, I'm thinking about getting a PhD. Before, I didn't even think about a PhD but now it's something that I'm considering. I'm just at a different place now."

MICHAEL: "I'M CREATING MY STORY"

When we met during one of our later interviews, Michael showed a sense of urgency and seemed as though he had a lot on his mind. He seemed this way through some of our phone conversations and text check-ins during this time as well. He seemed to be operating with a sense of urgency that required immediate results. He was a little late for the interview as he was spending some time with one of his younger brothers; he had focused on their relationship in the last year as he wanted to ensure that he offered his brother his perspective on navigating school as well as identifying and pursuing his personal interests. His brother was a year away from completing secondary school and Michael wanted to share some strategies for him to consider.

As we reflected back on his early college years, Michael talked about his first year of college as a tone setter that pushed and pulled him in different directions—academically, personally, and socially. He felt tested and taxed; he felt that he was on a learning journey. He also noted that his first year was consumed by trying to adjust to the institution by learning more about his college's context and developing his plan for success. In relation to his early college years, he explained: "Set in that tone. It was . . . first year was going to be some understandings; second year was gonna be, the plan being thought out and acted upon because now you have to think about a major. Therefore, the meat of what you're in college for is going to reveal itself. The first two years are the general education classes; that sophomore year was about setting up the work that you gotta put in." As revealed in his discussion, Michael took a systematic approach to his first two years of college where he tried to devise a system that would help him establish a plan for college success. In effect, he was working to create a map for his college years, how he would navigate various facets of the college environment, and how he could accomplish some of his goals.

His struggles in transitioning to college impacted his academic performance: he earned a 2.2 grade point average his first semester but improved to a 2.4 in his second semester. Although his GPA was not what he wanted it to be, Michael acknowledged the increase as improvement and as part of his adjustment, which helped instill some confidence in his ability to navigate the institution. In discussing his second-year performance, he expressed excitement: "Then I came back and my performances continued to improve; that's what I'm talking about, I was starting to hit a peak and my grades were starting to reveal that. When I saw the improvement, I knew what the results are because I know what a 3.0 is." Midway through his third year, Michael had improved his overall GPA from a 2.3 in his first year of college to a 2.9. With excitement in his voice and showing appreciation for his journey, Michael declared, "I was on my way."

Critical to Michael's turnaround and improvement was his discernment and self-reflection on his efforts and capabilities; what is more, he engaged in self-talk, sought out support and guidance from his mentors and peers, and developed close relationships with a few faculty members. Some of the experiences that he enjoyed about the liberal arts college he attended included its focus on critical thought and the ways in which he felt pushed academically and intellectually. "[This school] challenges the way you think. It gives you knowledge and wants you to see the wisdom." In addition to his support system, he shared that he was able to adjust quickly because of his learning and understanding of his college's ethos and focus, "The knowledge is what happened, the wisdom is why; that's how I feel [this school] pushed me."

Similar to his secondary school experiences, Michael identified that his first two years also were a period of self-discovery. As he adjusted to the college and the campus environment, he also felt that he was relearning how to be a college student and, even more importantly, the type of student he wanted to or could be. "It was just trying to figure out what type of student I was, how did I learn on this scale, what was the best way for me to learn. Being able to engage in academic discussions, heated academic discussions; being able to hold my own, being able to be a thinker and analyzing. You realize how much of a weapon your brain really is." Being engaged in an academic atmosphere where classes were centered on critical discussions resonated with Michael's budding intellectual interests. "A lot of my classes are discussion-based classes; you're thinking, processing information, rephrasing information, you just have to think."

As we discussed the academic challenges he experienced, Michael identified these as learning experiences. In fact, perhaps because of his early college experiences, he identified struggle as part of the process of understanding one's self and one's possibilities. In an attempt to overcome his challenges, Michael referred back to developing and trusting his plan and support system as critical to garnering his success. "It's trusting your plan, trusting the people that you have around you whose job is to make sure you succeed. Just trusting that and trusting the work you have to put in and understand that you're going to have some failures. You're not going to college and just rock out because if it was that easy then everybody would be doing it. So, just understanding that and then working accordingly." He received significant support from peers and also accessed some institutional resources, such as academic advising, tutoring services, and various student affairs professionals in the Black Cultural Center. Michael's narrative suggests that he accepted academic struggles as a reality of the educational journey: he felt he couldn't simply go to college "and just rock out" academically, but rather that he needed to develop a plan that could help him pursue his educational goals and prepare to respond to potential setbacks and challenges as well.

As we sat discussing his experiences in a retrospective, present, future point of view, I asked Michael to look back and put his experiences in perspective starting from the time he started secondary school. He responded with a lengthy and insightful reflection that focused on his interiorities:

> I've been learning who Michael Amari Williams is, what he's made of, what makes him smile—according to him. He's a strong individual. He's resilient, he's thoughtful, he's not heartless. He embraces defeat knowing that you can't win everything; he embraces the failure knowing eventually you have to get up. Somewhere down the line he built that relationship. And it's not because someone felt sorry but because it's his name and how he made Michael Amari Williams a name; that's not my father's name. I'm building on it.

Michael continued in his reflection and focused on the importance of building a foundation for character as well as his sense of self and how his life and experiences will contribute to the next generation. Here, he included a discussion of various family members including his son, Amare, and added:

> These past nine years, because we've talked about foundation, resiliency, these nine years have been the foundation to the man that I am becoming. It's what I stand on. This is my story that I can tell that will make me proud to tell it. Because I was born into a situation and I made the best out of it and now I'm in position to change a generation's life, period. Not a child, a generation. You understand what me going to school can do for Amare's [my son's] generation;

> Amare, Danai, my niece, my little brothers, them going to college and whoever else is next? We're already breaking that cycle. So these past nine years are what they are supposed to be. They've been my home because my life is my home. I've lived to overcome situations. I've lived to be a great person, loving son, great brother, great athlete. Just because you have life doesn't mean that you're living and just because you live doesn't mean that you've learned. Life is given but what you choose to do with it is important; I'm living. I'm living right now; I'm creating my story.

Clear in Michael's reflection is his personal development, the ways in which he believes he is continuing to come into himself, and the importance of his development, efforts, and accomplishments in relation to his family. Michael's statements that the years since he began secondary school "have been the foundation to the man that I am becoming" is connected to how he sees himself through the processes of these experiences. Additionally, his desire and focus on his ability to "change a generation's life"—including the life of his son and his niece, his siblings, and "whoever else is next"—reflects his belief that he can be and already is a change agent for both his family and community.

Summary

As first-generation college students, these young men identified completing college as an important milestone for themselves as well as their families and communities. Their status as first-generation students was prominent in a number of their experiences and contributed to their persistence efforts. In trying to make it through college, the young Black men discussed in this chapter identified a range of strategies that they called on to pursue and accomplish their educational goals. They each discussed the need for more focused efforts and greater investments in their academic endeavors as they navigated their college years. Whether it was trying to rebound from significant academic challenges or battling with stereotypes and lowered expectations, these young men were resolute in their desires to make it through college. Additionally, across each of their narratives the young men described ways in which their experiences continued to reveal their sense of self, their agency, and their educational desires.

Most notably, internal and external dilemmas were prominent in their decision making, strategizing, and efforts in navigating college. Internally, some of the dilemmas they highlighted in this chapter included Julius's professed "fear of failure," which Edwin also discussed in the previous chapter. While this sentiment was expressed explicitly by Julius, each of the young men discussed the fact that continuing to pursue their educational goals required them to face some of their fears and personal concerns. Another internal dilemma that was prominent in some of their experiences was trying to negotiate the academic rigor of their colleges. Their concerns about achieving well academically informed their study habits, time management, and academic strategies and focus. As the intensity of their courses increased, the young men reassessed how they approached their work and the time they committed to it so that their educational efforts were reflected in their academic performance.

The main external dilemma that these young men faced was their Black male racialized-gendered identities. Chris's concerns about navigating his college included how his intersecting identities of being a Black male from a lower socioeconomic background impacted how he could enmesh himself in college life and how he believed and experienced others' lack of concern for individuals from backgrounds similar to his. Similarly, Jamal held concerns about navigating the historically white institution he attended even before he enrolled, which, unfortunately, were affirmed throughout his college years. The combined impact of trying to navigate the academic demands of their respective colleges and having to cope with racism, microaggressions, profiling, and mistreatment were taxing for all these young men. That they experienced various racial battles on and off campus simply because they are Black males continues to reveal the prominence of their Blackmaleness and the ways in which they are repositioned by others. These experiences included belittling, stereotypes, dissonance, social avoidance, verbal harassment, and interpersonal animus and anti-Black racism. Their responses to these experiences were not about ignoring them and acting as if they did not exist, but rather were based on calculations that centered on the efforts and investments that they had made to their educational goals. Additionally, they all were keen on understanding the maldistribution of racial justice.

Extracting lessons from their early college experiences and activating plans that allowed them to rebound, overcome, persevere, push through, and create alternate pathways toward success reflected their maturity and growth and also revealed their educational urgency. As Julius noted in the quote that opens this chapter, all these young men knew they had to stay motivated regardless of the challenges and obstacles they faced and in spite of the hardships they experienced. A critical component of their striving was the support they received along the way and the support systems that helped sustain them throughout their college years. These young men had people who believed in them and people counting on them, both of which were translated into internal and external motivations. As a result, they maintained their aspirations and understood quite clearly that there was a shared interest in them pursuing their educational goals. Because college itself is challenging, because being young Black men in college is difficult and can be stressful, and because their personal journeys already had required particular forms of resolve and resilience, these young Black men had developed clarity in their educational desires. These young men were determined to complete college; in fact, Chris said it best when he shared, "I didn't just come [to college] just to come to school." Chris's declaration represents that of the group, as they all stated that completing college was part of the story that they were creating about themselves and their families and, at the same time, they identified their educational endeavors as ways to help create pathways for better futures for their families and community as well.

PART III

LESSONS

Chapter 9

"Sometimes the odds are just stacked against you"

Reassessing the Challenges That Make Education High-Stakes

> It's not easy! [laughs in frustration] It's not easy at all being a Black male. Sometimes you're a statistic, sometimes you're a murder rate . . . sometimes you're lost, sometimes you're blind. Sometimes the odds are just stacked against you—just to see how willing you are to get through the obstacles.
>
> —Michael

This study is based on the premise that Black boys and young men matter. Educators who believe Black boys and young men matter listen to and hear their stories; they develop social contexts and structures that ensure that their whole selves are valued and validated; they promote and support healthy self-conceptions and create opportunities for them to learn more about themselves; they develop relationships with them that accounts for multiple facets of their lives; and they create and sustain environments that allow for growth, development, and successes.

Those who truly know Black boys and young men are not surprised by their intellect and aptitude, but instead look for their brilliance. Those who truly know Black boys and young men embrace and encourage their brilliance, intellectual genius, and resourcefulness—even as they are developing, exploring, and learning to express these qualities, both individually and collectively. Those who truly know Black boys and young men understand that their past does not automatically determine, or overdetermine, their future. Those who truly know Black boys and young men understand that for far too many of them, they bear incredible costs because of their Black male identities, because of the neighborhoods that they reside in and must navigate, because of the schooling environments and other social institutions they must endure, and because of the ways that they are devalued perpetually across US society. Those who truly know Black boys and young men work to keep them positioned toward their possibilities—even through their struggles and missteps, through conditions that can constrain their lives and opportunities, and across contexts and experiences that can lead to self-doubts.

The main thrust of this study was to explore the lives and educational experiences of a select group of young Black men with particular attention to their pathways to college and the efforts they engaged in and sense making they used in trying to make it through college. In this study, I adopted a sociocultural perspective to examine these young men's lives, relying on their meaning making of interactions, experiences, and connections within and beyond school as contexts for understanding their educational journeys.

What Are the Challenges?

Based on the narratives and experiences presented in this study, young Black men face a number of high-stakes challenges in their lives that are apparent in and impact their educational journeys. As they attested, anti-Black racism continuously impacts their lives and how they make sense of their lifeworlds; importantly, the chances, costs, and circumstances that they must navigate are not some form of "paranoia" of their own minds, as James Baldwin discussed, but rather are a real social danger that accosts and confronts them across social institutions, interactions, spaces and places, and lived experiences.[1] In this section, I bring forward a multidimensional analysis that accounts for their experiences across several facets of their lives. The goal here is to bring into greater focus a cogent analysis of how they experienced and made sense of these facets and extracted lessons from them as well. In particular, I discuss the challenges they experience and try to navigate across four interconnecting dimensions: societal devaluing of Black boys and men; the neighborhood context; educational institutions; and mental health and wellness.

The Societal Devaluing of Black Boys and Men

Most prominently, the young men in this study identified the devaluing of Black life and various forms of anti-Black racism as detrimental to their psyche, sense of self, life chances and outcomes, and possibilities. The devaluing of Black life has incorporated both mediated messages and projections about Black boys and men as well as the continued and ongoing killing of Blacks boys and young men throughout the United States, such as Tamir Rice, Laquan McDonald, Trayvon Martin, Michael Brown, Jonathan Ferrell, and Daunte Wright, to name a few.[2] Young Black men regularly face alienation in a society that portrays them negatively, preys on their demise, and is complicit in their troubles and suffering. Moreover, as researchers have contended, Black boys and young men are "against the wall" partly because their Blackness continuously mars them as guilty.[3] As discussed throughout this work, several of the young men transformed the challenges that anti-Black racism and Blackmaleness presented them with and that confronted their lives. Julius's assessment, which was used to open the previous chapter, is useful to revisit again here. In speaking about his learning about being Black and male he asserted, "Learning how to be yourself. When you look at the stereotypes and statistics that are given to you it gets to you sometimes. If you don't stay powerful then you won't be powerful, not in this environment."

Pairing Julius's comment with the quote from Michael used at the beginning of this chapter is revelatory for several reasons. Based on the ways in which they are devalued across US society, Julius deemed it critical for Black boys and young men to engage in self-learning and self-defining practices. Both young men asserted that such an approach was important in helping them learn more about themselves, and perhaps even their place in the world, and also as an effort that could help them navigate society and social institutions more effectively. Further, they maintained that even a cursory glance at how they are framed within society makes their invisibilities apparent. That stereotypes and statistics could be "given to" Black boys and Black young men about who they supposedly are or what they potentially could be reduced to are attacks on their character and promise. These young Black men learned early on that their Blackmaleness marked them as "Other," and this othering was translated, understood, and experienced as difficulties ("It's not easy at all being a Black male"). As shown throughout this work, being Black and male placed these young men in precarious scenarios of harm, danger, and uncertainty and, because of how they were projected, (mis)seen, and treated by others, this created challenges that could confront them on an ongoing basis. As Michael attested, this risk could render them as "a statistic" where "the odds are just stacked against you." For too many young Black men, even beyond the stereotypes that marginalized them, these statistics and odds help inform the persistent societal devaluing and the perpetual denigration and exclusion that confronts their lives and humanity.

That Black boys and young men are accosted with being relegated to a "statistic" through societal projections and expectations on a routine basis reveals their marginal mattering and the critical nature of the stakes they face. As they discussed throughout and as Malik stated explicitly (as quoted in chapter 1), this marginalizing occurs from and within "everyday situations . . . that makes it hard to be a Black man in society." The everydayness of these "situations" and experiences inherently raises the stakes for Black boys and young men in their efforts to keep their humanity intact. Additionally, as Malik and several of the young men made clear, whether as projections, (mis)perceptions, stereotyping, or denial, society's interminable anti-Blackness means that too many people across society "don't give us a chance to be us." Their fight for dignity is both daunting and exhausting; the effects of these battles can disrupt and undermine their pathways, can diminish how they see themselves and relate to others, and can (continue to) arrest their development.

Not being able to be who they are manifests itself in numerous ways, such that Black boys and young men face additional and undue burdens and challenges in their lives, in schools and social institutions, and across society that contribute to how they are policed and surveilled, regardless of who they are. In fact, *who* they are is meaningless because their fate has been predetermined through punitive means and the threats of harm shroud their lives precisely because their humanity remains under constant attack. Moreover, *where* they are is insignificant as well since they encounter being repositioned and having their movements tracked constantly, from neighborhoods to public perceptions to social institutions. This surveillance and the attendant secondary policing of their presence and movements suggests over and over again that they are out of place and do not belong, as was exemplified by some of the young men's college experiences (e.g., Jamal's point that "there are some parts on campus [where] Black students aren't welcome").

Even places where they "should" belong, such as their home neighborhoods, sometimes are sites of contestations through interactions with community members, along with the police presence and activities in those neighborhoods (e.g., indiscriminate surveillance). And *how* they are, in relation to their behaviors and actions, is of little consequence because their personhood is invisible. Individually and collectively, this also means that too many Black boys and young men are held to different standards, as Paul asserted, "because of the stereotypes out there against us, the statistics that most of us are supposed to be in jail, not college. . . . You know, like not living past twenty-one and things like that." These dominant narratives not only produce burdens, misunderstandings, and challenges, they also are inherently violent and anti-Black, rely on tropes that criminalize and demonize Black boys and young men, and contribute to their feelings and sense that "sometimes you're lost."

As displayed in the narratives presented throughout this book, these young men know from firsthand experience and cultural knowledge that the odds continue to be stacked against too many Black boys and men in US society. This has a marginalizing and delegitimating effect. It deems their talents and capabilities invisible while also reducing and misconstruing their aspirations as doubtful, unlikely, and questionable. Even further, though, the societal devaluing of Black boys' and young men's lives also construes their becoming as improbable and impossible. The devaluing of Black boys and young men across the wider society means that they are disregarded and unworthy and considered as disposable.

The Neighborhood Context

Within the neighborhood, all of these young men discussed experiencing grave difficulties that impacted their schooling experiences, their physical and mental health and well-being, and their self-perceptions. That a number of these young men said they "had to get out" of the neighborhood helps shed light on the gravity of the circumstances that they faced. Quite clearly, these young men asserted that navigating the neighborhood was wrought with challenges; particularly, their narratives suggest that because of the conditions of their neighborhoods, which included economic depravity and lack of access to quality resources, staying in these environments placed them at increased risk of distress, discomfort, affliction, and injury—physically, emotionally, mentally, and spiritually.

The structural and material conditions of the neighborhoods they traveled, navigated, and are connected to are important because they relate to how these young men thought about themselves and contribute to how they made sense of relationships and opportunities. Also, what they learned through experience was that in the eyes and imaginations of others, Black boys' and young men's past, present, and future selves are transfixed by the perilous conditions of their neighborhoods and some of the activities of other youth. As Chris, Jamal, and several others attested, they felt overly scrutinized and experienced multiple types of surveillance that repositioned them as "guilty" by association. Regardless of neighborhood or locale, these young Black men contended that they were always already under surveillance; and, at the same time, being in or traveling through specific neighborhoods made the scrutiny they faced even more stringent.

Each of these young men translated neighborhood peril and the various troubles that it produced, such as strained interpersonal relationships between Black boys and men along with hyperpolicing and stereotyping, as another critical challenge that they faced and were confronted by during their adolescent years. Further, they identified getting out of the neighborhood—and even out of the city—as a powerful motivating force that informed their educational desires. As an example, some of these young men declared that being able to continue to pursue their educational goals meant that they did not succumb to structural violence and did not get caught up by or in affiliations or associations that could restrict their educational focus or personal goals. In one sense, while they were able to stay on their educational pathways to college, they didn't consider themselves "winners" from a dichotomous positioning standpoint. Rather, they remained actively aware of the disadvantages they faced in their home neighborhoods, which included significant structural racism exacerbated by social inequities, economic blight and depravity, and interpersonal conflicts, which also contributed to police surveillance, illegal and illicit activities, and negative impacts on their life outcomes. These young men had knowledge of and proximity to ways in which Black youth could get "caught up" in gang activities and risk being relegated to negative statistics simply because of the neighborhood they lived in or navigated.[4] The contentions by the young men in this study that they "didn't want to be a statistic," needed to be both cautious and aware in navigating neighborhoods because they knew "bullets don't have names," and were always already under surveillance because they experienced "having police around there, harassing people—especially kids" all speak to some of the high-stakes challenges and conditions they had to navigate.

The difficulties that were present and that they faced in their neighborhoods, both in their home and school communities, challenged and confronted these young men's sense of self, schooling experiences, and personal aspirations. Each of these young men, in their own ways, translated the challenges they bore within the neighborhood context as temporary, and they used them as motivation to inform and strengthen their educational desires. For instance, as Chris stated (quoted in chapter 2), "At some point, I know I didn't think I would make it to eighteen [years old]. Not because I was engaged in illegal or illicit activities, but you just didn't know if you would make it there in environments like those." Similarly, as Michael explained, the neighborhood "made me feel like I *had* to go somewhere because of those things, it was a must!" (chapter 3). Moreover, even beyond experiences or activities that could affect them personally, they also used a critical lens to make sense of how the structural conditions of the neighborhood affected families. For instance, in reflecting on the school neighborhood, which is where he lived, Paul stated, "It was hard, it was rough; it was dangerous. A neighborhood I'm pretty sure most people don't want to raise their family. A neighborhood that's corrupted, neighborhood that government don't really care about." These realities impacted how these young men thought about their lives and their futures and also informed the precautions they needed to take, decisions regarding peer relationships, and the activities that they engaged in.

For the young Black men in this study, who negotiated segregated urban geographies every day, particularly during their secondary school years, navigating and engaging with the school's neighborhood (and, potentially, adjoining neighborhoods) functioned as real challenges to their physical and psychosocial health, well-being, and security. Moreover, navigating this environment often created tensions and challenges for their schooling experiences and educational aspirations. Given that the participants in this study successfully navigated neighborhood threats and matriculated to college, it is no surprise that their narratives centered on educational desires and using education as a tool for contributing to their families. Chris and Michael make this point quite clear. Chris explained, "For me, providing for my family and getting out, I thought that getting out was my way of providing for my family. I thought that getting out was what I needed to help change my trajectory." Michael made a very succinct statement: "My favorite part about living there is making it out." That they saw neighborhood peril, interpersonal violence, and potential lack of opportunities within the community as disruptions is apparent, and it clearly informed some of their educational and personal motivations.

While young men such as Chris and Michael took this approach, the point here is not to suggest that one cannot "make it there" or that other Black youth do not do well in these same environments. Rather, their meaning making reflects how they perceived and reacted to their circumstances, environment, and understanding at a specific point in their lives. To Paul's point that he lived and attended school in a "neighborhood that [the] government don't really care about," and because he perceived that the government didn't care about his home and school neighborhood, he anticipated little change or improvement in resources, opportunities, and outcomes for young people like himself. Overwhelmingly, these young men contended, realized, and experienced government neglect, state-sanctioned violence, and other structural forces as very real reasons why it might be difficult or unlikely to overcome some of the high-stakes challenges they experience in economically deprived, underresourced, and state-neglected neighborhoods.

Educational Contexts

As the young men discussed their educational journeys, they shared observations and experiences that shed light on some of the dilemmas they faced in educational settings. They were quite clear about their secondary school choices and the meaningful experiences and relationships that they believed had helped get them on and keep them on a college-going pathway. As they reflected on their educational journeys, these young Black men expressed keen awareness about some of the educational challenges they faced, such as schooling options, and how some of the trials they faced and saw in the neighborhood were apparent in some of the local schools as well—such as potential gang violence or physical altercations. In our conversations, they talked at length about what they perceived as potential drawbacks and limitations to attending certain schools and what attending these schools might mean even as they continued to build their own educational aspirations and goals. As first-generation students, they faced a number of potential barriers, which included a lack of family knowledge about college, inequality of neighborhood resources, and the potential and real psychological impact of societal devaluation and standardized testing results.

As it relates to critical moments and experiences in their secondary school years, several of the young men's experiences are noteworthy. As Chauncey discussed concerning his educational journey, there were significant differences in the schools he attended. At the private secondary school he attended initially, he noted a lack of focus on supporting students' college going. His affirmation is quite telling: "Believe it or not, [Arnold High] wasn't big on trying to get people to college—unless you were big on sports or something. So I'm glad I got up outta there anyway" (chapter 2). Given the small Black student population and that many of the Black male students participated in athletics, he surmised that preparing Black students for college academically did not seem to be a clear focus of the school. Without doubt, the circumstances that led to his eventual decision to depart from the school provided him with a very real perspective on educational neglect and personal disregard. As several other young men discussed, they needed to adjust their academic orientations in efforts to improve their academic performance. It is significant that each of the young men affirmed the importance of learning the schooling "system" at Ellis Academy (especially the academic standards and college-going focus), they acknowledged the need for developing positive relationships with their teachers (to aid in their adjustments, learning, and development), and they attested to the need for a caring, understanding, and supportive schooling environment that could help transform their aspirations into realities.

Even more broadly, each of these young men identified pursuing higher education as a considerable trial to be faced. In this regard, especially as first-generation students, they had to contend with their own lack of knowledge of how to access higher education and acknowledged the lack of college-going capital in their families as a limitation. Further, they identified "getting to" college as a way to change the trajectories and expand their families' histories. For these young men, securing a college degree was identified as a personal, familial, and communal goal and responsibility. This lack of college knowledge is important to these young men's meaning making and matters in how they thought about neighborhood schools and their peer networks as well. For instance, the fact that some of their peers did not pursue college provides another context for understanding assessments of local schools and their decisions to attend Ellis Academy. Moreover, the antagonisms and negative social interactions that impacted the neighborhood also were rife in some of the local schools as well. Thus, these young men's attestations that the neighborhood dynamics and their lived experiences informed and motivated their educational experiences and desires is important. For instance, Chauncey offered that he was motivated by "really just wanting to get away."

As it relates to aspiring to college, as mentioned, a number of points within these young men's journeys identify the critical context of their experiences. First, each of these young men identified pursuing college as a significant educational desire. They tied college to personal success ("the standard to succeed") and saw it as necessary for future job prospects and life satisfaction ("I was told that college would be hard and it's hard to get a job in this world without having a bachelor's degree"). Second, and importantly, each of these young men also noted a significant knowledge gap in accessing higher education. This sentiment was expressed most clearly in reflective statements that affirmed a significant need to bridge the gaps between aspirations and knowledge. There are significant consequences that this gap creates that ultimately lead to two prominent outcomes. On the one hand, lacking college knowledge serves as a significant barrier for pursuing and accessing college. For instance, as the young men revealed, college "was a fairy tale," "I didn't even know how I'm going to get there," "I didn't really know anything about college outside of athletics like football and basketball," and "I didn't think I was going to college [laughing in recollection]; not me, un uh. I didn't even know how to get to college!" On the other hand, the popularity of the dominant narrative that Black boys "don't care about education" fundamentally dismisses their aspirations, ignores their needs, and denies them support. Clearly, Black boys' and young men's intersecting identities and lived experiences play a critical role in what they believe as possible for themselves and their futures.

During their college years, these young men faced some educational difficulties and dilemmas that stretched and strained them in a number of ways. From transitioning to college and adjusting to the academic and social life on campus to learning about campus culture and navigating the institutional environment, these young men's college years were full of experiences that required them to constantly assess and stay centered on their educational desires. I focus on three specific areas of their college years that mattered greatly to their experiences and how they tried to negotiate them. First, each of these young men had interpersonal experiences that undermined and threatened their sense of belonging on campus. These experiences included interactions with faculty and staff at various points in college as well as with other students and even community members. Some of these interactions included various types of aggressions, Black misandry, and even racial battle fatigue.[5]

Second, each of these young men had to learn to cope with, manage, negotiate, and respond to academic difficulties that ultimately created internal dilemmas. As a result of these experiences, they talked about feeling discouraged, overwhelmed, stressed, and even doubtful of their ability to rebound from and overcome the litany of challenges they faced in college. Moreover, it is very likely that their first-generation status also contributed to the effect of these experiences. Here I call on a few excerpts from the narratives offered in part 2 of this book that speak directly to these high-stakes challenges. For instance, Edwin acknowledged, "I wasn't sure how far I was gon' make it; I wasn't sure if I was college material," and Paul asserted, "Yeah, I doubted myself but I just had to keep on going and keep on believing in myself." Likewise, after several setbacks that led to his family picking him up from college midway through one of his semesters on campus, Chauncey questioned, "How did I even get here?" Finally, the compounding impact of these experiences revealed two important points. On the one hand, these experiences shook their self-beliefs and tested their mental fortitude, support systems, and persistence efforts throughout their college years. On the other hand, these experiences and a number of others meant that the daily decisions they had to make about continuing to persist revealed the complexities of their college journeys and the educational trials they faced.

Mental Health and Wellness

Each of these challenges contribute to how Black boys and young men see themselves in the world and can inform their sense of self and their health and well-being. As discussed throughout this book and highlighted in this chapter, these Black young men were confronted by a range of high-stakes challenges that are multidimensional and multispatial, encompassing dominant and deficit-based narratives, disparate treatment and repositioning in public discourse, ill-informed and uncaring projections, misrepresentations, straining environments, and hostile social institutions. Collectively, these trials create a series of weights that these Black young men, and so many other Black boys and men, carry with them in their lives that ultimately taxes them psychosocially, emotionally, mentally, and spiritually. Again, I invoke Michael's words from the beginning of this chapter: "It's not easy at all being a Black male. Sometimes you're a statistic, sometimes you're a murder rate. . . . Sometimes you're lost, sometimes you're blind. Sometimes the odds are just stacked against you."

Several of these young men endured emotionally and psychological agonizing experiences throughout their educational journeys. These experiences run the gamut of academic, personal, social, and familial distress and even stressors within their communities. Navigating, responding to, and coping with these harrowing and agonizing experiences is taxing and places tremendous stress on these young men. Thus, part of the reason why the stakes is high relates to the multidimensional costs associated with education. Black boys and young men are damned and condemned by others if they choose not to pursue higher education; for instance, they are labeled as oppositional and defiant or even perhaps as antischool. They experience both internal and external dilemmas in wanting to contribute to their families and their future selves knowing that a lack of higher education can create a number of limitations for social mobility and professional opportunities. Moreover, in pursuing educational attainment, they must navigate miseducation, educational neglect, racial battles, stereotypes, and disparate treatment. These costs make clear Black suffering and spirit murder in educational contexts.

I recall these young men referring to stress and depression-like experiences during our conversations and, in transparency, it was not until conducting rounds of analysis in writing this book project that I became even more aware of how prevalent they referred to issues that impacted their mental health and well-being. In writing across several chapters of this work, I am still struck by the weight that these young men carried and endured. Their statements, such as "I almost felt depressed sometimes," "I low key went through a depression for a minute," and "it was depressing because I didn't feel that smart," all are striking. Their statements and experiences reflect another dimension of the stakes they face. Considerations must be given to how Black boys and men internalize, express, and share about their experiences. Along the same lines, racial battles and various forms of stress that relate to race, gender,

Blackmaleness, academics, and social experiences impacted these young men's educational experiences. Combining such statements with their lived experiences that they offered throughout this work provides great depth about their health, well-being, and meaning making. Considered together, these young men offer critical insights into their emotionality, interiorities, and vulnerabilities. These insights also speak powerfully to the importance of their sense of self, their relationships, and the various types of support they received.

To both recognize and affirm the humanity of Black boys and young men requires acknowledging the adverse effects of racism, anti-Blackness, and educational neglect. This call has been raised by a number of scholars who argue for advancing social and racial justice, counseling competencies, and meeting the needs of Black boys and young men.[6] Additionally, researchers continue to note that Black college men experience both school-related and non-school-related stressors that can impact their mental health and health behaviors, their sense of self, and their educational engagement.[7] Some of these young men identified stressful life events, beyond the traditional stressors that college students might experience (e.g., classes, finances, and romantic relationships), such as racism and anti-Blackness, racial stereotyping and profiling, school-related interactions, denigrations, and educational neglect as major concerns that led or contributed to stress. Moreover, these experiences are amplified given the denigrating views and treatment of Black boys and men in wider US society—and globally. Some of these young men felt personally connected to a number of Black boys and men who were shot, killed, and injured at the hands of law officials, in public domains, and even in or near educational institutions. All these experiences, including experiences during their youth, contribute to how Black boys and men think about themselves, develop coping strategies, attempt to navigate social institutions, consider cost-benefit analyses for their efforts, and pursue their educational desires.

Summary

The high-stakes challenges for Black boys and men are complex, multidimensional, and multispatial. Additionally, as discussed in this chapter and throughout this book, these troubles are interconnected and impact their lives, livelihoods, and educational journeys and are compounded by their intersecting identities (e.g., race, gender, class, first-generation status). Overwhelmingly, each of these challenges, individually and collectively, affect their educational experiences and how they think about and engage with school. More importantly, though, these trials ultimately influence how they think about themselves, their efforts and aspirations, and their possibilities. Taking account of the stakes that Black boys and men encounter in their lives provides important insights into their sense of self, educational desires, motivations, and the pathways they choose.

Chapter 10

Looking Forward

Addressing the Stakes for Black Boys and Young Men

This study examined the educational journeys of a select group of young Black men, primarily focusing on their pathways to college, their college transitions, and the efforts they engaged in while trying to make it through college. Many researchers characterize several aspects of what these young men offer about their college preparation as predictors of attrition. Examining how young Black men make meaning of their aspirations and academic preparation for college is meant to signal the need for practitioners, researchers, and others to consider the spectrum of preparation they need, from their academic engagements and prominent experiences to the often untaught, soft skills needed to contribute to their academic, social, and cultural preparation, college knowledge, and college-going mindsets. Additionally, these meanings provide a salient context for what the young men considered, expected, and experienced in their educational journeys. As this study has suggested, we need to give more attention to the context of Black young men's lives, which has the potential to provide a broader picture of their educational experiences. Part of what I am arguing for is not reducing their education to a prediction of whether they will "succeed" or "fail" but rather transforming how researchers and even educators think about what constitutes success and drawing out the myriad factors that can influence their experiences and put them in an even better position to thrive. As is evident from what the young men in this study shared, it is not simply the academic subject matter that is critical for student learning, development, and engagement but also the interactions, messages, encouragement, information, and knowledge, together with the educational opportunities, support, guidance, and care they are afforded.

While this study centered on Black young men's educational journeys, I was also able to provide analysis of the wider social and cultural significance of their personal efforts in and for their families and communities. Moreover, I was able to examine how they navigated and negotiated sociocultural and educational contexts in trying to pursue and achieve some of their goals. In doing so, this book considers the structural, social, and cultural challenges in Black boys' and young men's lives, personal development, and educational journeys. Here, critical race theory and the concept of educational urgency have been used to argue that, rather than continuously confronting Black boys and young men with deficit-laden perspectives and low expectations that problematize them, we must consider their educational desires, determination and sense of empowerment, and efforts to create their own stories. This involves examining how social structures and social institutions act on them and, along with their agency, resources, identities, sense of self, and relationships, play a role in their goals, aspirations, and possibilities.

As discussed throughout this study, Black boys and young men face a number of social, personal, and academic risks and challenges during their educational journeys—all of which increase the stakes of their journeys. In other words, the high-stakes challenges they face can make their journeys more perilous and difficult and also make it all the more crucial to persist. And, given Black boys' and young men's intersecting social identities (e.g., social class, sexuality, etc.), not only can these high-stakes challenges further the marginalization they experience, but they also can be intensified as well.[1] Through centering Black males' voices and experiential knowledge, this research serves as a powerful counternarrative that can help researchers, educators, and stakeholders think differently about Black boys' and young men's promise and potential. Students endured a number of difficulties that ranged from personal and family dilemmas to societal challenges and educational setbacks, all of which threatened their educational pathways and achievement. Most concretely, students also perceived these experiences and Blackmaleness as challenges that threatened their sense of self, socioemotional well-being, educational trajectories, and life outcomes.

This chapter builds on and extends the discussion from the previous chapter. First, I center my focus on two primary domains that bring back into focus some of the critical points raised throughout this study. Additionally, at the heart of my argument is the need to counter and rewrite narratives about Black boys' and young men's educational experiences, educational successes, and possibilities.[2]

Responding to and Navigating the Challenges: Agency and Educational Desires

As discussed throughout this book, the stakes that these young Black men experience are real, ongoing, and multifaceted. They are also paradoxical in a number of ways. Stakes is high because these young men need and desire educational attainment for themselves, their families, their communities, and their futures as Black men. Yet because they are Black young men, structural and cultural forces consistently threaten their lives and possibilities, can disrupt and limit their educational opportunities, and can have negative impacts on their sense of self and health and well-being. The findings from this study relate to the ways in which Blacks suffer in schools, demonstrate how Black boys and young men are taxed by Blackmaleness in their daily lives, and speak powerfully to these young men's educational desires. Researchers note that too many Black boys and young men are dismissed and written off, experience affronts to their intellectual abilities, carry considerable burdens in pursuing their educational goals, and are routinely "at risk" of stereotyping, miseducation, controlling images, and racism.[3]

That resistance and resilience continue to be prominent or even distinguishing components of Black boys' and young men's educational narratives is problematic for a number of reasons. At minimum, their need to call on and activate resistance and resilience relays some of the troubles and challenges they face in their educational journeys. In addition, Black resilience can be used to project exceptionalism and peddled into deficit framing by using it against other Black youth who do not achieve in the same ways—albeit for a variety of very different reasons. Moreover, the concept of resilience can be denigrated by institutions, school personnel, stakeholders, policy makers, and news media who encourage yet demean Black youth for their "grit."[4] Inherently, suggestions that Black youth need to show more grit or should shoulder a "no excuses" mantra may be intended to encourage their persistence; the problem, of course, is that those who achieve differently are framed in culturally deficient ways and as lacking what it takes to succeed. Such a discourse is lazy, dishonest, and misguided. Greater attention is needed to place Black boys and young men's lives and educational journeys in perspective. We should not (just) celebrate a handful of individual young men for defying the odds; what is needed is twofold: seeing the odds and what constitutes success through their eyes and, at the same time, working to dismantle the structures that create the odds.

The young men in this study, alongside many of their peers, learned from their early years that educational success and even educational aspirations in some cases were not expected. These experiences relate to the high stakes of their efforts and the depth of troubles in their lives and educational journeys. Black boys and young men are routinely confronted by low expectations and deficit perspectives, but to be confronted by such ideologies and views does not negate their educational aspirations and successes. In fact, these viewpoints can be translated into external motivating factors that fuel their educational efforts and, in some cases, inform Black boys' and young men's attempts to prove others wrong.[5] Still, for those who do perform well, stories and discussions about them often individualize them and rely on exceptionalizing their accomplishments. These perspectives, along with several other stimuli such as family histories, support, and commitment, strengthened their drive to excel in ways that allowed them to challenge and resist denigrating views and assert their meanings for being young Black men. Additionally, as presented throughout this work, their aspirations, agency, resilience, and persistence exemplify their educational desires, their willingness to continue pursuing their personal and educational goals, and the value they place on education in their lives.

Most prominently, these young men responded to and navigated various challenges and difficulties by activating their agency, maintaining their faith and aspirations, and pursuing their educational desires. I see their agency and educational desires as connected and I use these terms specifically to refer to how these young men worked diligently to "create their own stories." These young men demonstrated a high-level of self-efficacy and activated agency in educational, familial, communal, and other social contexts to overcome challenges and barriers embedded in institutions, ideologies, and various structures that threatened to impede their progress. Their narratives demonstrate that motivation is a multidimensional construct. They connected their educational motivations to their internal drive and determination to be successful. Additionally, a number of multiple external factors contributed to their motivation and educational desires, such as their families (parents and siblings in particular) as well as relationships with peers and significant adults (such as teachers and mentors). That they believed in the benefits of education and connected their educational attainment to their futures and understandings of success speaks to their educational desires, how they value education, and the opportunities they pursued.

Across their educational journeys, these young Black men demonstrated commitment and the desire to excel academically. While their status as the first generation to attend college created some barriers, they were agentic in pursuing and attaining precollege experiences that they believed could help prepare them to be academically successful once in college. During their secondary school years, their agency was evident in their persistence efforts to perform well academically and included taking rigorous course loads and participating in college-related activities (e.g., summer immersion programs). Additionally, they attributed their persistence efforts to their funds of knowledge as well as social capital in the form of support systems (e.g., family, friends, teachers). The connections they had with individuals during and beyond their secondary school years meshed well with the new relationships they developed once in college to provide critical social and emotional support, financial or material assistance, guidance, and encouragement. These forms of support proved critical because they allowed them to navigate college more smoothly. That is, even though they experienced struggles during college, the sage advice, holistic support, and encouragement they received helped minimize the negative impact so that rather than feeling alienated and isolated, they garnered social and cultural capital. Also, this support helped them bounce back from challenges and strengthened their resolve to pursue their higher education goals. During their college years, they activated agency and their educational desires to motivate themselves to stay focused academically—even as many of them faced academic setbacks, maintained rigorous course schedules, navigated challenging social interactions and campus cultures, and had to respond to and overcome personal difficulties.

In addition to navigating sometimes inhospitable educational environments, these young men also had to cope with societal misperceptions and social degradation, both individually and collectively. Here, their agency and aspirations also are notable. As these young men negotiated a number of experiences and tensions, particularly related to their Blackmaleness, part of the skills and acumen they developed and refined involved the motivation to both manage and counter the prevalent narratives regarding their abilities and exceed expectations. In a broader sense, whether it was strategizing ways to get away from neighborhood troubles, maintaining their athletic ambitions, desiring to give back to and contribute to their families and communities, or pursuing their educational goals, their personal aspirations all required drive, focus, commitment, and persistence. Their aspirations demanded effort to maintain and keep them in view and also required constant reassessment and refinement. Thus, keeping their goals, aspirations, and desires intact as well as holding on to their self-efficacy and faith helped them respond to and navigate a number of the tribulations they faced. In these ways, these young men continuously affirmed their mattering and sense of self and benefited greatly from strong support systems that included their families, communities, and a cadre of institutional agents. For these young men, their families, friends, peers, siblings, mentors, and school-based personnel provided personal, emotional, spiritual, educational, and financial support throughout their educational journeys. Additionally, some individuals actively encouraged and engaged in behaviors to motivate and sustain them. Thus, along with their own efforts, these young men were embedded in, gained support and inspiration from, and were substantiated by their "village."

Restructuring the Conditions and Improving Opportunities

> I guess it's gon' be 99.9 percent of people going to college. Every time somebody say something about ACT scores I used to be so ashamed. But, now that I have a [college] degree I just say, "I got a 15!"
>
> —Edwin

The findings from this study make clear the need to restructure both the conditions that Black boys and young men experience in their daily lives and the opportunities afforded to them. As education scholar Bianca Baldridge has argued, not only are greater attention and efforts needed in removing the deficit ascribed to Black youth, to rely on "deficient rhetoric and 'needing-to-be-fixed' framing of Black and poor youth denies their agency."[6] Similarly, there is a need to create more equitable learning environments and disrupt racialized distortions of Black youth. These distortions create misrecognitions that too often negate who they are, who they understand themselves to be, and their possibilities.[7] Leaving the conditions that Black youth face intact perpetuates anti-Blackness and is predicated on Black suffering. These conditions rely on majoritarian stories of Black inferiority along with cultural and structural racism and the narratives that are called on about Black men's and boys' lives, achievements (or lack thereof), and outcomes.

That these young men did not succumb to some of the neighborhood challenges is an important accomplishment. Still, even as I make this statement, I remain mindful of and want to draw, or redraw, attention to the need for Black boys' and young men's comprehensive mattering. How many dreams, aspirations, and hopes have died and been denied in environments like the ones that these young men had to navigate? That a number of their peers, those who attended Ellis Academy and others who attended different schools, were not college goers or had some of their opportunities blocked or denied requires much greater attention. Thus, what is clear from these young men's narratives is the need to connect educational policies with social policies and programs. And specifically related to schools, the legacies of anti-Blackness and Black suffering contribute to miseducation and educational malpractice. Continuing to ignore the conditions that Black youth are confronted by and must navigate is derelict and plays a part in and furthers institutional betrayal.

A few points of consideration regarding the need to create change. First, to restructure the conditions, we need a massive overhaul of how Black boys and young men are positioned in US society (and abroad) and across social institutions. If the current (and historical) public imageries and narratives remain intact, then Black boys and young men will continue to be viewed as incapable, their goals and aspirations will be relegated as improbable, and they themselves will be repositioned as both disposable and undeserving. What we know from too many cases is that such renderings and perspectives denigrate and diminish Black boys and young men and also subject them to additional burdens, challenges, setbacks, and troubles. Being young, Black, and male is designated as a socially devalued identity. As the lives of Tamir Rice, Trayvon Martin, Jordan Davis, Kendrick Johnson, Kalief Browder, Jordan Edwards, Stephon Clark, Ahmaud Arbery, and others among a list too long to include here continuously reveal, the misperceptions and disparaging views of Black boys and young men expose them to various forms of violence, both individual and institutional. In like manner, while I name a number of Black boys and young men who have been killed, we also know that violence and anti-Blackness can manifest themselves in other forms, such as social death and nonbeing.[8] Undoubtedly, the projections and misperceptions negatively impact their lives and the opportunities afforded to Black boys and young men.

Second, and along the same lines, there is a great need to restructure educational opportunities so that teaching and related practices (such as discipline) do not rely on and perpetuate Black suffering, that position Blackness as both a problem and peripheral to education, and that alienate Black students from themselves. Such an approach can allow greater attention and action related to calls for advancing social justice and affirming the humanity of Black youth. Also, this restructuring should move away from high-stakes testing, such as the SAT or ACT, that can block and limit access to higher education and also can contribute to educational inequities. For instance, researchers have argued that the high-stakes testing movement has created harm for Black K–12 students by increasing student apathy and the severity of punitive discipline policies.[9] Students are often reduced to their test scores on standardized assessments like the SAT and ACT and these scores weigh heavily in decisions about and the "worthiness" of students' college admissions, yet colleges continue to overlook, undermine, and underappreciate the wealth of skills and assets that these students bring with them to college campuses. These tests also ignore what young people like Jamal, Michael, Malik, Chris, Edwin, Julius, Chauncey, and Paul demonstrated on a routine basis across their educational journeys: they have the desire, drive, agency, skills, perseverance, and aptitude to persist in their educational endeavors.

In making connections to high-stakes testing, I point to the statement from Edwin that opens this section. As he shared throughout his narrative, Edwin developed serious self-doubts about his ability to get to college; even once in college, he questioned his ability to compete academically with his college peers and persevere to graduation. These self-doubts and internal dilemmas informed his transition strategies and academic engagement efforts; they also created mental blocks that were difficult for him to overcome. He went from believing that he had "always been smart" during his secondary school years to wondering "Am I smart enough?" during his college years. The key factor in his internal dilemma was his ACT score—and what this score is supposed to represent or convey. That Edwin graduated from college in four years is a testament to his aptitude and abilities and also reflects the opportunities he was afforded, the philosophies he enacted, the centrality of his faith, the support he received throughout his college years, and his educational desires. Restructuring educational opportunities could provide greater access to higher education for young people who demonstrate their capabilities even if they do not perform well on standardized tests. This restructuring is centered on the importance of a school culture that contributes to students' academic preparation, skill acquisition, and personal development while also being respectful of their cultural backgrounds and needs. It also is concerned with centering more humane and humanizing pedagogies and caring practices that help redefine success—especially beyond high-stakes testing.

If we are serious about educating Black boys and young men, then that means we need to create educational, social, and community environments that empower them. Secondary schools must be nurturing environments that enhance Black boys' sense of self, belongingness, aspirations, and educational outcomes. Additionally, they must be attentive to students' educational journeys, such as college going, which includes helping them prepare for college admissions, providing them with information to make informed decisions about college types and fit, and equipping them with preparation and skills that will help them matriculate to and navigate college successfully.[10] These environments must be developed and sustained to meet the needs and support the educational possibilities of Black boys and young men. There is a grave need for schools to improve the practices, resources, messaging, support, and opportunities that they use with and afford to Black boys and young men. Also needed in these environments are opportunities for strong, positive, and supportive relationships to develop and flourish—among their peers and with teachers and staff. Part of what we know about effective schools and effective teaching is that teaching and praxis occur in ways that are culturally relevant, person-centered, and include what bell hooks described as an engaged pedagogy whereby one teaches "in a manner that respects and cares for the souls of our students."[11] Even further, such an approach can help enhance achievement levels of Black boys and men across various educational contexts.[12] Additionally, Black boys and young men need educational contexts that value and validate them, focus on their promise and potential, enhance their mattering and possibilities, and support their self-actualization.

Third, there is a critical need to restructure both community and educational environments along with alleviating social pressures in the ways that they each create additional burdens for Black boys and men. In particular, the points I raise here are related specifically to the ways in which navigating these environments and pressures weigh on and negatively impact their mental health and wellness. As discussed, these young men experienced mental anguish due to a particular type of policing, surveillance, and interpersonal violence in their home and school neighborhoods and across society writ large for Black families and communities along with other Black boys and men. They also experienced agony due to worrying about ACT scores, in considering whether accusations of plagiarism could result in being kicked out of college, and in dealing with racism and anti-Blackness on campus. The related interactions and experiences weighed on their psyches, produced depression-like effects, and created feelings of isolation and alienation. While any of these experiences are troublesome in their own right, the compounding effect of these experiences can be severe, induce poor health and wellness (mental, physical, and spiritual), and diminish both relationships and outcomes. As researchers have identified, these types of experiences can contribute to and exacerbate stressors that Black boys and men must navigate in their educational endeavors and in their lives.[13]

As made plain throughout this study, stakes is high for these young men precisely because of the institutional neglect and structural racism they experienced in their home communities, the challenges they faced in navigating the neighborhood, the precariousness they experienced in accessing and acclimating to college, and the challenges, trepidations, and racial battles they endured during their college years. Additionally, stakes is high because of the permanence of race and anti-Black racism that they must negotiate on a daily basis. As discussed, the fact of Blackness is stamped on Black boys and young men in ways that makes their lives much more difficult, limits their ability to be or become themselves, and relegates them as "bad boys," "beyond love," in trouble, or even as "a statistic"—any of which are realities that continuously confront and threaten their lives.[14] The idea, notion, and realities of "being a statistic" too often marks Black boys and young men as disposable; even further, these realities not only encompass a number of negative possibilities for their lives (e.g., miseducation, isolation, suffering, and violence) but also help reveal how they are burdened with a societal expectation of Black male failure.

Final Thoughts

Given the experiences and high-stakes educational journeys documented in this study and the challenges Black boys and young men continue to face and endure, it is essential for educators, practitioners, researchers, policy makers, and leaders across community, educational, and political realms to activate even higher levels of commitment to, and support of, better-quality opportunities for Black boys and young men. In particular, that Black boys and young men should or are expected to shoulder the weight of these challenges or that the stakes of their everyday experiences and decisions are so high is both unreasonable and unsurprising. The general sentiment that Black boys need to be "fixed" and the dominant narratives that misrepresent their realities continue to devalue their lives and futures and reveal their marginal mattering and social death. The narratives that Black boys "don't care about school" or even suggesting they would do better if they "just cared more about school" are short-sighted, ahistorical, and antithetical to their realities. And by realities, I'm referring to the multidimensionality and materiality of the high stakes they face—especially as discussed throughout this work—and the idea that, as other researchers have noted, they are "against the wall" and "doomed" while also being relegated to the status of "faces at the bottom of the well" and "nobodies."[15]

Future research would do well to consider the broader context of Black boys' and young men's lives to help uncover and provide insights into how contexts matter in their educational journeys and personal development. It is unreasonable to place expectations on Black youth suggesting that the vast majority will be able to navigate the litany of challenges they face across environments, institutions, systems, and interpersonal interactions while also keeping their educational goals, personal aspirations, and health and wellness intact. Of course, I recognize and know that a number of Black boys and young men create some of their own troubles through some of their own dispositions, attitudes, and behaviors. Still, I firmly believe that there is a great need to explore Black boys' and young men's educational experiences beyond school walls to understand other forces and factors that impact their daily lives. Such an approach not only provides a broader context from which to appreciate their experiences, but also helps researchers and educators have a better sense of actions, decisions, coping strategies, and even aspirations of Black boys and young men. Also, paying closer attention to the sociocultural and even political contexts of their lives (national, local, and communal) can provide fertile ground for more humanizing research. Relatedly, this approach also can help improve our pedagogy, praxis, and policies by focusing more on improving the conditions of their lives. At the heart of this approach is creating healing policies that expand opportunities for better health and wellness, life chances and circumstances, and outcomes of Black youth.

While each of the young men in this study discussed the importance and critical roles that their support systems played in their educational journeys and personal development, there are still greater issues that must be addressed. For instance, although a great deal of attention has been given to the "need" for mentors in the lives of Black boys and young men and there are a number of tangible benefits for positive mentoring experiences, the greater issue at hand is the uneven, inequitable, and anti-Black social structures and social institutions that these boys and young men must navigate. If we are serious about educating them and improving their life outcomes, then it is both critical and urgent that we see the crisis in its proper context. I argue that the more accurate reality is that we are in a prolonged societal crisis, given the ongoing neglect, educational malpractice, anti-Blackness, and institutional racism that continuously accosts the lives, experiences, and futures of Black youth.

Additionally, we must continue to engage in methodological approaches that provide better ways of seeing and knowing our youth—especially those who experience marginalization, racism, trauma, betrayal, and harm or those who navigate a range of hostilities and inequities in social institutions. Future research with Black boys and men must investigate ways that bring their efforts to the forefront of analysis such that we better appreciate their resistance, resilience, persistence, and development. The longitudinal design of the current study contributes well in this regard. One of the clear benefits of prolonged engagement in the field, conducting multiyear studies, or coordinating longitudinal research projects is to develop a broader context to understand people's experiences, understandings, and meaning making at different points in time in their lives and journeys. Another benefit includes opportunities to explore how they act on, respond to, and pursue their goals and aspirations—or even setbacks and challenges—at multiple points throughout that time in their lives. There are clear benefits here that include learning and taking account of changes, growth, shifts, and varied perspectives.

Such a research approach has the promise to develop more robust data that can provide a fuller picture and understanding of our participants' lives and experiences.

Finally, the choices of research approaches—both the theories that inform our analyses and the methods that inform how we collect data—are critical as well. There is a great need to use theories and frameworks that are culturally sensitive, culturally congruent, and grounded in people's experiences and sense making. Similarly, we must be culturally sensitive in our methodological approaches as well, particularly related to who we partner with, the questions we ask, and the goals of our work. Moreover, research approaches that combine methodological traditions (e.g., mixed methods) or include youth as partners who shape the direction of the research both have the potential to provide rich insights about who they are, their ongoing and developmental processes for understanding and navigating their lifeworlds, and how different social, cultural, political, and environmental dimensions matter to their educational efforts and goals. How we, as researchers, approach our work with Black boys and young men matters just as they and their lives and stories matter. Clearly, the stakes is high.

Appendix

Research Study and Methods

The research that makes up the data for this book project is part of a larger, seven-year longitudinal study that focuses on the educational experiences of a selected group of young Black men across their secondary and postsecondary school years and how the young men make sense of their lives and personal experiences as well. In the present study, I focus on the lives and educational journeys of eight young men; this decision was made primarily because they had completed the most interviews (both quantity and length of time) and, as a result, their narratives allowed for the most comprehensive view possible of who they are as well as their experiences and meaning making. The thrust of my qualitative longitudinal project was to explore young Black men's pathways to college. I primarily wanted to explore and understand the efforts and strategies they deployed in their college years. In order to do so, I argued that their precollege years could prove vital in establishing a context for their educational journeys, on the one hand, and their motivations and aspirations, on the other hand. That is, I didn't take their college going for granted; I was interested in (a) why they wanted to attend college and (b) how they believed they were able to matriculate to higher education. Given that I was interested in young men who transitioned to college, there are a number of young men whom I did not include in this study because they did not matriculate to college.

Given my use of critical race theory in developing the study and the ways in which race and racism continue to impact the lives, livelihoods, and life outcomes of Black boys and men, I took a critical race methodological approach in this research.[1] I examine these young men's narratives as critical race counternarratives, an approach taken for four primary reasons. First, my approach appreciates these young men's narratives as experiential knowledge that is both valid and meaningful. Second, my approach humanizes the struggles they face, especially because of the permanence of race and racism in the United States and the impact of their Black male identities.[2] Third, these narratives challenge the dominant stories told about Black boys and men. And fourth, my approach focuses on these students' intersecting identities, the material conditions of their lives, and the structures and institutions that act upon them.

Studying the experiences of Black students holds both theoretical and methodological significance, as it allows for examining how institutional and instructional practices impact their belonging and mattering in school as well as investigating their behaviors, performance, and outcomes.[3] As O'Connor, Lewis, and Mueller suggested, these investigations are important because they provide opportunities to (a) examine race as an element of educational settings and institutional practice and policies as much as it is what students bring with them to schools and (b) investigate how Black students—Black male students in the current research—view, begin to understand, and negotiate their racialized social locations in considering their educational experiences.[4] Furthermore, in line with the literature discussed previously regarding Black males' schooling experiences, they encourage the belief that research on Black education needs to analyze how race intersects with gender and social class.

Ellis Academy

All these young men attended Ellis Academy [a pseudonym], a college preparatory, ninth through twelfth grade school located in an urban, low-income community in a major US city. Designed as a single-sex charter school, Ellis Academy opened its doors in the mid-2000s and accepts any male student in the district regardless of previous academic performance, test scores, or location in the city.[5] The graduation rate of Black males has increased steadily within the district, from nearly 40 percent and 30 percent in the state and district, respectively, in 2000/2001 to 60 percent and 40 percent, respectively, for the 2011–2012 cohort of students.[6] These early data were used to accentuate the need for focused efforts to improve the graduation and college matriculation of Black boys. Thus, the single-sex design of Ellis Academy was based on contemporary research and realities that revealed the low rate of high school graduation for Black boys, especially in high-need, urban communities. In 2010–2011, the school's student body included approximately 550 students. As a result of residential segregation patterns, the school comprised a student body that was 100 percent Black boys, and about 75 percent of the students were eligible for the federal free and reduced lunch program.

Student Participants

The larger study was comprised of twenty college-aged young Black men who all attended and graduated from Ellis Academy. Initially, I conferred with Ellis Academy's college counselor to generate a list of students who had graduated from Ellis during the year I developed the study and also the previous year and were enrolled in college. Given my focus on educational journeys and pathways to college, I used a purposive approach to identify and recruit students who (a) were either in college or college-bound and (b) lived within driving distance from my primary locations. I reached out to students using email, text, and Facebook communication. I successfully recruited twenty young men to participate in the larger study and concentrated on eight of the young men in particular as the focus of this book project. All the young men were aged eighteen or nineteen when I began the interviews. Regarding their backgrounds, beyond the details I described in chapter 1, these young men all had siblings, ranging from two to seven in number; seven lived with at least one parent; and one lived with a great-aunt and great-uncle. Seven of the young men were first-generation college students, and they all began their college tenures at four-year institutions.

Study Design and Data Collection

The longitudinal design of the study was structured to target four main domains: secondary school experiences, pathways to college, college experiences, and postcollege plans and experiences. The project included data collection that spanned seven years and used ethnographic observations and numerous individual interviews. The ethnographic observations were conducted in the neighborhood where Ellis Academy is located; here, I wanted to document some of the material conditions of the neighborhood that these young men had to navigate during their secondary school years. These data included field notes, observations, and photo documentation. These data provided a context for understanding some of the young men's discussions of their out-of-school time with particular attention to navigating the neighborhood or in their declarations that they "needed to get out" of the neighborhood (as discussed in chapter 2).

Individual interviews were in-depth and semistructured, and the follow-up interviews were generally based on the young men's offerings and responses. The structure of my interviews followed a framework similar to that discussed by qualitative researchers such as education scholar Milagros Castillo-Montoya, who described the interview protocol refinement (IPR) framework as a four-phase process for systematically developing and refining an interview protocol.[7] Similar to the IPR framework, I developed a six-phase approach, which included: (1) familiarizing myself with existing research on Black boys' and young men's schooling experiences; (2) developing research questions that aligned with contemporary discussions; (3) ensuring that interview questions aligned with the research questions; (4) constructing an inquiry-based conversation that allows for in-depth communication; (5) receiving feedback on interview protocols; and (6) piloting the interview protocol.

The open-ended response gave the young men a wide spectrum in which to recall, reflect, and share their thoughts and experiences. In-depth interviews can allow participants an opportunity to make sense of their experiences from their own vantage points.[8] These interviews were ongoing throughout the study, and with the exception of three interviews to follow up immediately on our conversations, which lasted for 20, 25, and 35 minutes, each interview conversation lasted at least 1 hour. In total, these eight young men participated in 63 interviews for a total of nearly 150 hours.

I divided the initial interview guides into two main sections: secondary school experiences and college experiences. Within each of these main sections, I developed subsections to focus in on specific aspects of their experiences and developed new subsections based on our collective discussions. For instance, in talking with these young men about their secondary schooling experiences and their pathways to college, aspects of the school neighborhood were mentioned in several instances as the neighborhood impacted their sense making and schooling. In response to the young men making general reference to "challenges in the neighborhood" or specific reference to "gangs and gang activity" in the neighborhood, I "added a selection of questions to investigate their thoughts, meaning-making, and experiences in the neighborhood explicitly."[9] Similarly, based on their discussions of their experiences with Black male teachers (including instructors, staff, coaches, and mentors) at Ellis Academy, I developed a subset of questions to explore "students' reflections on, perceptions of, and experiences with adult Black males during their secondary school years . . . whom they identified as 'fathers'—students used language such as 'he was like a father to me' or 'he was a father-figure.' "[10]

The overwhelming majority of our interviews occurred at a mutually agreed on location, which most often was a local café, library, or restaurant. I recorded and transcribed each interview and read and reread each transcript to help inform the upcoming interview with each young man and also various aspects of these ongoing interviews—such as the neighborhood and Black male teachers. Additionally, various aspects of the interviews also asked them to make meaning of their Black male identities: as a young man, as a student, as a community member, and through a number of their relationships as well—such as with male peers, teachers, and within their families.

In investigating their educational journeys, I also explored various aspects of the young men's lives. First, a foundational aspect of the study takes a phenomenological approach to the students' life histories, and thus explores a range of experiences within schooling contexts that informed their decisions, peer associations, academic performance, identity development, and educational aspirations.[11] Given the structure of the study, the first interview occurred early in the young men's college career, primarily during the summer after graduating from Ellis Academy or very early during their first year of enrollment in college. These interviews focused specifically on the young men's experiences at Ellis Academy and, where appropriate, their transition to college. The second interview focused primarily on the young men's early college experiences, such as their transitions to college. Second, dividing the interviews across multiple sessions allowed for me to focus strategically on particular segments of the young men's lives and educational experiences.

Data Analysis Procedures

All data were transcribed and analyzed to address the study's two central research questions: (1) How did these selected young Black men account for their lived experiences and schooling in successfully matriculating to college; and (2) How did these selected young Black men account for progressing through their college years? I took a grounded theory approach to understanding and interpreting the data as it was not salient to me what issues, concerns, or prominent points might derive from the interview questions, especially given my sociocultural approach to examine aspects of their lives and educational experiences. Thus, I followed K. Charmaz's guide on grounded theory research. Data analyses were ongoing during data collection, and I wrote extensive field notes after conducting the interviews as well as analytic memos to "make sense of the data" and gain further insight into the young men's lifeworlds.[12]

I performed an analysis of the data using Charmaz's guide by conducting initial coding. I tried to keep the codes as similar to the data as possible and looked for actions in the data. These initial codes remained open to allow new ideas (or even new codes) to emerge and so I could learn while coding. The goal in this phase was to ensure that the initial codes fit the data. Next, I performed line-by-line coding. This form of coding prompts the researcher to remain open to the data, "to see nuances in it" and identify where it "sparks new ideas" to pursue, such as the salience of Black male identities, navigating the neighborhood, college-based messages and aspirations, transitioning to college, the importance of noncognitive factors in their education (e.g., spirituality/faith, motivation, and determination), or responding to academic or personal setbacks.[13] Additionally, the line-by-line coding provided an opportunity to read the entire narrative from the interview in comparison with the line-by-line coding. Here, I separated the data into categories and then reread the transcripts and in some cases recoded into additional codes.

After line-by-line coding, I engaged in a constant comparative method where I compared data against data in order to find overall similarities and differences.[14] I summarized each of the excerpt files and their codes to bring coherence and meaning to the data. In the end, I renamed categories as themes and I identified a number of major themes in these young men's (a) pathways to college (aspirations, messages, and schooling experiences) and (b) college experiences from the interview data, each with its own set of subthemes. The next step was focused coding, which can help to "synthesize and explain larger segments of data."[15] The final step was theoretical coding. These codes helped me specify relationships between categories from the focused coding—such as negotiating and responding to neighborhood and schooling experiences, interpreting and internalizing college-based messages, pursuing information, experiences and knowledge as a way to "prepare" for college, navigating the transition to college, pursuing college degree attainment, and learning about the self. Using theoretical coding, I worked to develop a single coherent story from the data, which is how these young men pursued their educational desires amidst the high-stakes challenges they faced along the way.

In taking a grounded theoretical approach, the goal was to allow the theory to emerge from the data. Since coding is an emerging process, I used a constant comparative method of going back to the data and forward into analysis to gather further data and refine the "emergent theoretical framework."[16] For example, I did not begin the interviews with questions looking for educational urgency. My questions about these young men's college aspirations and educational desires, at various points in our interviews, were intended to establish a context to understand and appreciate their narratives and sense making. By going back and forth to the data (e.g., schooling experiences, the messages and support they received, the challenges and struggles they endured, and their efforts to continue pursuing their educational desires), educational urgency as a theoretical frame was developed inductively.

Trustworthiness and Quality of Evidence

Consistent with methods of maintaining rigor and accuracy in qualitative research (i.e., credibility, transferability, and dependability), I followed several steps, as outlined by K. Bhattacharya.[17] First, trustworthiness was built into the study's longitudinal design; the ongoing and follow-up interviews required that I stay familiar with the data and allowed me to develop additional questions (or even subsets of questions) for upcoming interviews. Second, in my efforts to build and extend this research collaboration, and also as a form of member checking, I engaged the young men in ongoing discussions about primary results, emerging themes, and research notes; I also engaged them in conversations about my interpretations and understanding of data, and they were invited to respond and offer further insights throughout the study. Importantly, these member checks helped keep the young men's voices at the center of the study during data collection and analysis and in writing as well. Third, I wrote reflexive memos, which included reflections on my own positionality, assumptions, and beliefs. And fourth, I used peer debriefing, whereby I called on peers to aid in probing my thinking about these young men's narratives and to add credibility to the findings and trustworthiness of the research design.

Research Positionality

I take an unapologetically Black inquiry approach to my research work, which is framed by Black subjectivity—accounting for the influence of a researcher's prior knowledge, experiences, and perspectives in the research process.[18] And, at the same time, I also know that reflexivity is critically important to both interpretation and reflection, especially for research in Black communities. As scholars have noted, reflexivity requires that researchers consider how their background, personal values, and experiences can impact what they observe and analyze.[19]

Several aspects of my identities and experiences are prominent in this research. First and foremost, the impetus for this work grew out of my own experiences in attending public schools, associating with peers who held a range of varying interests, trying to make sense of my life and how I could navigate my social worlds, and continuously reflecting on what educational attainment could mean for my life—and my future. I am a first-generation college graduate, and as I look back at my journey, I see that it is filled with efforts to "create my own story." I was raised in multigenerational households, I grew up in all-Black communities on the South Side of Chicago, and, with the exception of one school year, I attended public K–12 schools that were located in hypersegregated communities. These experiences and others shaped my perspectives and ways of knowing as I transitioned to college, and they fueled my own educational desires. During my college years, they also informed my decisions to major in African and African American Studies and to engage in volunteer work in several local communities, and they influenced the first major research study I ever conducted ("Black Student Experiences at Predominantly White Institutions," under the direction of Edgar Epps). What I learned in my own lived experiences, in my coursework, from relationships and related experiences, and through reading and research all motivated me to continue these studies in my master's program in African and African American Studies at Clark Atlanta University.

I entered graduate studies, including my doctoral program, with serious interest in wanting to better understand Black life in the US context and abroad. Throughout my studies (including those during my professional career as an educator), I constantly reflect on my own educational journey, from the schools I attended and the relative experiences in each context to institutional cultures, relationships, coursework and opportunities. Additionally, my studies, learning, and growth were connected to my community work and serving as a youth worker. As an educator, through teaching within the community as well as secondary and postsecondary contexts, I engage a philosophy of Black education.

Quite simply, not only do I fundamentally believe that Black youth matter, but I also believe in their brilliance, creativity, beauty, becoming, and possibilities. My scholarship regarding Black boys' and men's lives and experiences, as well as my broader activism and service to and in Black communities, aligns with those of a long cadre of scholars who continue to reveal the important epistemological knowledge birthed and sustained in Black communities. And, importantly, I learned valuable lessons in my own family, particularly from the work and efforts in how family members (particularly my grandmothers, father, and several aunts and uncles) saw, curated, sustained, and valued relationships. Their ways of knowing made deep impressions that I carry with me today and that also influence my praxis, activism, and research. I have deep concern and a vested interest in Black boys' and men's lives, education, and well-being. Not only do I have professional experiences that keep me in close proximity with Black boys and men, as well as other youth of color, but I also work with them in a number of capacities, from educational institutions to athletics to community spaces.

I have a deep commitment to educational access, racial equity, and racial healing for Black youth and youth of color. As it relates specifically to Black boys and men, my research profile and the studies that I conduct are primarily centered on their lives and lifeworlds. Focusing on education is centered in my work as I see it as an important vehicle for which to learn about oneself as well as to better understand the contexts of our lives. Schooling also is a major socializing agent and Blacks have a complex history with formal educational spaces, contexts, and institutions within the United States.[20] Even further, given my own investments in education (both formally and informally), I see this as an important domain to care for, guide, support, and build up Black boys and men.

Given this context, I approached my study as a youth worker, as an educator, as an individual who continues to volunteer and serve in Black communities in several locales, and as a Black man who mentors and works with many young adults of color. These roles and my identity influenced the data collection process and I am keenly aware of how my identity and positionality inform how I read and interpret my research. As a result, I take a culturally sensitive approach to my research that relies on these young Black men to speak from their own viewpoints and experiential knowledge.[21]

Conducting Research, Sustaining Relationships, and Remaining Accountable

While the research I present in this book is focused on these young men's lives and experiences, this study is based on relationships. My use of a longitudinal qualitative research approach meant that I needed to keep in contact with these young men over a sustained period of time. Given my own background, profile, and experiences, I connected with these young men in a number of ways. Parts of their stories and journeys connect well with my own life and, given my roles and experiences as an educator and youth worker, their sharing provided me with great insights about their experiences, accomplishments, needs, and desires. In this study, and across the broader spectrum of my research, it is important for me to think beyond research. Thus, I never considered these young men as "subjects" but rather as participants and, in some ways, as partners and coresearchers as they invited me into their spaces, led some of our conversations, and pointed me in the direction of useful inquiries. Most importantly, they invited me into their lives and have kept me there.

As a result of our connections, I had many conversations with these young men that were not interviews or about research at all. We have had many conversations about Black history, popular culture, sports, and movies and film in addition to family, politics, contemporary issues, and the Movement 4 Black Lives. Given our exchanges and conversations, our relationships have grown in numerous ways. I have served as a mentor, confidant, advisor, and coach; they have asked me for advice, support, and guidance on a number of occasions related to education, relationships, personal experiences, aspirations, and professional work endeavors. That I chose to invest in them and serve in these roles never seemed like a choice I needed to make. Throughout this study and far beyond it, I continue to wear multiple hats, including researcher, educator, mentor, community member, and youth worker; each of these connect with and inform my relationships with them. Further, my research study served as a bridge for our relationships, as our communications and connections provided a sense of understanding, helped us build trust, and brought us closer together.

As I see it, the way in which they view me and the roles they have allowed me to play speak to the quality of our relationships; these roles also speak to our proximity and the investments I've made in their lives. For instance, we both hold mutual appreciation and respect for the time we have invested in each other. As they shared at various points, they appreciated the opportunities to reflect on their experiences and contribute to my work. They appreciated that they could share parts of their lives where they did not feel like they would be judged or placed on trial for some of their actions and decisions, which contributed to the ways in which they think about and see me. Additionally, how they view me and how I matter in their lives also speaks to our relational trust: they trusted me to listen to and hear their stories, they trusted me as a caretaker of their experiences, they trusted my perspectives of them, and they trusted me with their interiorities. At the heart of my work is relationships; I believe that these young men know that I value and care about them deeply.

Finally, part of what this study facilitated, especially given the ways that Black boys and young men are repositioned in the national lexicon, required that I take a culturally sensitive approach to my research.[22] I relied on these young Black men to speak from their own viewpoints and I viewed their experiential knowledge as legitimate, relevant, and necessary for analyzing, understanding, and reporting their stories and experiences. Given my approach, I constantly practice sharing my research with participants—at various stages of the writing process as well as in the published form—and I continue to share with these young men (and a number of others with whom I am connected) my professional work and efforts. Specifically related to the larger research project and this book, my sharing is not simply as a form of member checking but also as a measure of accountability and as a way to ensure that they have access to my writing. Without doubt, conducting this study has sharpened my teaching, research, and praxis in multiple ways. As a result, I carry these young men with me in many respects and their impact on me and my work is ongoing.

Notes

Notes to the Introduction

1. I borrow the phrase "stakes is high" from the hip-hop group De La Soul's fourth studio album of the same name, which includes a title song as well.

2. The larger study is comprised of twenty young Black men. In this book project, I focus on the eight young men who completed the most interviews and, as a result, I have a more robust collection of interview data. I firmly believe that the breadth and depth of these data allow me to offer a fuller view of these young men, their lives, perspectives, and educational experiences.

3. See Brooms (2019b), p. 57.

4. As an example, Complete College America (CCA) was started as part of then-President Barack Obama's national educational campaign; CCA's stated mission reads, "Established in 2009, Complete College America is a bold national advocate for dramatically increasing college completion rates and closing institutional performance gaps" (see https://completecollege.org/our-work/). The CCA homepage declares, "American dreams are powered by college completion."

5. Chimamanda Ngozi Adichie (2009) noted several dangers that are laden within stories; she suggested, "The single story creates stereotypes, and the problem with stereotypes is not that they are untrue, but that they are incomplete. They make one story become the only story." As it relates to school discipline practices and policies, researchers not only identify that Black boys and young men are disciplined in disproportionate ways, they also reveal how these practices are based on stereotypes and labels, negatively impact their educational aspirations, and disrupt and undermine their educational pathways (see Duncan, 2002; Ferguson, 2000; Fitzgerald, 2015; T. Howard, 2014; C. James, 2012; Polite & Davis, 1999; Toldson, 2008, 2011; Wood et al., 2018).

6. Mutua (2006) used the term *Blackmaleness* to convey the ways that the combined impact of being both Black and male relegates Black boys and men to denigrating views and suspicions on a routine basis. Mutua argued that these views and ideologies narrow their life opportunities because they are "oppressed

because they are both Black and men; that is, Black men are oppressed by gendered racism" (p. 6). Relatedly, James and Lewis (2014) contended that Blackmaleness signifies "both a personal journey and social reality, tethering the life chances of Black males to an inescapable but navigable milieu of ideological, institutional, and individual inopportunity that all Black males must masterfully traverse or face the certain consequences of disenfranchisement" (p. 105; also see Brooms, 2017a; Brooms & Perry, 2016; Brown, 2018; Young, 2018). As it relates to the persistent practice of rendering Black boys and men as criminal and weaponizing legal action and state-sanctioned violence against them, the Scottsboro Boys, the killing of Emmett Till, and the Central Park Five stand as some of the more egregious cases.

7. See Mirza (2006), p. 144. I discuss the theoretical approach of this study in the next chapter, where I explain how I aim to expand Mirza's conceptualization.

8. My point here about the "wealth" of Jamal's community, as well as the community of each of the young men in this project, is in reference to Tara J. Yosso's (2005) community cultural wealth framework, which recognizes and identifies multiple forms of cultural capital that students of color bring with them into educational settings. Yosso identified six types of capital that are nurtured by communities of color and collectively form cultural wealth: aspirational, familial, linguistic, navigational, resistance, and social. In regard to Jamal's experience, he relied on and deployed his cultural capital through his family, aspirations, and navigational skills. Several researchers have used community cultural wealth to detail Black college men's experiences (e.g., see Brooms & Davis, 2017a; McGowan & Pérez, 2020).

9. With a perspective centered in critical theory, Solórzano and Yosso (2002) have argued that critical race methodology can challenge racism, expose deficit-informed research, and serve as a form of resistance. Furthermore, critical race methodology in education "generates knowledge by looking to those who have been epistemologically marginalized, silenced, and disempowered" (p. 36). Moreover, critical race methodology contextualizes these Black men's experiences in the past, present, and future.

10. Solórzano and Yosso (2002), p. 26.

11. See Scheurich and Young (2004).

12. For a critical discussion of counternarratives, see L. Bell (2003), Huber (2008), Solórzano and Yosso (2002).

13. See Solórzano and Yosso (2002), p. 37; see also Solórzano and Delgado Bernal (2001).

14. Here, my reference to "Black youth's schooling experiences" is intentional as I wish to speak to a broad range of experiences. In particular, many of the issues that are referenced here impact Black youth across multiple backgrounds. Overwhelmingly, Black youth are repositioned within school settings

because of low or lowered expectations, high rates of discipline and punishment, and the imposing weight of deficit perspectives that limit their opportunities and support (e.g., see Baldridge, 2014; Clark, 2020; Epps, 1995; Farmer, 2010; Lindsey, 2018; McCready, 2010; Morris, 2015; Tyson, 2003; Venzant Chambers & McCready, 2011).

15. See Snyder (2018).

16. See Snyder (2018). For instance, Ron Suskin's (1998) biographical novel about the life of Cedric Jennings, *A Hope in the Unseen*, is a prime example of this form of storytelling; the book focuses on Jennings's last years of high school and first years of college.

17. See Toldson (2015), p. 105.

18. The definition and analysis I put forward here regarding anti-Blackness are derived from a range of work that reveals how US policies, laws, and practices reconstruct Blacks as nonbeings, subhumans, and socially dead (Fanon, 1952/1967; Wilkerson, 2020; Wynter, 1994). Even more particularly, Blacks are rendered as: condemned and constantly repositioned at the lower rungs of society (D. Bell, 1992a; Browne, 2015; Coates, 2015; Du Bois, 1903/2005; Fanon, 1952/1967; Hartman, 1997; Moten, 2013; Muhammad, 2011; Sharpe, 2016; Yancy, 2008); undeserving of justice in the law (M. Alexander, 2010; D. Bell, 1992b; Foreman, 2017; Miller, 2021); uneducable (Kunjufu, 2004; C. Woodson, 1933/2011); and as part of the US-based racial contract (Mills, 1997). For instance, critical scholar Christina Sharpe (2016) articulates representations of Black life as the "orthography of the wake." Sharpe illustrates how Black lives are consumed within and animated by the afterlives of slavery. Additionally, scholars note that anti-Blackness manifests within both secondary schooling and higher education (e.g., see Dancy et al., 2018; Du Bois, 1939; Dumas & ross, 2016; Duncan, 2002; Goff et al., 2014; Lofton, 2021; Love, 2016; Moten, 2013; Mustaffa, 2017; Tichavakunda, 2021; Williams et al., 2019; Wun, 2016) and within education policy and discourse (Dumas, 2016; King, 1992, 2005).

19. In addition to Baldridge (2014, 2019), a number of scholars call for the need to reimagine Black youth in school settings and within their communities as well (e.g., see Carey, 2015, 2019b; Dancy, 2014a; Dumas, 2014; Dumas & Nelson, 2016; Ginwright, 2009; Hucks, 2014; Jett, 2019; O. Johnson, 2018; Love, 2016; Toldson, 2015; Weiston-Serdan, 2017; Wright & Counsell, 2018).

20. Legal scholar Patricia Williams (1987) conceptualized the term *spirit murder* to denote the psychological trauma, affects, and injuries that racism and the disregard of Black life induces. Additionally, several scholars have used the concept to investigate Black youth's schooling experiences (e.g., see Bryan, 2021; Carter Andrews et al., 2019; Jett, 2019; Love, 2016, 2019).

21. In our conceptualization (Clark, Wint, and Brooms, 2020), we note that a possibilities framework necessarily resists and rejects the "single story" of Black boys and young men as uninterested in or uncaring about their education;

as opposed to viewing them as continuously being in danger of stereotyping or at risk of punishment in schools, we argue viewing and appreciating Black boys in their possibilities can position them for better educational successes and contribute to their health, well-being, and development. Thus, in some ways, Black boys' and young men's educational efforts can be seen as their own efforts of activating their agency and affirming their possibilities.

22. See Hardeman (2018).

23. In particular, Du Bois (1903/2005) spoke of Blacks' "double consciousness," which he articulated as a "two-ness" of being "an American, a Negro" or the internal conflict of being "African" and "American." In discussing this "two-ness," he asserted that they represented "two warring ideals in one dark body, whose dogged strength alone keeps it from being torn asunder" (pp. 16–17). For Du Bois, the Black struggle and striving was both to navigate this duality, which had been created by colonization and enslavement, and to shed the distinctiveness of inferiority that enslavement, subjugation, and anti-Black racism relied on.

24. Relative to the references made here, see Robinson (2017); Smith et al. (2016); A. Woodson (2017); C. Woodson (1933/2011); Wright et al. (2016). Robinson's (2017) experiences are noteworthy for several reasons, partly because he had been failed by schools continuously and because he felt he lived in a world that held an antagonistic perspective of him. The main title of his work, "Me against the World," speaks to this antagonism; he wrote, "I felt restrained and warehoused in a special education system that is designed to segregate and ghettoize, and to contextualize the term 'ghetto' to my experiences, I was placed in an isolated area within the school (i.e., basement), which usually does not lead to liberating racialized minority students throughout the US school system" (p. 749). Further, as historian Ibrahim Kendi (2016) has argued, Blacks have been "stamped from the beginning" by racist thinking, structural racism, and racial violence that have helped fuel the persistent ideology of Black inferiority.

25. Education scholar Jawanza Kunjufu has discussed the attempts to destroy and dehumanize Black boys across a series of books that span four volumes. Additionally, he complemented this work with research on the importance of developing positive self-images among Black children as well as identifying and offering strategies on successfully guiding Black boys into manhood (see Kunjufu, 2004, 2013).

26. In her conceptualization of community cultural wealth, Yosso (2005) noted that individuals may harbor or hold onto aspirations even in "without the means to make such dreams a reality" (p. 77). My uses of social capital (networks of people and community resources) and cultural capital ("a sense of group consciousness and collective identity"; Franklin, 2002, p. 177) here are connected to Yosso's community cultural wealth model as well.

Notes to Chapter 1

1. In his seminal essay, Franz Fanon (1952/1967) articulates the struggles and constraints that Blacks experience in trying to rationalize their Blackness in an irrational system of racism and race prejudice. Although written through the lens of the colonial context, Fanon's "fact of Blackness" thesis and theorizing connects well with Blacks in the US context, especially given the ways in which they are subjugated. For Fanon, the "fact of Blackness" also alluded to the constant and ongoing negotiation that Blacks pursue, sometimes even against their will, of attempting to assert their humanity. Fanon's argument builds on Du Bois's (1903/2005) concept of double consciousness; whereas Du Bois articulated Black subjugation as a problem created by whiteness, Fanon analyzed the socially constructed idea of Blackness as the contrived representation of evil. The image of Black inferiority was necessitated to "rationalize" European colonization, and attempts by indigenous peoples to assert Black identity are still construed through the white gaze and preestablished white-centric parameters. (For further discussion, also see D. Bell, 1991; Chesler et al., 2005; hooks, 1995; Rajack-Talley & Brooms, 2018.)

2. For instance, sociologist Nikita Carney (2016) argued that youth of color played an active role in debates on Twitter following the killings of Michael Brown and Eric Garner in 2014. Using a qualitative textual analysis of selected Twitter posts following the nonindictments of officers in the killings of Brown and Garner, Carney found that activists and youth in general "subtly and effectively shifted the conversation away from a debate over the meaning of these hashtags (#BlackLivesMatter versus #AllLivesMatter) as mutually exclusive and toward a call for collective action" (p. 195). Similarly, in regard to social media and discussions of college campuses, scholar-practitioner Jamal Mazyck (2013) noted, "Social media has created a space for students to connect and participate in national conversations that tackle concerns related to race, identity and representation on college campuses."

3. As an example, although the killings of a number of Black boys and men, such as Mike Brown and Philando Castile, to name just a few, made national headlines, the #SayHerName campaign was started to raise awareness of how anti-Black and state-sanctioned violence impacted Black women and girls, such as Sandra Bland, Reika Boyd, and Renisha McBride (see Crenshaw et al., 2015; Lindsey, 2018).

4. See Hucks (2014), p. 4.

5. See legal scholar Athena Mutua's (2006) work on the multidimensionality of Black males' masculinities. Mutua argued that Black males face a specific form of gendered racism precisely because of their Black male identities. In a qualitative study of twenty-five Black men, Brooms and Perry (2016) found that

participants in the study believed that many Black boys and men faced physical violence from police and other actors because of their Blackmaleness. Along the same lines, Simone Drake (2016) has contended that Blackmaleness repositions Black boys in the US lexicon and imagination, "From the mainstream media to policy makers to scholars working at the intersection of race and gender, Black boyhood is a landscape of tangled pathologies and pipelines and, ultimately, certain unavoidable doom" (p. 447). Also see scholarship whose primary aim centers on Black boys' and men's lived experiences (e.g., E. Anderson, 2008; Brown, 2018; Curry, 2018; Glynn, 2013; hooks, 2004; Young, 2018).

6. For recent critical studies that discuss the surveillance of Blackness, see Browne (2015) and Hill (2016).

7. Elizabeth Alexander (2020) contends that the Trayvon Generation, by which she means the young people who grew up in the past twenty-five years, always knew the stories of police brutality, anti-Black violence, and racism: "They always knew these stories. These stories formed their world view. These stories helped instruct young African-Americans about their embodiment and their vulnerability. . . . These stories instructed them that anti-Black hatred and violence were never far."

8. The films *Boyz in da Hood* and *Menace to Society* were critical media productions in the 1990s as they leaned on some of the popular discourse of young Black men as threats to their communities and themselves. Sealey-Ruiz and Greene (2015) argued that popular media images that position or feature Black boys and young men as "out-of-control gangsters etch powerful negative images into viewers' minds. These images influence the perceptions that teachers have about their students, and imagining them as dangerous (similar to characters played in popular film) supports the existence of school policies that lead to a school-to-prison pipeline for these students" (p. 67).

9. See Carey (2019b), p. 373. Carey defined the marginal mattering of Black boys and young men as "the type of baseline, minimal recognition that implies their insignificance, as signaled by individuals (e.g., peers, educators, the general public) and institutions (e.g., schools) around them" (p. 375). Although not conceptualized in mattering, several empirical studies also reveal how Black boys and young men (re)negotiate their marginalizing related to education (e.g., see Baldridge et al., 2011; Brooms, 2020b; P. Johnson & Philoxene, 2018; Wright et al., 2020); additionally, several studies examine young Latino men's experiences and decisions along with those of Black boys and young men (e.g., see Hines et al., 2019; Howard et al., 2019; Huerta, 2015).

10. My reference to the negations faced by high-achieving Black male students is reflected in two studies in particular. Jett's (2019) study showed that even Black young men who were among the highest achievers in their schools faced denigration and questions about their intellectual fortitude. Similarly, McGee and Martin's (2011) study also revealed how young Black men feel that they have to overperform in order for their academic merit to garner respect.

11. A plethora of studies across varies disciplines reveal these challenges and the continued denigration of Black boys and young men (e.g., see Brooms, 2017a; Carey, 2019b; Clark, 2017; Davis, 2006; T. Howard, 2013; McGee, 2013; Oeur, 2016; Richardson et al., 2014; Rogers & Way, 2016; Warren, 2005; Wright et al., 2016; Young, 2018).

12. See Baldwin (1963/1992), Coates (2015), Drake (2016), and Du Bois (1903/2005).

13. I mention these Black boys and young men very specifically because several of them were of elementary or secondary school age when they were killed and, as a result, did not have the opportunity to transition to college and were denied opportunities to pursue adulthood). Browder (age twenty-two), the oldest among those I name, had what I consider an experience that is both exceptional and routine; exceptional because of the multiple failures of the criminal justice system and routine because his Blackness was rendered as nothingness. With the exception of Browder, these incidents reached the headlines because each of these Black boys was gunned down in what some considered to be callous ways. For instance, twelve-year-old Tamir Rice was shot and killed by police within two seconds of them arriving on the scene. Police were called to the scene because Rice was playing with a toy pellet gun at a local park in Cleveland, Ohio. Several details from callers were not relayed by dispatch to the two police officers at the scene, such as a 911 caller twice reporting the weapon as "probably fake."

14. See the *Schott 50 State Report* (Schott Foundation for Public Education, 2015), which identified a variety of disparities that Black boys face in secondary school and criminal justice institutions. Also see Love (2016) for a poignant discussion of anti-Black violence in education. Along the same lines, sociologist Victor Rios (2006, 2011) has contended that a "youth control complex" functions to delimit the lives and livelihoods of Black and Latino boys across multiple institutions. In his ethnographic study, Rios found that Black and Latino boys experienced hypercriminalization from both the juvenile justice system and from noncriminal justice structures traditionally intended to nurture, including the school, the family, and the community center. Additionally, studies such as those by Bryan (2020, 2021) have offered a critical investigation of how Black boys are criminalized in their play, while studies such as those by Porter (1997) and Kunjufu (2004) have discussed the denigration of Black boys within schools. Other studies also have revealed how Black boyhood is challenged and denigrated (e.g., see Carey, 2015; Dancy, 2014b; Drake, 2016; Dumas & Nelson, 2016; Robinson, 2017). Finally, Brooms and Perry (2016) and Brooms and Clark (2020) have discussed how people rationalize and make sense of the killing of Black boys and men.

15. Sociologist Alford Young (2018) has argued that Black males are doomed by the material conditions of their lives in tandem with the denigrating views held about them.

16. For instance, Hotchkins (2016) has revealed the bevy of racialized microaggressions that Black males face in K–12 education. As discussed earlier, Black boys and young men's marginal mattering confront them across social institutions (e.g., schools and juvenile justice system) and can be seen as part of the "youth control complex." According to Rios (2006), the youth control complex is "an ecology of interlinked institutional arrangements that manages and controls the everyday lives of inner city youth of color" which has taken "a devastating grip on the lives of many male youth of color in the inner city" (p. 52). Also, research on navigating hostile neighborhood environments (Brooms, 2019b; McGee, 2013; Perry et al., 2015), marginality (Brooms, 2020b; Carey, 2019b; Jenkins, 2006; Noguera, 2008), and interpersonal challenges (E. Anderson, 1990, 2008; Brooms & Perry, 2016; Rios, 2006, 2011) are critical to explore as well when attempting to make sense of Black male youth's experiences.

17. As an example of the multispatial challenges faced by Blacks, Lofton and Davis (2015) found that Black students and parents faced systemic inequalities in their home, school, and community. In particular, across their interviews with thirty-eight Black students and twenty-six parents who lived in a poor Black neighborhood, the researchers contended that out-of-school time provided a context for distinct struggles and experiences that strongly influenced students' educational experiences. As an example, several participants acknowledged the negative associations attributed to the Black community and shared the denigrating comments used to describe their neighborhood. The researchers noted, "These stereotypical images of their neighborhood had negative consequences on the African American students," the town had a history of racial tension, and both students and parents were confronted currently by police brutality (p. 221). Similarly, Posey-Maddox (2017) found that middle-class Black parents experienced microaggressions that often were "multispatial and cumulative, occurring both within and across the various fields that parents traversed in their daily lives and influencing parents' sense of belonging in and connection to community and educational institutions" (p. 16). According to Posey-Maddox, these multispatial microaggressions included negative racialized experiences, which typically took a toll on parents. Finally, English and colleagues (2020) found that Black US youth reported over five experiences of racial discrimination per day, and these occurred in multiple dimensions, including individual and vicarious, online and offline, and teasing and general discrimination experiences. They noted that amount of racial discrimination experienced can be used to predict short-term increases in depressive symptoms.

18. See Baldridge et al. (2011); Christian (2005); Douglas (2016); Graham and Robinson (2004); T. Howard (2008); Jenkins (2006); Noguera (2008); C. Wright et al. (2016). It is important to note Baldridge et al.'s (2011) argument for the need to adopt an intersectional approach to studying Black males, which should allow researchers to be able to "understand how the social constructs of race and gender mutually construct and reinforce one another" (p. 123).

Relatedly, O'Connor (2020) posed a challenge to education researchers to "think more deliberately about how our analytical foci (i.e., who and what we gaze upon), as well as our methods (i.e., how we gaze), can flatten the identity and experience of racially minoritized folk as well as the topography in which they operate" (p. 478).

19. See M. Alexander (2010); Kendi (2016); Miller (2021); Muhammad (2011); Wilkerson (2020).

20. A great deal of research makes this point abundantly clear, as evidence shows that Black boys and young men are underserved in schooling contexts across a number of countries (e.g., see Christian, 2005; Cobbett & Younger, 2012; Graham & Robinson, 2004; C. James, 2012; Jenkins, 2006; Warren, 2005; Wright et al., 2016; Wright et al., 2020).

21. Research is replete with examples of the points raised here about Black boys and young men's ability to achieve academically in spite of the challenges they face. For instance, Wright and colleagues (2016) found that a group of Black male youth in the United Kingdom used resilience and various forms of capital to transform school "failure," while in a previously published work I found that young Black men benefited significantly from the supports they received in school as they struggled to overcome some of the obstacles they faced (Brooms, 2019b). Research literature reveals that some of Black boys' and young men's resilience is informed by their resistance to stereotypes (Hrabowski et al., 1998; Rogers & Way, 2016) and that they continue to achieve at high levels even as they face scrutiny and uneven opportunities within secondary schools (Jett, 2019).

22. For research engaging conversations about the troubles and challenges that Black boys and young men face, see Baldridge et al. (2011); Davis (2003); T. Howard (2013); Jett (2019); McGee (2013); Noguera (2008); Wright et al. (2010). For research on particular challenges that Black boys and young men face in urban education and environments, see Brown (2018); Christian (2005); Duncan (2002); T. Howard (2008); Kunjufu (1986); Noguera (2008); Oeur (2016); Shedd (2015). These challenges include disproportionate discipline and unsupportive and uncaring schooling environments (Ferguson, 2000; Kunjufu 2004; Polite & Davis, 1999), stereotypes and multiple forms of anti-Blackness (Brooms, 2020b; C. James, 2012; Rogers & Way, 2016), and exclusion (Davis, 2006; Wright et al., 2016).

23. For instance, see Baldridge (2014); Baldridge et al. (2011); Brooms (2019b); Douglas and Arnold (2016); Kunjufu 1986); Lewis-McCoy (2016); Noguera (2003, 2008); Polite and Davis 1999); White and Cones 1999).

24. A few key sociological studies include works by Elijah Anderson (1990, 2008), and Alford A. Young (2004, 2018). Also see Wilson (2010), who argued for considering both cultural and structural factors that impact Black life.

25. See Noguera (2003), p. 438.

26. See E. Anderson (2008); Mincy (2006); Young (2004, 2018).

27. See Hurd et al. (2013); Perry et al. (2015); Robinson et al. (2011). Moreover, and specifically related to the experience that Chris had with the public transit employee, sociologist Gwendolyn Purifoye (2015) found that Blacks may be contested by racial hostilities on public transportation that often are masked as "nice-nastiness"—a type of micro-level interaction or "individual expression that combines expressions of politeness with disdain and distancing" (p. 287).

28. See Sampson (2012).

29. For instance, Patton and colleagues (2016) found that Black boys adopt a number of "hardiness scripts," which "emphasize their perceived control over their individual experiences with violence as an explanatory framework," as coping responses to community violence (p. 640). They contended that these scripts proved useful for understanding the boys' behavioral responses particularly because they demonstrate their agency in trying to overcome challenging situations in their neighborhood environment (also see Harding, 2010; Stewart et al., 2007; Swanson et al., 2003; Toldson, 2008).

30. As examples, see Allen (2017); Brooms (2019b); Douglas and Arnold (2016); T. Howard (2014); Howard and Associates (2017); M. James (2010); Jett (2016, 2019); Kumah-Abiwu (2019).

31. See Allen (2015), p. 216.

32. A burgeoning research agenda uses asset-based frameworks to shift the discourse on Black boys' and young men's academic identity, achievement, and successes (see Allen, 2015; Brooms, 2019a, 2020b; Davis, 2003; Harper & Davis, 2012; Howard et al., 2019; Jett, 2019; Kumah-Abiwu, 2019; Moore & Lewis, 2014; Oeur, 2016; Rogers & Way, 2016; Whiting, 2006; Wright & Counsell, 2018).

33. See Wright et al. (2016).

34. For further reading, see the studies listed here, which are just a portion of the vast array of existing research: on racism and racial microaggressions (Robertson & Chaney, 2017; Smith et al., 2016); hostile campus climates (Brooms, 2017a; Harper, 2015); and college environments rife with anti-Black policies and practices (Abrica et al., 2020; Dancy et al., 2018). Additionally, see Cuyjet (2006) for a robust discussion of Black men's college experiences; this edited volume engages conversations pertaining to academic experiences, identity development, and social engagement and also offers profiles of Black Male Initiative programs across nine chapters.

35. Smith et al. (2016) noted that Black misandry, defined as an exaggerated pathological aversion toward Black boys and men, informed the stereotypical tropes used to confront Black college men in their study: the criminal/predator stereotype, the ghetto-specific stereotype, the nonstudent but athletic stereotype, and the anti-intellectual stereotype. Being confronted by these stereotypes on an ongoing basis made these students' college experiences much more stressful. In addition, philosophy scholar Tommy J. Curry (2017, 2018) articulates Black

misandry as well. For instance, Curry (2018) contended that Black boys and men often are reduced to a "perpetrator-only view" even while societal violence and white vigilantism exploit and assault Black lives: "Black males are ultimately the cause of the communal and interpersonal violence that most threatens Black women children, and non-conforming Black peoples" (p. 3).

36. Studies repeatedly demonstrate the stereotyping, racism, and violence that Black men experience in college, which often undermines their academic engagement, sense of belonging, and educational outcomes (for example, see Abrica et al., 2020; Brooms, 2017a; Brooms & Davis, 2017b; Harper, 2015; S. Johnson, 2019; Johnson-Ahorlu, 2013; Mustaffa, 2017; Robertson & Chaney, 2017; Smith et al., 2007; Smith et al., 2011). For instance, in their study of twelve Black male students at a predominantly white institution, Robertson and Chaney (2017) found that the students experienced racism and racial microaggressions that included verbal assaults along with a minimization of their culture and heritage. Even when a few of the students did not experience it directly themselves at the institution, they knew racism "still exists here" and perceived racial slights as something that "comes with the territory" of being Black male students on campus (pp. 268–269).

37. For further reading, see the studies listed here, which are just a portion of the vast array of existing research: on strong academic performance (Cuyjet, 2006; Palmer & Wood, 2012; Robertson & Mason, 2008); the importance of peer relationships (Strayhorn, 2008, 2017); benefits they accrue from mentorship and relationships with faculty (Brooms, 2020a; Brooms & Davis, 2017b); and their engagement experiences as well (Brooms, 2017a; Clark & Brooms, 2018; Druery & Brooms, 2019).

38. See Warde (2008), p. 68. Additionally, other research is pertinent as well. Researchers find that a "village" approach, where having multiple people committed to their development and success, contributes significantly to Black men's achievements in higher education (Beale et al., 2019; Burt et al., 2019; Martin et al., 2010; Palmer & Gasman, 2008).

39. See Brooms and Davis (2017b).

40. See Brooms (2017a).

41. For research on supportive college environments, see Brooms (2017a); Palmer and Strayhorn (2008); Wood et al. (2015); Wood and Williams (2013); also see Robertson and Mason (2008) for a discussion of Afrocentric student development. Research on Black men's peer group in college abounds, see Brooms and Davis (2017b); McGowan (2017); Strayhorn (2017); for research on the benefits of Black male-centered programs, see Clark and Brooms (2018); Druery and Brooms (2019).

42. See Watkins et al. (2007), p. 108.

43. While more research is needed in these areas that account for the stressors that Black students continue to experience in higher education, particularly

during their college years, several studies have contributed important insights (see Fleming, 1981; Goodwill et al., 2018; Greer & Brown, 2011; S. McClain & Cokley, 2017; K. McClain et al., 2016; Steele & Aronson, 1995; Watkins et al., 2007).

44. Brown and Donnor (2011) identified the need for "new narratives" about Black males' schooling experiences that could replace the "same old stories" that routinely point to underachievement and other deficit-centered narratives. Also see Brooms (2017a), Harper (2015), and Young (2004) on centering Black men's lives and experiences in qualitative research.

45. A number of scholars have discussed, theorized, outlined, and written about how Black pain and suffering are predicated on anti-Blackness, which positions Blacks into the lower rungs of society (e.g., see Browne, 2015; Du Bois, 2005; Harris, 2020; Hartman, 1997; Kendi, 2016; Moten, 2013; Sharpe, 2016). The suffering manifested in this Black repositioning can be defined by Sexton's (2011) argument that "Black life is lived in death" (p. 29).

46. These studies continue to show that Black men are denigrated by institutional culture, racism, and stereotypes, and in social interactions as well, across various institutional types—though most prominently at four-year predominantly and historically white institutions (e.g., see Brooms, 2017a; Smith et al., 2007; Smith et al., 2011; Smith et al., 2016) and also across two-year colleges (Abrica et al., 2020). For studies that discuss how institutions act on individuals, see both Dancy et al. (2018) and Squire et al. (2018) for poignant and timely analyses regarding the plantation politics and neoliberal racism in higher education. As Chesler, Lewis, and Crowfoot (2005) maintained, there is a great need to challenge racism in higher education and promote justice.

47. For more in-depth discussions of these intersections, see Delgado (1995); Delgado and Stefancic (2011); Solórzano and Yosso (2002).

48. See Delgado (1995), p. xiv. With regard to the permanence of race, see D. Bell (1992a).

49. Derrick Bell (1980) argued that the *Brown vs. Board of Education* decision to end racial segregation in public schools was reflected in interests by both Blacks and whites; for Blacks, the decision provided greater educational access while for whites, and the US government in particular, it helped strengthen Cold War foreign relations, helped assuage critiques about race relations domestically, and could be used in efforts to demonstrate the US commitment to equality (p. 523). Bell expounded on this theory in later work as he noted that certain conditions must be met for white intervention or action; he contended that "when whites perceive that it will be profitable or at least cost-free to serve, hire, admit, or otherwise deal with blacks on a nondiscriminatory basis, they do so. When they fear—accurately or not—that there may be a loss, inconvenience, or upset to themselves or other whites, discriminatory conduct usually follows" (1992a, p. 7). Relatedly, Lofton (2021) found that Black students in racially diverse schools faced multiple systemic inequalities that often keep them

in lower-track classes. He argued that a racial caste system is sustained in and manifested through a nexus of home, school, and community.

50. This phrase is borrowed from the main title of Derrick Bell's (1992a) critical work on the permanence of race and racism in the United States.

51. Legal scholar Kimberlé Crenshaw (1991) has made significant contributions to our understanding of critical race theory and to how Black women are marginalized within US society.

52. See Solórzano and Yosso (2002).

53. Delgado (1995), p. xiv.

54. See Ladson-Billings (1998), p. 14.

55. See Ladson-Billings (2000), p. 272.

56. See Brooms (2017a) for a specific use of CRT in analyzing Black men's college experiences and T. Howard (2008, 2014) for a critical race theory perspective of Black boys in K–12 settings. Howard (2014) attested that CRT has the potential "to enable a discourse to take place in the educational research community that has occurred in Black homes, neighborhoods, churches, barber shops, and communal gatherings for years" (p. 55). CRT is an important framing as it allows for interrogating how race matters in educational settings and experiences and also recognizes other forms of oppression, such as class and gender, which necessarily have important connections and implications for Black boys and young men as well (e.g., see Allen, 2015; Brooms, 2020b; Duncan, 2002; T. Howard, 2008; Jett, 2019; Reynolds, 2010). Lori D. Patton (2016) also offered three critical propositions in examining CRT within the context of US higher education; specifically, higher education: (1) is rooted deeply in in racism/white supremacy, which is still apparent in the current time; (2) is entangled with imperialistic and capitalistic efforts that intensify the intersections of race, property, and oppression; and (3) serves as venues through which "formal" knowledge production grounded in racism/white supremacy is generated. For broader discussions about the utility of CRT, also see Delgado (1995); Gillborn (2015); Ladson-Billings (1998); Ladson-Billings and Tate (1995); Lynn and Dixson (2013); Lynn and Parker (2006); Solórzano and Yosso (2006). Also see Diamond (2018), who offered a potent and needed interrogation of race and white supremacy in the sociology of education.

57. See Mirza (2006), p. 144.

58. Mirza and Reay (2000), p. 521.

59. Mirza and Reay (2000) maintained that Black female social action "occupies a theoretical blind spot" and argued that Black women educators "are marginal in research on Black supplementary schooling" even though they played critical roles in social transformation through community building, visions of Blackness, and radical pedagogical practice (p. 525).

60. For instance, in previous work I found that young Black men's educational urgency allowed them to resist and reject one-dimensional projections of them (e.g., "I didn't want to be a statistic"; see Brooms, 2020b).

61. Here, I'm specifically thinking about the ways that Black boys and young men reveal and demonstrate their agency and rely on an ecology of hope that encompasses personal efforts along with family, community, and school (see Brooms, 2020b; Duncan-Andrade, 2009; Harmon et al., 2020; S. Johnson, 2019; Rogers & Way, 2016; Wright et al., 2016).

62. Venzant Chambers and McCready (2011) contended, "the notion of 'making space' is meant to capture the social, cultural, geographical, and psychological dynamics of a strategy African American students can employ to respond to and/or cope with their marginalization" (p. 1356).

63. For example, see Baldridge et al. (2011); Brooms (2019b); Hrabowski et al. (1998); Wright et al. (2010).

64. For instance, see Arbouin (2018); Brooms (2017a); Cornell and Kessi (2017); Warmington (2014); Williams et al. (2021); Wright et al. (2020).

65. See Edwards (2019).

66. A number of scholars acknowledge the importance of learning from Black boys and young men's own ways of knowing to understand their educational experiences, meaning making, and perspectives (Douglas, 2016; Goings & Shi, 2018; Robinson, 2017). It is important that scholars also help bring into greater focus the ways in which educational contexts can procure greater agency and possibilities (see Baldridge et al., 2011). Additionally, see Clay (2019) for an excellent discussion of Black resilience and Quigley and Mitchell (2018) for a critical assessment of "what works" in designing educational and mentoring interventions for Black boys and young men.

67. In his study of Black males' schooling experiences, Hucks (2014) focuses on the contextual factors "that have influenced the cross-generational schooling experiences and achievements" of Black males and reveals "both the continuities and discontinuities that have been underexplored in past research" by using their voices "to suggest directions for educational reform and future research" (p. 5). Hucks found several factors that were critical to their resilience, namely: lessons learned from older males in the family, negative incidents with teachers, the threat of racism, peer buffers versus peer perpetrators (urban masculinity), and the threat of violence in the community.

68. See Ladson-Billings (2006), p. 5.

69. See James D. Anderson's seminal work on Black education in the South, *The education of Blacks in the South, 1860–1935* (1988). Also see Jarvis Given's recent critical study of Black education through the lens of the pioneering work of Carter G. Woodson, *Fugitive Pedagogy* (2021).

70. See hooks (1995), p. 59.

Notes to Chapter 2

1. This narrative has been popularized by highly public figures who use various occasions to chide Black boys and young men for their ways of being—

from their style of dress to their cultural ethos. A number of researchers have explored the inherent tensions in these narratives (see, for instance, Brooms, 2017a, 2017b; Carey, 2019b; Dumas & Nelson, 2016; Evans-Winters & Bethune, 2014; Harper & Davis, 2012; L. Howard, 2012; T. Howard, 2008; Howard & Associates, 2017; Howard et al., 2019; Jett, 2019; Ladson-Billings, 2011; Nelson, 2016; Rogers & Way, 2016; Toldson & Johns, 2016).

2. The Schott Foundation for Public Education releases reports on the status of education for Black males, which also have included Latino males over the past several publications (e.g., see Schott Foundation for Public Education, 2015). In like manner, the Congressional Black Caucus Foundation has supported reports on the status of Black boys as well (see Toldson, 2008, 2011).

3. In a study with a colleague examining ideology and identity among white male teachers, we found that the ideology of meritocracy was used to place Black boys' supposed underachievement on they themselves; that is, Black boys did not do well in school in part because they didn't care enough about their education or even because, supposedly, their families and communities did not value education (Rogers & Brooms, 2020). Some of these conversations have been engaged by research intended to highlight the disparities in opportunities afforded to Black students (e.g., see Emdin, 2016; Love, 2019).

4. Research continues to show that Black boys and young men often are "written off" and not expected to achieve intellectually, and they are denigrated as well (see Allen, 2017; Brown, 2017; Davis, 2006; Holzman, 2008; Wright et al., 2016; Young, 2018). Related to the pressures and challenges that some youth face in their neighborhoods and how they try to navigate them, some researchers help unpack and clarify their experiences, decision making, and agency (e.g., see Brooms, 2019b; Huerta, 2015; Polite & Davis, 1999; Richardson & St. Vil, 2015; Robinson, 2017).

5. This research has examined these Black young men's sense making regarding ways in which they value education, their secondary schooling experiences, the importance of relationships that they developed, how they navigated various arenas of their lives (e.g., the neighborhood effect), and educational aspirations (see Brooms, 2014, 2015, 2017b, 2019a, 2020b).

6. In my discussion here, I use the phrase "hoop dreams" intentionally to refer to the 1994 film *Hoop Dreams*, which followed the basketball experiences and aspirations of two Black male adolescents, William Gates and Arthur Agee. Gates and Agee lived in Chicago and attended school in a northern suburb to play for a highly praised basketball program, which they believed could help them pursue their postsecondary basketball goals (S. James, 1994). Sociologist Reuben May (2007) provides critical insight into how Black adolescent males pursue the allure of social status and athletic prominence through playing basketball. Through an ethnographic account, May shows how these male youth bank on the allure and financial, social, and cultural potential of the game through their hard work, their steadfast dedication to practice (even during leisure time), and

the team's successes. May reveals the "double-edged sword" of hoop dreams for many of the Black male youth in his 2007 study *Living through the Hoop*. Additionally, sociologist Scott Brooks (2009) also shows how basketball provides Black males with education and opportunities well beyond athletics. In following the lives of two Black males, Brooks argues that they garner success not through a mythic "natural athleticism," but rather through extreme discipline, intentional effort, and a focus on personal goals.

7. In some of my previous work, I use a qualitative research approach to discuss the neighborhood effect as it relates to Black boys' and young men's educational experiences (see Brooms, 2019b). Other researchers also reveal how youth of color have to navigate complex neighborhood dynamics that can impact and disrupt their educational experiences, their growth, and their development (e.g., see Oliver, 2006; Perry et al., 2015; Rendón, 2014; Shedd, 2015; Spencer et al., 2003; Stewart et al., 2006; Wallace, 2018).

8. May (2007) provides a detailed discussion of Black boys' and young men's basketball aspirations and how they develop and pursue basketball identities. Relatedly, Brooks (2009) details the efforts that some Black young men engage in to pursue basketball opportunities and improve their plight in the highly competitive basketball leagues in inner-city communities such as those in Philadelphia. Additionally, scholars note that Black male students' sports participation can contribute to their educational expectations, college attendance, and educational attainment (see Cooper, 2016; Harris, 2014; Harris et al., 2014; Harrison et al., 2010). In a historic event, on the heels of winning the 2012 NCAA championship, the five starting players of the University of Kentucky's men's basketball team, all of whom were Black males, declared themselves eligible for the National Basketball Association draft. In assessing this collective announcement, even while acknowledging the potential personal and professional benefits of such aspiration, David Pate (2012) argued that greater attention is needed in assessing the long-term perspective of Black young men's holistic development; he noted, "Too many young black men are encouraged to perfect their 'balling' skills but not their academic skills."

9. Lofton and Davis (2015) argued that such acts of betrayal can undermine trust, damage relationships, and even inflict trauma. As a result, they contended, "Another distinct phenomenon that many African American students and parents must confront is the institutional betrayal they witness in their schools, communities, and society in general" (pp. 222–223). Further, studies show that Black males are routinely targeted in school and even viewed as dangers to the school environment (Allen, 2017; Ferguson, 2000; Ginwright, 2009; T. Howard, 2014; Jenkins, 2006; Noguera, 2008; Polite & Davis, 1999; Wright et al., 2016). This narrative is rooted in anti-Blackness and Black misandry, which render Black males as threats—to themselves and others—which then, based on this racial logic, "warrants" their policing, surveillance, and criminality. Additionally, Langtiw and Heidbrink (2016) contended that removing Black youth from public

spaces, such as schools, is a form of betrayal and structural violence. They argued that "violence, inculcated in public policies and institutional practices, negates the humanity of Black youth and actively and routinely removes them from family, community and the nation" (p. 41). In their analysis, they asserted that structural violence constitutes institutional betrayal trauma, since institutions brandish harm on those who depend on them for security, safety, and care or that fail to prevent harm being perpetuated against them.

10. Building on W. E. B. Du Bois's (1935) seminal text, which affirmed a sympathetic touch between teacher and student as an imperative for Black education, and given the ongoing challenges that Black male youth experience in educational settings, Terry and colleagues (2014) used qualitative data from a two-year study of single-sex educational spaces in two Los Angeles County high schools to explore the viability of such spaces for Black males. They argued that when all-male spaces effectively function as counterspaces, "sites where deficit notions of people of color can be challenged and where a positive collegiate racial climate can be established and maintained (Solórzano et al., 2000, p. 70), that center on meeting "the growing educational and social needs of Black males in schools" (p. 689), they can enhance Black males' schooling experiences.

11. Ovink (2016) argued that college-for-all is a pervasive culture that "largely ignores economic, racial/ethnic, and gendered constraints on college attendance, to the detriment of first-generation and underrepresented groups" (p. 13).

12. Williams and colleagues (2019) argued that HBCUs collectively suffer from anti-Blackness in public policy—and, by extension, public discourse—which too often ignores the contributions of HBCUs for Black students and families. They found that the HBCU presidents they interviewed maintained that HBCUs are critical in cultivating students' leadership abilities and development, expanding educational opportunities for students with financial barriers, and tapping into the potential of students with prior academic challenges. They concluded, "The narratives presented disrupt and complicate pervasive negative depictions of HBCUs and foster a more nuanced understanding of their modern contributions" (p. 586). Similarly, in considering the contributions of these institutions, Albritton (2012) argued that the HBCU history "is deeply rooted in the Black community's commitment to racial uplift and community empowerment." The significance of this commitment continues to be relevant today given the ongoing "sociopolitical policies and practices that deemed Black men and women incapable of succeeding as learners because of the unfounded belief that their race made them inferior and unable to appreciate the benefits of postsecondary education" (p. 311). Finally, in a study of fifty alumni from twenty different institutions, education scholar Jennifer Johnson (2017) found that the primary reasons why these "twenty-first century students" chose HBCUs was due to the desire to be in a predominantly Black environment, the reputation of academic programs, and cost/financial aid. Thus, across a variety of studies, HBCUs are

highly desirous given their unique culture and traditional practices, academic programs and opportunities, and welcoming environments (see Freeman & Thomas, 2002; Mobley, 2017; Mobley & Johnson, 2015; Palmer et al., 2010; Palmer & Wood, 2012).

13. Dancy, Edwards, and Davis (2018) contended that anti-Blackness is constitutive to the US settler colonial state and also manifests within higher education as a form of plantation politics at historically white institutions (HWIs). They identified three specific dimensions in which anti-Blackness is manifested in higher education: (a) interpretations of Black labor through colonial arrangements; (b) the relationship between labor, ownership, and education; and (c) the institutionalization of Black suffering. In regard to Black suffering particularly, they argued that HWIs are spaces where physical insecurity continues, albeit to a lesser degree than in previous times, and where "psychological and economic vulnerabilities persist" (p. 188). Additionally, the continued defunding of HBCUs "exposes the state's commitment to Black vulnerability" (p. 188).

14. For instance, a vast score of recent and ongoing research shows that Black students as well as other students of color are frequently marginalized on the campuses of predominantly and historically white institutions (e.g., see Fischer, 2010; Fleming, 1984; Hurtado et al., 2015; S. Johnson, 2019; McClain & Perry, 2017). As an example, in their study of 345 African, Caribbean, and Black American college students, Thelamour, George Mwangi, and Ezeofor (2019) found that students who identified strongly with their Blackness felt less connected to their college campuses. Relatedly, studies show that students vary in their understanding and analysis of race and racism (e.g., see Johnston-Guerrero, 2016; Linley, 2018). For instance, in a qualitative study of 40 college students at two West Coast public research universities, Johnston-Guerrero (2016) found that students' precollege experiences and campus contexts influenced race-related patterns in their experiencing of and learning about race. Students' racial meanings informed the ways in which they refuted postracial claims and how they saw race mattering (or not) on multiple levels (e.g., the interpersonal, institutional, and systemic).

15. As an example, survival in impoverished Black communities requires that individuals often rely on each other to meet some of their needs and garner support (see Pattillo, 2012; Stack, 1974; Young, 2004).

16. Here, I relate these young men's fugitivity to the concept of flight from oppressive conditions as a key strategy of resistance and survival (see McKittrick, 2011; Roberts, 2015).

Notes to Chapter 3

1. Emdin and Lee (2012), while discussing the ways in which the term developed in both educational and political discourse, defined the Obama effect

as "the potential of Obama's presence and visibility to be a tool for sparking the interest and participation in previously closed fields among populations who resonate with the President's many hybridized identities" (p. 14).

2. In his study of Black and Latino high school boys' college-going processes, Carey (2016) contended that this college-going familial capital is "transferred through lessons, values, practices, and beliefs, that serve as rationale, motivation, and support for securing postsecondary educational attainment" (p. 718). Similarly, Kiyama (2010) identified educational ideologies and funds of knowledge as critical for supporting college aspirations among Mexican American families. Also see Brooms (2017a); Huerta et al. (2018); Jett (2016); Knight et al. (2004).

3. For instance, see Brooms (2017a), Freeman (2005), and Mwangi (2015). Specifically, in a previous study, which focused on the college experiences of forty Black men, I identified family support as well as family history to inform and inspire their college aspirations and expectations (Brooms, 2017a). College, then, for a number of Black youth, is not simply an individual venture but rather one that the encompasses dreams, aspirations, and needs of one's family and community. Relatedly, George Mwangi's (2015) metasynthesis of research literature revealed the importance of focusing on diverse and underrepresented student populations and acknowledging the various ways in which families and communities are involved in students' access to college.

4. Wilson (1987) maintained that the deep changes in the economy combined with the departure of the Black middle class to remove an important "social buffer" that could have prevented joblessness from moving people into the underclass, which weakened critical social institutions such as churches and schools at the same time as businesses and recreational facilities. Thus, Wilson argued, the combined effect of labor market changes and departure of the middle class created "social isolation" and "isolation effects" that undermined social mobility and advancement.

5. For instance, Rendón (2014) found that some youth's educational experiences can be disrupted or even undermined due to urban violence and peer ties. Some individuals are pulled into altercations and disagreements because of these ties and, therefore, are "caught up" in various entanglements of peer and youth associations and negotiations. Along the same lines, I have found that some young Black men use a collective approach of "sticking together"—that is, developing deep bonds with their Black male peers—to help provide physical and psychological safety from neighborhood violence and to support their educational goals (Brooms, 2019b).

6. Stevie "DJ View" Johnson's 2019 dissertation album is a critical representation of scholarship media, and particularly the utility of hip-hop in inviting and creating space for Black college men's unapologetic voices and knowledge. Johnson contended that the study was centered on "Black male collegians theorizing Blackness and expressing their anti-Black experiences at HWIs"

(p. 81). Given its expressive elements and possibilities, Johnson maintained that hip-hop, as used by his study participants to develop their own album (*The Space Program*) and author their experiences through lyrics, could help the men liberate themselves. In speaking about the power and centrality of hip-hop to his work, Johnson stated, "The research seeks to disrupt anti-Blackness and organize through the fugitive space of Hip-Hop (using the creation of a Hip-Hop album as a fugitive tool) in hopes of actualizing Black male collegians' agency, or, more specifically, their radical self-determination and self-knowledge" (p. 19). Along the same lines, Washington (2018) asserted that hip-hop culture, particularly rap music, offers a broad repository of artists, songs, albums, and lyrics that can be useful to counseling Black boys and men. In speaking about its utility, Washington noted, "Rap music, as an expression of Hip-Hop culture, can function as part of a conceptualizing lens through which counseling professionals might achieve greater insight into Black males' worldviews, contextual experiences, and short- and long-term aspirations" (p. 99). Much like S. Johnson, Washington, and others, I see great utility and benefits of engaging hip-hop in working with Black boys and men and learning about their lives, and I agree that they may see it as a form of expression that contributes to their knowledge and sense making.

7. In this opening line, Skyzoo particularly noted "looking for luck" and "dreaming" and, as mentioned, this sentiment was expressed by a number of the young men in this study. In our conversations, we consistently talked about hopes and the ways that our efforts could align with our aspirations. Given that our conversations were dynamic and our relationships continue to grow and be sustained, these young men often inquire about my work, teaching, and research. More importantly, though, they inquire and care about my health, well-being, and personhood. As a result, I continue to talk about and share with them my progress, activities, goals, and aspirations.

8. In a study of forty-nine Black college students, Holland (2011) found that peers served as positive influences in advocating academic engagement and plans to pursue education beyond high school, often served as college "advisors" in helping guide their peers' knowledge and decisions about higher education, and provided academic and social support. Similarly, using ethnographic and survey data from a three-year study in the Los Angeles Unified School District, Tierney and Venegas (2006) found that students positioned in peer counselor roles can offer critical social capital to other students and also help to cultivate a college-going identity. As it relates to school culture and family, researchers find that both the capital and the identity contribute to the nexus of support that is often needed to make college going a stronger reality for Black male students (see Brooms, 2014, 2020c; Carey, 2016; Farmer-Hinton, 2008; Freeman, 2005).

9. As an example, in her study of Mexican American families, Kiyama (2010) found that despite educational limitations within some of the families, they still maintained a sense of college as a realistic goal through their educa-

tional ideologies and social networks. Kiyama noted that among the families, "Thoughts about educational choices were often found at two ends of the spectrum. Either families' college knowledge was limited to the local institutions, or families wanted their children to attend the most prestigious institutions" (p. 341; also see Brooms & Davis, 2017a; Carey, 2019a; George Mwangi, 2015; Knight et al., 2004).

Notes to Chapter 4

1. For instance, see Brooms (2014, 2017b, 2020b, 2020c).

2. See Kunjufu (2013), p. 33.

3. For instance, Reid and Moore's (2008) work is noteworthy here, as they found that students in their study clearly identified specific preparation that they believed helped with college success, such as certain classes and teachers that helped prepare them academically. They also found that close connections with teachers provided important social capital that helped encouraged and support students' college aspirations and preparation. Research also indicates that lack of college planning and success for first-generation Black males can impact their career development as well (Owens et al., 2010).

4. See Brooms (2017b); Fergus et al. (2014); Howard and Associates (2017); Michael-Chadwell (2014); Milner (2007); Rogers and Way (2016).

5. For instance, see Carey (2018); Noguera (2003); Palmer et al. (2009); Reid & Moore (2008).

6. See Noguera (2003), p. 436.

Notes to Chapter 5

1. For instance, Hines and colleagues (2019) found that Black and Latino males faced a number of challenges to college going and persistence as first-generation collegians. In particular, they found that participants experienced limited social and navigational capital connected to college enrollment and that inequitable schooling experiences made their college going and persistence more difficult.

2. A number of studies substantiate the links between young Black men's self-authorship and their academic self-efficacy, personal and social adjustment, and sense of self in higher education (Amechi, 2016; Clark & Brooms, 2018; Strayhorn, 2014). For instance, in Amechi's (2016) study of the higher education experiences of Black male alumni of foster care, he found that students' poor academic performances created dissonance, which called into question their way of knowing. Students reported several critical self-authoring strategies, such as

maintaining a positive self-identity during their college years and establishing positive, supportive, and meaningful relationships with faculty and peers as important factors that helped facilitate academic self-efficacy and success in college.

3. Researchers note that young Black men's peer relationships play a vital role in their educational experiences and provide critical forms of support that contribute to their academic, social, and personal selves (see Brooms, 2017a; Brooms & Davis, 2017b; Carey, 2019a; Strayhorn, 2008; Thelamour et al., 2019).

4. My previous research showed that as some Black college men made sense of their status and positioning at historically white institutions, their experiences of alienation not only were connected to feelings of isolation, but also revealed how this relative positioning created stressors and burdens for them (Brooms, 2017a). It is important to note that students experience alienation in both academic and nonacademic spaces and that peer relationships can be important to their sense of belongingness and ability to navigate these challenging experiences (see Robertson & Chaney, 2017; Smith et al., 2016; Strayhorn, 2018).

5. A number of scholars make clear the importance of space and place for Black students in college, particularly at historically and predominantly white institutions and even at Minority Serving Institutions as well (e.g., Hypolite, 2020; Serrano, 2020; Tichavakunda, 2020). For instance, in a study of Black and Latino men's experiences at a Hispanic-Serving Institution, Serrano (2020) found that the Pan-African Studies Department and the Latin American Studies program provided students with a positive campus racial microclimate on campus, which he identified as an academic homeplace. Importantly, these homeplaces "not only provided services" to students, in terms of programs and activities, but also "most importantly, fostered a community of resistance to hostile environments and racism on campus" (p. 2). Tichavakunda (2020) conceptualized Black place making within higher education as a way to provide "tools to better engage with and understand the expansiveness of Black student life" (p. 4). As opposed to simply focusing on challenges or even counterspaces that Black students develop on campus, which often dominate discourses about their experiences, Tichavakunda focused on exploring how Black students create and sustain communities; a Black place-making analysis can help better equip stakeholders to create transformative changes in higher education and take account of sites of belonging, mattering, joy, and community.

6. In his study of Black and Latino boys' college-going dilemmas, Carey (2019a) combined social cognitive theory with "college-going internal and external dilemmas" to investigate how these youth developed self-appraisals and assessed their own "cognitive and noncognitive factors that both supported and would likely obstruct them from accessing and eventually achieving postsecondary education success" (p. 383). Findings revealed that participants' perceptions of their skills, academic and social needs, and expected familial contributions contributed to their college-going dilemmas.

7. P. D. Johnson's (2016) work identified "somebodiness" as a significant finding in the psychological functioning of Black men. In particular, the researcher found that somebodiness "meant having a sense of worth, purpose, and community" (p. 336). The men in Johnson's study wished to "discover their purpose and make something productive out of their lives, and they yearned to help others, especially African American youth in the community" (p. 336). The participants talked about teachers as key people in their lives who nurtured their sense of somebodiness by using an engaged and affirming pedagogy, teaching life skills, understanding barriers that they faced, and offering support for their educational goals.

8. Extending research from other scholars who discuss the significance of Black men in the lives of Black youth (e.g., M. Johnson, 2013; Richardson, 2009) and especially those within educational contexts (Brooms, 2017b; Brown, 2009; Lynn, 2002, 2006), I conceptualized and found that *otherfathers* contribute significantly to the development of Black male youth (Brooms, 2017b). In particular, the students in this study noted that learning from Black male teachers was valued highly by students because these experiences provided them with insider perspectives and key insights on being Black and male, provided opportunities to learn more about how race and gender could matter in their lives, and provided students with unique opportunities to learn more about themselves. Through otherfathering—expressed as holistic care, support, parenting, modeling, and life coaching—students' learning enhanced their critical consciousness and connected to their racial and gender identities as well.

9. In other published research, I have found that interactions and relationships with faculty contributed to Black college men's sense of belonging and helped strengthen their persistence efforts as well (Brooms, 2020a; Brooms & Davis, 2017b). Along the same lines, research shows that students of color benefit academically and personally from mentoring and bonding with faculty members (see Chang, 2005; Goings, 2017; Hurtado et al., 2015; Wood, 2014; Wood & Turner, 2012).

10. Jack (2018) discussed the difficulties that these students experienced in navigating the norms in a new institutional setting and particularly focused on how elite colleges are failing "disadvantaged" students.

Note to Chapter 6

1. Research shows the benefits that young Black men can accrue through engaging in programs and events that help them learn more about college-going plus connecting with their college-aged peers. For instance, in one study I found that Black young men's participation in college summer programs exposed them to firsthand college experiences and a wide variety of peers (Brooms, 2020c). Additionally, see Tichavakunda and Galan's (2020) study, which assessed how the

summer before college mattered in the experiences of 33 first-generation, urban high school students. Their findings indicated a variety of factors that contributed to students' college enrollment, including college readiness, college-based interactions, and social capital. Most prominently, their findings indicated that summer bridge programs and summer classes at prospective institutions mattered greatly in providing important social capital and can help bridge students' lack of knowledge as well as the unreliable and inconsistent college advice available to them.

Notes to Chapter 7

1. See Yosso's (2005) conceptualization and discussion of community cultural wealth and discussion of how it can support students and communities of color in navigating various educational contexts and pursuing their goals. In like manner, some researchers have used the concept of community cultural wealth to examine and analyze Black students' educational experiences as well (e.g., see Brooms & Davis, 2017a; Hines et al., 2019; Jayakumar et al., 2013; Lane & Id-Deen, 2020; McGowan & Pérez, 2020).

2. See Brooms (2017a); Brooms and Davis (2017b); Luedke (2017); Palmer and Gasman (2008); Strayhorn (2017, 2018).

3. Collegiate 100 is a national program of the 100 Black Men of America, Inc. The program provides mentoring and guidance for Black men in college (see https://100blackmen.org/).

Notes to Chapter 9

1. Baldwin contended, "The years I lived in Paris did one thing for me: they released me from that particular social terror, which was not the paranoia of my own mind, but a real social danger visible in the face of every cop, every boss, everybody" in the United States (Baldwin & Peck, 2017, p. 88).

2. As I stated throughout this work, the discussions with these young men about their lives and current events were robust and included a wide range of topics. In specifically discussing the ongoing killings of Black people, the overwhelming majority of the points they raised were about their age proximity to some of the Black young men and men who were killed, the grotesque nature of the killings (e.g., the nine individuals killed while worshipping at the Mother Emanuel AME Church in Charleston, South Carolina in 2015), and some that received significant public attention. To the point regarding mediated messages, numerous scholars assert that negative portrayals of Blacks in general and Black boys and men in particular, though not new, have damaging effects that impact

their lives (e.g., see M. Alexander, 2010; Brooms & Perry, 2016; Brown, 2018; Brown & Donnor, 2011; Kumah-Abiwu, 2020; Muhammad, 2011). For instance, Kumah-Abiwu (2020) argued that, "the criminalization of Blackness has become a powerful force in shaping the American society, especially in the current era of social media explosion. Media images of Black male criminality and negative depictions as 'brutish' and 'predators' have become the norm that continues to permeate the consciousness of the society" (p. 77).

3. Sociologist Elijah Anderson (2008) argued that young Black men are "up against the wall" because "Being Black and male in this country is to hold second-class citizenship" (p. 17). Also, in a different project, I argued that they are "innocent until proven Black" given that "the violence propagated against Black males and the imagery used to misinform perspectives" are tributes to the attacks and violence levied against Black humanity (Brooms, 2016).

4. The point I raise her about how Black boys and young men can be entangled in neighborhood challenges should be considered within the context of the various disadvantages discussed previously, such as lacking significant economic opportunities. Rendón's (2014) study examined how urban violence and peer ties contributed to Latino young men's high school noncompletion. These youth drew upon male peer youth for protection from urban violence and, ultimately a number of these students got "caught up" in activities and behaviors that were undermine school completion (e.g., being truant or helping friends fight in physical altercations). Rendon found that some of these young men "with ties to gang and crew peers were constantly 'watching their back'" which easily "distracted these youth from school" and often "absorbed youth into gang and crew behavior in direct and consequential ways that impacted school completion" (Rendón, 2014, p. 71). Other researchers also demonstrate how involvement in street-oriented life or gang activities and affiliations can impact young men's schooling experiences and engagement (Huerta & Rios-Aguilar, 2021; Johnson et al., 2010; Miller, 2021; Oliver, 2006; Patton et al., 2016; Rankin & Quane, 2002; Richardson et al., 2014). Importantly, Jones' (2010) work details how inner-city violence impacts Black girls as well. Finally, as R. Johnson (2015) found using a nationally representative sample, Black boys' and young men's early contact with the criminal justice system through juvenile arrests create pervasive limits on their college enrollment.

5. Scholars have discussed a range of macro- and microaggressions that Black male students face in higher education (see Brooms, 2017a; Burt et al., 2020; Robertson & Chaney, 2017; Strayhorn, 2017) and also racism and anti-Blackness which can have a negative impact on their educational focus and academic performance (Abrica et al., 2020; Arbouin, 2018; Brooms & Davis, 2017b; Burt et al., 2019; Cuyjet, 2006; Johnson-Ahorlu, 2013; Mustaffa, 2017; Tichavakunda, 2021). Also, as it relates to Black misandry and racial battle fatigue, these experiences generate (or further extend) feelings of isolation and

alienation on campus, can siphon energy away from academic endeavors, and threaten Black male students' persistence efforts (for instance, see Brooms, 2017a; Smith et al., 2007; Smith et al., 2011; Smith et al., 2016).

6. Researchers maintain that how Black boys and young men are imagined, seen, and (mis)perceived all play critical roles in the educational opportunities they are afforded and the disparate treatment they too often receive (for instance, see Brooms, 2020b; Bryan, 2020; Clark et al., 2020; Duncan, 2002; Goff et al., 2014; Hotchkins, 2016; James & Lewis, 2014; Jenkins, 2006; Kumah-Abiwu, 2020; McGee, 2013; Robinson, 2017; Sealey-Ruiz & Greene, 2015; Toldson, 2008). Thus, scholars continue their call for racial and social justice. For instance, Smith and Smith Lee (2020) asserted that accurately and appropriately recognizing the pain of Black boys and men is "essential to transforming systems levels responses to it" (p. 209). Relatedly, scholars have highlighted the need for improving counseling through school-community collaborations and social justice (Grimmett et al., 2017; Moore-Thomas & Day-Vines, 2010; Washington, 2010; Washington & Henfield, 2019). For instance, given the ways that anti-Blackness is predictable, Washington and Henfield (2019) argued for an ecological understanding of oppression among counselors and counselor educators. Importantly, in situating their discussion within the Black Lives Matter movement, they contended that counselors too often underappreciate how systems of oppression constrain life chances and outcomes for Black people: "By underappreciating this relationship, counselors fortify these systems, which belies the claim counseling is politically neutral or that a counselor's work with clients can be compartmentalized from the sociopolitical terrain where it unfolds" (p. 151). As a result, they called for re-envisioning the counseling profession through pedagogy, research, and advocacy that improves cultural competence, centers in social justice, and is rooted in the plight of oppressed people.

7. See Goodwill et al. (2018); Watkins (2006); Watkins et al. (2007); Watkins et al. (2010). Additionally, research on role strain and risks is important to consider as it sheds light on how various scenarios and experiences impact Black men's life cycle (e.g., see Bowman, 1989; Hucks, 2014; Rowley & Bowman, 2009).

Notes to Chapter 10

1. Here, I'm calling specific attention to various constructions of Black masculinities and gender performances among Black boys and young men (Laing, 2017; McCready, 2010; Mutua, 2006; Venzant Chambers & McCready, 2011), as well as the range of stereotypes that "operate to categorize, essentialize, and disenfranchise young Black male students as they navigate and negotiate the school system" (C. James, 2012, p. 471; also see Brooms, 2017a, 2020b; Davis, 2006; Ferguson, 2000; Kunjufu, 2004; Noguera, 2008).

2. As it relates to countering, rewriting, or even developing new narratives about Black boys and young men, I join a number of colleagues and scholars who help to amplify these needs (e.g., see Amechi, 2016; Baldridge et al., 2011; Brown & Donnor, 2011; Carey, 2019b; Goings et al., 2015; Howard et al., 2019; Hucks, 2014; Rogers & Way, 2016).

3. The points I raise here are grounded in findings from a number of recent qualitative studies that explore Black boys' and young men's schooling experiences in the United States and abroad (see Allen, 2017; Brooms, 2020b; Brown, 2017, 2018; Bryan, 2020; Carey, 2019a; Jett, 2019; Kumah-Abiwu, 2019; Robinson, 2017; Rogers & Way, 2016; Wright et al., 2016) as well as several earlier studies (Christian, 2005; Cobbett & Younger, 2012; Duncan, 2002; Ferguson, 2000; Graham & Robinson, 2004; T. Howard, 2013; C. James, 2012; McGee, 2013).

4. A growing cadre of scholars discuss the inequities that contribute to "grit" and "no excuses" discourses or that burden youth with the responsibility to achieve regardless of the inequities they face, which are important critiques and contributions (see Baldridge, 2014; Carey, 2019b; Clay, 2019; Dumas & Nelson, 2016). For instance, Carey (2019b) argued that Black boys' and young men's success, "be it academic, artistic, or athletic, is heralded as proof that social forces like racism can be overcome through innate talent, stick-to-itiveness, and grit" (p. 379).

5. A number of researchers have documented the incredible efforts of Black boys and men to prove their intellectual abilities within educational contexts (see Allen, 2105, 2017; Brooms, 2017a, 2020b; Harmon et al., 2020; Harper, 2015; Jett, 2016; McGee & Martin, 2011; Moore et al., 2003). For instance, Moore et al. (2003) contended that the "prove-them-wrong approach" for the Black male students in their study was based on working harder to reach personal goals in efforts to prove critics wrong when they doubt one's ability to perform.

6. See Baldridge (2014), p. 465.

7. O'Connor (2020) argued the need for better assessing and understanding how racialized micro-interactions produce and reify educational stratification and inequality. In speaking specifically to racialized distortions, she contended, "Black and Brown bodies are not only subject to distortion when we fail to analyze how they are institutionally placed at risk as per cultural biases and social group conflicts over power and access that get articulated on the ground each day" (p. 477; also see Du Bois, 1935; Dumas & Nelson, 2016; Epps, 1975; Givens, 2021; King, 2005; Lofton, 2021; C. Woodson, 1933/2011; Wright & Counsell, 2018).

8. I invoke the lives and memories of these Black boys precisely because they were named by the young men in this study and their killings impacted how these young men thought about themselves, their own lives, and the lives of their friends and close associates (see also M. Alexander, 2010; Brooms & Clark, 2020; Brooms & Perry, 2016; Brown, 2017; Bryan, 2021; Dancy, 2014a; Evans-Winters & Bethune, 2014; Goff et al., 2014; Jenkins, 2006; Love, 2016;

Miller, 2021). In addition, a number of scholars discuss the prominence of anti-Blackness and Black social death (e.g., see Fanon, 1952/1967; Moten, 2013; Sexton, 2011).

9. Thompson and Allen (2012) identified four specific harms that Black students experience related to high-stakes testing: (1) limited improvement in test scores and dropout rates; (2) an increase in student apathy; (3) more punitive discipline policies and pushing of more youth into the prison pipeline; and (4) a narcissistic education system. Also see Donnor and Shockley (2010); Epps and Morrison (2003); Polite and Davis (1999).

10. See Brooms (2014, 2019a); Carey (2019a); Fergus et al. (2014); Hines et al. (2019); Knight and Marciano (2013); Reid and Moore (2008).

11. See hooks (1994), p. 13. Moreover, scholars continue to discuss the importance of improving educational environments, including teaching, to enhance opportunities and successes for Black boys and men (e.g., see Arbouin, 2018; Baldridge et al., 2011; Carey, 2019b; Davis, 2003; Fergus et al., 2014; Kunjufu, 2013; Ladson-Billings, 2011; Milner, 2007; Nelson, 2016; Rogers & Brooms, 2020).

12. For instance, recent work highlights the need to understand and reverse underachievement by Black boys and young men, especially those in urban schools (Fergus et al., 2014; Ford & Moore, 2013; Moore & Lewis, 2014; Toldson & Johns, 2016; Whiting, 2006).

13. For instance, although they primarily discussed Black college men's coping strategies, Goodwill et al. (2018) found that the participants in their study identified "strained interpersonal relationships, academic difficulties, racism, and discrimination" among a host of other stressors that negatively impact Black men's health and well-being (p. 542). Even further, scholars note increases and growing problems of mental distress and suicide among Black boys and young men (see Griffith et al., 2013; Joe et al., 2018; Watkins, 2006; Watkins et al., 2010), which makes it even more incumbent on us to understand and have in place protective factors, such as social support from peers, family support, religion, private esteem, and access to care (see Reed & Adams, 2020; Joe et al., 2018). Black boys and men also write about dealing with and navigating stress, depression, and mental health issues in their own writing as well (e.g., see Coates, 2015, and Laymon, 2018, for two recent examples of critical texts).

14. My references here related to a range of scholarship that identifies the ways in which Black boys suffer in school. For instance, Ferguson (2000) contended that Black boys are constructed as "bad boys" through inequitable school discipline practices that routinely identify their youthful behaviors as "bad." Similarly, Duncan (2002) found that the school discipline practices examined in his study pushed Black boys outside of caring networks and relegated them as "beyond love," while Noguera (2003, 2008) contended that a variety of factors converge to create troubles for Black boys. Finally, in other published work, I

present findings on how Black boys make meaning of and navigate the notion of "being a statistic" as connected to their lives and schooling experiences. Most prominently, they related "being a statistic" to a number of negative possibilities for their lives, including interpersonal violence, being denied educational opportunities, and structural racism (see Brooms, 2020b).

15. My references here are to several works that focus explicitly on the lives of Black boys and men (see E. Anderson, 2008; Young, 2018) and also relate to work presented more broadly on the impacts of racism on Black life (see D. Bell, 1992a; Hill, 2016; Muhammad, 2011).

Notes to the Appendix

1. Solórzano and Yosso (2002) defined critical race methodology as a theoretically grounded approach to research that includes five characteristics: (a) it foregrounds race and racism in the research process; (b) it challenges traditional research paradigms and theories used to explain the experiences of students of color; (c) it offers a liberatory or transformative solution to racial, gender, and class subordination; (d) it focuses on the intersecting experiences of students of color (e.g., race, gender, and class); and (e) it uses an interdisciplinary knowledge base (e.g., including elements of Black/Africana Studies, education, sociology, history, and law) to better understand the experiences of students of color. (For further discussion of critical race methodologies, see DeCuir-Gunby et al., 2019; Huber, 2008; Parker, 2015; Parker & Lynn, 2002).

2. In multiple works, Derrick Bell (1991, 1992a, 1992b) advances the argument that racism is here to stay in the United States and that Blacks will continue to suffer greatly because of it. For instance, he argued that Blacks' racial status "in this country has been a cyclical phenomenon in which legal rights are gained, then lost, then gained again in response to economic and political developments in a country over which blacks exercise little or no control" (1991), p. 80. Also, as noted in the text, I couple my point here with the realities of these young men's Black male identities. Researchers acknowledge and identify that Black students are challenged in navigating neighborhoods in their schooling efforts, some of which is connected to structural racism and overpolicing (e.g., see Harding, 2010; Lofton & Davis, 2015; Wallace, 2018), while some is related specifically to their Black male identities (Brooms, 2019b; Jenkins, 2006; Oliver, 2006; Richardson & St. Vil, 2016). Finally, a plethora of research shows that Black boys and men carry a significant burden due to their Blackmaleness (e.g., see Brooms & Perry, 2016; Curry, 2017; Mutua, 2006). In trying to make sense of the constant and ongoing trifling of Black men's lives, sociology scholar Alford Young Jr. (2018) argued that too many Black men battle extreme disadvantage, especially socially and economically, and expend a great

deal of energy in both fighting for survival and struggling for dignity. According to Young, the overarching challenges they face involve constantly negotiating a society that labels them a "problem" and creates a damning portrayal of Black men as beyond hope while simultaneously ignoring their voices.

3. For excellent discussions of researching Black students' schooling experiences and centering race in research, see O'Connor, Lewis, and Mueller (2007) and Tillman (2002).

4. O'Connor, Lewis, and Mueller (2017).

5. There is a robust discussion of Black male academies as single-sex institutions (e.g., see Epps, 1995; Fergus et al., 2014; Leake & Leake, 1992; Mitchell & Stewart, 2013; Quigley & Mitchell, 2018). Two recent texts offer important interrogations of the politics, structuring, and ideologies that inform how these schools operate (Lindsay, 2018; Oeur, 2018).

6. See Schott Foundation for Public Education (2004, 2015).

7. See Castillo-Montoya (2016).

8. See Bhattacharya (2017); J. Johnson (2002).

9. See Brooms (2019b), pp. 62–63.

10. See Brooms (2017b), p. 3.

11. See Moustakas (1994) for a discussion of phenomenological studies.

12. See Charmaz (2006), p. 15.

13. See Charmaz (2006), pp. 50–51.

14. See Strauss and Corbin (1998).

15. See Charmaz (2006), p. 57.

16. See Charmaz (2006), p. 23.

17. See Bhattacharya (2017).

18. See Clark and Brooms (2021) for a discussion of centering Blackness in education research.

19. See D'Silva et al. (2016).

20. A number of research works have explored Blacks' experiences and relationships with US educational institutions (see J. Anderson, 1988; Ballard, 1973; Du Bois, 1935; Epps, 1973; King, 2005; Wilder, 2013; C. Woodson, 2011).

21. See Tillman (2002).

22. By "culturally sensitive research approach," I invoke Linda Tillman's (2002) Black-centered framing in particular to inform my own work. Tillman contended that culturally sensitive approaches "include the connectedness of the researcher to the research community" (p. 6). Tillman situated her framing in historical roots of Black-centered research (e.g., W. E. B. Du Bois, Anna Julia Cooper, and Carter G. Woodson) and identified five dimensions: culturally congruent research methods, culturally specific knowledge, cultural resistance to theoretical dominance, culturally sensitive data interpretations, and culturally informed theory and practice.

References

Abrica, E. J., Garcia-Louis, C., & Gallaway, C. D. J. (2020). Antiblackness in the Hispanic-serving community college (HSCC) context: Black male collegiate experiences through the lens of settler colonial logics. *Race Ethnicity and Education, 23*(1), 55–73.

Adichie, C. (2009). The danger of a single story [Video]. *TED: Ideas worth spreading*. https://www.ted.com/talks/chimamanda_adichie_the_danger_of_a_single_story

Albritton, T. J. (2012). Educating our own: The historical legacy of HBCUs and their relevance for educating a new generation of leaders. *Urban Review, 44*(3), 311–331.

Alexander, E. (2020, June 15). The Trayvon generation. *New Yorker*. https://www.newyorker.com/magazine/2020/06/22/the-trayvon-generation

Alexander, M. (2010). *The new Jim Crow: Mass incarceration in the age of colorblindness*. The New Press.

Allen, Q. (2015). "I'm trying to get my A": Black male achievers talk about race, school and achievement. *Urban Review, 47*(1), 209–231.

Allen, Q. (2017). "They write me off and don't give me a chance to learn anything": The positioning, discipline, and resistance of Black male high school students. *Anthropology & Education Quarterly*, 48(3), 269–283.

Amechi, M. H. (2016). "There's no autonomy": Narratives of self-authorship from Black male foster care alumni in higher education. *Journal of African American Males in Education*, 7(2), 18–35.

Anderson, E. (1990). *Streetwise: Race, class, and change in an urban community*. University of Chicago Press.

Anderson, E. (2008). *Against the wall: Poor, young, Black, and male*. University of Pennsylvania Press.

Anderson, J. D. (1988). *The education of Blacks in the South, 1860–1935*. University of North Carolina Press.

Arbouin, A. (2018). *Black British graduates: Untold stories*. Trentham.

Baldridge, B. J. (2014). Relocating the deficit: Reimagining Black youth in neoliberal times. *American Educational Research Journal, 51*(3), 440–472.

Baldridge, B. J. (2019). *Reclaiming community: Race and the uncertain future of youth work*. Stanford University Press.

Baldridge, B. J., Hill, M. L., & Davis, J. E. (2011). New possibilities: (Re)engaging Black male youth within community-based educational spaces. *Race Ethnicity and Education, 14*(1), 121–136.

Baldwin, J. (1992). *The fire next time*. Vintage. (Original work published 1963)

Baldwin, J., & Peck, R. (2017). *I am not your Negro: A major motion picture*. Vintage.

Ballard, A. B. (1973). *The education of Black folk: The Afro-American struggle for knowledge within America*. Harper & Row.

Beale, T., Charleston, L., & Hilton, A. A. (2019). Black male college persistence: A phenomenological collective of familial and social motivators. *Journal of Research Initiatives, 4*(3), 1–18.

Bell, D. A. (1980). *Brown v. Board of Education* and the interest-convergence dilemma. *Harvard Law Review, 93*(3), 518–533.

Bell, D. A. (1991). Racism is here to stay: Now what? *Howard Law Journal, 35*, 79–93.

Bell, D. A. (1992a). *Faces at the bottom of the well: The permanence of racism*. Basic Books.

Bell, D. A. (1992b). Racial realism. *Connecticut Law Review, 24*(2), 363–379.

Bell, L. A. (2003). Telling tales: What stories can teach us about race and racism. *Race Ethnicity and Education*, 6(1), 3–28.

Bhattacharya, K. (2017). *Fundamentals of qualitative research: A practical guide*. Routledge.

Bowman, P. J. (1989). Research perspectives on Black men: Role strain and adaptation across the adult life cycle. In R. L. Jones (Ed.), *Black adult development and aging* (pp. 117–150). Cobb & Henry.

Brooks, S. N. (2009). *Black men can't shoot*. University of Chicago Press.

Brooms, D. R. (2014). "Trying to find self": Promoting excellence and building community among African American males. In J. L. Moore III & C. W. Lewis (Eds.), *African American male students in PreK–12 schools: Informing research, policy, and practice* (pp. 61–86). Emerald Group Publishing.

Brooms, D. R. (2015). "We didn't let the neighborhood win": Black male students' experiences in negotiating and navigating an urban neighborhood. *Journal of Negro Education, 84*(3), 269–281.

Brooms, D. R. (2016). Innocent until proven Black: A eulogy for Black males . . . but, can we live? https://reimaginingmagazine.com/project/innocent-until-proven-black/

Brooms, D. R. (2017a). *Being Black, being male on campus: Understanding and confronting Black male collegiate experiences*. SUNY Press.

Brooms, D. R. (2017b). Black otherfathering in the educational experiences of Black males in a single-sex urban high school. *Teachers College Record, 119*(11), 1–46.

Brooms, D. R. (2019a). "I was just trying to make it": Urban Black males' sense of belonging, schooling experiences, and academic success. *Urban Education, 54*(6), 804–830.

Brooms, D. R. (2019b). "We had to stick together": Black boys, the urban neighborhood context, and educational aspirations. *Boyhood Studies: An Interdisciplinary Journal, 12*(1), 57–75.

Brooms, D. R. (2020a). "Helping us think about ourselves": Black men's sense of belonging through connections and relationships with faculty in college. *International Journal of Qualitative Studies in Education, 33*(9), 921–938.

Brooms, D. R. (2020b). "I didn't want to be a statistic": Black males, urban schooling and educational urgency. *Race Ethnicity and Education*, 1–19. https://doi.org/10.1080/13613324.2020.1803821

Brooms, D. R. (2020c). Preparing Black males for collegiate success: Exploring Black males' experiences in precollege summer programs. In A. R. Washington, R. Goings, & M. S. Henfield (Eds.), *Creating and sustaining effective K–12 school partnerships: Firsthand accounts of promising practices* (pp. 23–43). Information Age.

Brooms, D. R., & Clark, J. S. (2020). Black misandry and the killing of Black boys and men. *Sociological Focus, 53*(2), 125–140.

Brooms, D. R., & Davis, A. R. (2017a). Exploring Black males' community cultural wealth and college aspirations. *Spectrum: A Journal on Black Men, 6*(1), 33–58.

Brooms, D. R., & Davis, A. R. (2017b). Staying focused on the goal: Peer bonding and faculty mentors supporting Black males' persistence in college. *Journal of Black Studies, 48*(3), 305–326.

Brooms, D. R., & Perry, A. R. (2016). "It's simply because we're Black men": Black men's experiences and responses to the killing of Black men. *Journal of Men's Studies, 24*(2), 166–184.

Brown, A. L. (2009). "Brothers gonna work it out": Understanding the pedagogic performance of African American male teachers working with African American male students. *Urban Review, 41*(5), 416–435.

Brown, A. L. (2017). On Black males in history, theory, and education. *Race, Gender & Class, 24*(1–2), 107–119.

Brown, A. L. (2018). From subhuman to human kind: Implicit bias, racial memory, and Black males in schools and society. *Peabody Journal of Education, 93*(1), 52–65.

Brown, A. L., & Donnor, J. K. (2011). Toward a new narrative on Black males, education, and public policy. *Race Ethnicity and Education, 14*(1), 17–32.

Browne, S. (2015). *Dark matter: On the surveillance of Blackness*. Duke University Press.

Bryan, N. (2020). Shaking "the bad boys": Troubling the criminalization of Black boys' childhood play, hegemonic White masculinity and femininity, and "the school playground-to-prison" pipeline. *Race Ethnicity and Education, 23*(5), 673–692.

Bryan, N. (2021). Remembering Tamir Rice and other Black boy victims: Imagining Black playcrit literacies inside and outside urban literacy education. *Urban Education, 56*(5), 744–771.

Burt, B. A., Roberson, J. J., Johnson, J. T., & Bonanno, A. (2020). Black men in engineering graduate programs: A theoretical model of the motivation to persist. *Teachers College Record, 122*(11), 1–45.

Burt, B. A., Williams, K. L., & Palmer, G. J. M. (2019). It takes a village: The role of emic and etic adaptive strengths in the persistence of Black men in engineering graduate programs. *American Educational Research Journal, 56*(1), 39–74.

Carey, R. L. (2015). Desensationalizing Black males: Navigating and deconstructing extreme imageries of Black males and masculinities. In K. Fasching-Varner & L. Hartlep (Eds.), *The assault on communities of color: Exploring the realities of race-based violence* (pp. 153–158). Rowman & Littlefield.

Carey, R. L. (2016). "Keep in mind . . . you're gonna go to college": Family influence on the college going processes of Black and Latino high school boys. *Urban Review, 48*(5), 718–742.

Carey, R. L. (2018). "What am I gonna be losing?" School culture and the family-based college-going dilemmas of Black and Latino adolescent boys. *Education and Urban Society, 50*(3), 246–273.

Carey, R. L. (2019a). Am I smart enough? Will I make friends? And can I even afford it? Exploring the college-going dilemmas of Black and Latino adolescent boys. *American Journal of Education, 125*(3), 381–415.

Carey, R. L. (2019b). Imagining the comprehensive mattering of Black boys and young men in society and schools: Toward a new approach. *Harvard Educational Review, 89*(3), 370–396.

Carney, N. (2016). All lives matter, but so does race: Black lives matter and the evolving role of social media. *Humanity & Society, 40*(2), 180–199.

Carter, P. L. (2003). "Black" cultural capital, status positioning, and schooling conflicts for low-income African American youth. *Social Problems, 50*(1), 136–155.

Carter Andrews, D. J., Brown, T., Castro, E., & Id-Deen, E. (2019). The impossibility of being "perfect and White": Black girls' racialized and gendered schooling experiences. *American Educational Research Journal, 56*(6), 2531–2572.

Castillo-Montoya, M. (2016). Preparing for interview research: The interview protocol refinement framework. *Qualitative Report, 21*(5), 811–831.

Chang, J. C. (2005). Faculty student interaction at the community college: A focus on students of color. *Research in Higher Education*, *46*(7), 769–802.

Charmaz, K. (2006). *Constructing grounded theory: A practical guide through qualitative analysis*. Sage.

Chesler, M., Lewis, A., & Crowfoot, J. (2005). *Challenging racism in higher education: promoting justice*. Rowman & Littlefield.

Christian, M. (2005). The politics of Black presence in Britain and Black male exclusion in the British education system. *Journal of Black Studies*, *35*(3), 327–346.

Clark, J. S. (2017). *This is a Black–White conversation: Navigating race, class, and gender at an urban school*. [Unpublished doctoral dissertation]. University of Louisville.

Clark, J. S. (2020). Ring the alarm: Black girls in the discourse on the school-to-prison pipeline. *Du Bois Review*, *17*(1), 147–163.

Clark, J. S., & Brooms, D. R. (2018). "We get to learn more about ourselves": Black men's engagement, bonding, and self-authorship on campus. *Journal of Negro Education*, *87*(4), 391–403.

Clark, J. S., & Brooms, D. R. (2021). Unapologetic Black inquiry: Centering Blackness in education research. In C. E. Matias (Ed.), *The handbook of critical theoretical research methods in education* (pp. 303–318). Routledge.

Clark, J. S., Wint, K. M., & Brooms, D. R. (2020). Recentering the possibilities for Black boys in the preK–12 educational context (unpublished paper).

Clay, K. L. (2019). "Despite the odds": Unpacking the politics of Black resilience neoliberalism. *American Educational Research Journal*, *56*(1), 75–110.

Coates, T. (2015). *Between the world and me*. Spiegel & Grau.

Cobbett, M., & Younger, M. (2012). Boys' educational "underachievement" in the Caribbean: Interpreting the "problem." *Gender and Education*, *24*(6), 611–625.

Cooper, J. N. (2016). Excellence beyond athletics: Best practices for enhancing Black male student athletes' educational experiences and outcomes. *Equity & Excellence in Education*, *49*(3), 267–283.

Cornell, J., & Kessi, S. (2017). Black students' experiences of transformation at a previously "white only" South African university: A photovoice study. *Ethnic and Racial Studies*, *40*(11), 1882–1899.

Crenshaw, K. (1991). Mapping the margins: Intersectionality, identity politics, and violence against women of color. *Stanford Law Review*, *43*(6), 1241–1299.

Crenshaw, K., Ritchie, A. J., Anspach, R., Gilmer, R., & Harris, L. (2015). *Say her name: Resisting police brutality against Black women*. African American Policy Forum, Center for Intersectionality and Social Policy Studies.

Curry, T. (2017). *The man-not: Race, class, genre, and the dilemmas of Black manhood*. Temple University Press.

Curry, T. J. (2018). Killing boogeyman: Phallicism and the misandric mischaracterization of Black males in theory. *Res Philosophica*, *95*(2), 1–38.

Cuyjet, M. J. (Ed.). (2006). *African American men in college*. Jossey-Bass.

Dancy, T. E., II. (2014a). The adultification of Black boys: What educational settings can learn from Trayvon Martin. In K. J. Fasching-Varner, R. E. Reynolds, K. A. Albert, & L. L. Martin (Eds.), *Trayvon Martin, race, and American justice* (pp. 49–55). Springer.

Dancy, T. E., II. (2014b). (Un)doing hegemony in education: Disrupting school-to-prison pipelines for Black males. *Equity & Excellence in Education*, *47*(4), 476–493.

Dancy, T. E., II, Edwards, K. T., & Davis, J. E. (2018). Historically white universities and plantation politics: Anti-Blackness and higher education in the Black lives matter era. *Urban Education*, *53*(2), 176–195.

Davis, J. E. (2003). Early schooling and academic achievement of African-American males. *Urban Education*, *38*(5), 515–537.

Davis, J. E. (2006). Research at the margins: Dropping out of high school and mobility among African American males. *International Journal of Qualitative Studies in Education*, *19*(3), 289–304.

DeCuir-Gunby, J. T., Chapman, T. K., & Schutz, A. (Eds.). (2019). *Understanding critical race research methods: Lessons from the field*. Routledge.

Delgado, R. (Ed.). (1995). *Critical race theory: The cutting edge*. Temple University Press.

Delgado, R., & Stefancic, J. (2011). *Critical race theory: An introduction* (2nd ed.). New York University Press.

Diamond, J. B. (2018). Race and white supremacy in the sociology of education: Shifting the intellectual gaze. In J. Mehta & S. Davies (Eds.), *Education in a new society: Renewing the sociology of education* (pp. 345–362). University of Chicago Press

Donnor, J. K., & Shockley, K. (2010). Leaving us behind: A political economic interpretation of NCLB and the miseducation of African American males. *Journal of Educational Foundations*, *24*(3–4), 43–54.

Douglas, T. M. O. (2016). *Border crossing brothas: Black males navigating race, place, and complex space*. Peter Lang.

Douglas, T. M. O., & Arnold, N. W. (2016). Exposure in and out of school: A Black Bermudian male's successful educational journey. *Teachers College Record*, *118*(6), 1–36.

Drake, S. C. (2016). A meditation on the soundscapes of Black boyhood and disruptive imaginations. *Souls*, *18*(2–4), 446–458.

Druery, J. E., & Brooms, D. R. (2019). "It lit up the campus": Engaging Black males in a culturally enriching environment on campus. *Journal of Diversity in Higher Education*, *12*(4), 330–340.

D'Silva, M. U., Smith, S. E., Della, L. J., Potter, D. A., Rajack-Talley, T. A., & Best, L. (2016). Reflexivity and positionality in researching African-

American communities: Lessons from the field. *Intercultural Communications Studies*, *25*(1), 94–109.

Du Bois, W. E. B. (1935). Does the Negro need separate schools? *Journal of Negro Education*, *4*(3), 328–335.

Du Bois, W. E. B. (1939). The position of the Negro in the American social order: Where do we go from here? *Journal of Negro Education*, *8*(3), 551–570.

Du Bois, W. E. B. (2005). *The souls of Black folk*. Dover. (Original work published 1903)

Dumas, M. J. (2014). Losing an arm: Schooling as a site of Black suffering. *Race Ethnicity and Education*, *17*(1), 1–29.

Dumas, M. J. (2016). Against the dark: Antiblackness in education policy and discourse. *Theory Into Practice*, 55, 11–19.

Dumas, M. J., & Nelson, J. D. (2016). (Re)imagining Black boyhood: Toward a critical framework for educational research. *Harvard Educational Review*, *86(1)*, *27–47*.

Dumas, M. J., & ross, k. m. (2016). "Be real Black for me": Imagining BlackCrit in education. *Urban Education*, *51*(4), 415–442.

Duncan, G. A. (2002). Beyond love: A critical race ethnography of the schooling of adolescent Black males. *Equity and Excellence in Education*, *35*(2), 131–143.

Duncan-Andrade, J. M. R. (2009). Note to educators: Hope required when growing roses in concrete. *Harvard Educational Review*, *79*(2), 181–194.

Edwards, B. (2019, March 15). #BlackBoyJoy: Detroit high school senior accepted into 41 colleges. *Essence*. https://www.essence.com/news/blackboyjoy-detroit-high-school-senior-accepted-into-41-colleges/

Emdin, C. (2016). *For white folks who teach in the hood . . . and the rest of y'all too: Reality pedagogy and urban education*. Beacon Press.

Emdin, C., & Lee, O. (2012). Hip-hop, the "Obama effect," and urban science education. *Teachers College Record*, *114*(2), 1–24.

English, D., Lambert, S. F., Tynes, B. M., Bowleg, L., Zea, M. C., & Howard, L. C. (2020). Daily multidimensional racial discrimination among Black U.S. American adolescents. *Journal of Applied Developmental Psychology*, 66, 1–12.

Epps, B. D., & Morrison, H. R. (2003). "Leaving no child behind": Examining issues of school reform and social justice. In C. C. Yeakey & R. D. Henderson (Eds.), *Surmounting all odds: Education, opportunity, and society in the new millennium* (vol. 1, pp. 251–270). Information Age.

Epps, E. G. (1973). Education for Black Americans: Outlook for the future. *School Review*, *81*(3), 315–330.

Epps, E. G. (1995). Race, class, and educational opportunity: Trends in the sociology of education. *Sociological Forum*, *10*(4), 593–608.

Evans-Winters, V., & Bethune, M. C. (Eds.). (2014). *(Re)teaching Trayvon: Education for racial justice and human freedom*. Sense.

Fanon, F. (1967). *Black skin, white masks.* (C. L. Markmann Trans.). Grove Press. (Original work published in French 1952)

Farmer, S. (2010). Criminality of Black youth in inner-city schools: "Moral panic," moral imagination, and moral formation. *Race Ethnicity and Education, 13*(3), 367–381.

Farmer-Hinton, R. L. (2008). Social capital and college planning: Students of color using school networks for support and guidance. *Education and Urban Society, 41*(1), 127–157.

Fergus, E., Noguera, P., & Martin, M. (2014). *Schooling for resilience: Improving the life trajectory of Black and Latino boys*. Harvard Education Press.

Ferguson, A. A. (2000). *Bad boys: Public schools in the making of Black masculinity*. University of Michigan Press.

Fischer, M. J. (2010). A longitudinal examination of the role of stereotype threat and racial climate on college outcomes for minorities at elite institutions. *Social Psychology of Education, 13*, 19–40.

Fitzgerald, T. D. (2015). *Black males and racism: Improving the schooling and life chances of African Americans*. Routledge.

Fleming, J. (1981). Stress and satisfaction in college years of Black students. *Journal of Negro Education, 50*(3), 307–318.

Fleming, J. (1984). *Blacks in college: A comparative study of students' success in Black and White institutions*. Jossey-Bass.

Ford, D. Y., & Moore, J. L. (2013). Understanding and reversing underachievement, low achievement, and achievement gaps among high-ability African American males in urban school contexts. *Urban Review, 45*(4), 399–415.

Foreman, J., Jr. (2017). *Locking up our own: Crime and punishment in Black America*. Farrar, Straus and Giroux.

Franklin, V. P. (2002). Introduction: Cultural capital and African-American education. *Journal of African American History, 87*(2), 175–181.

Freeman, K., & Thomas, G. E. (2002). Black colleges and college choice: Characteristics of students who choose HBCUs. *Review of Higher Education, 25*(3), 349–358.

George Mwangi, C. A. (2015). (Re)examining the role of family and community in college access and choice: A metasynthesis. *Review of Higher Education, 39*(1), 123–151.

Gillborn, D. (2015). Intersectionality, critical race theory, and the primacy of racism. *Qualitative Inquiry, 21*(3), 277–287.

Ginwright, S. A. (2009). *Black youth rising: Activism and radical healing in urban America*. Teachers College Press.

Givens, J. R. (2021). *Fugitive pedagogy: Carter G. Woodson and the art of Black teaching*. Harvard University Press.

Glynn, M. (2013). *Black men, invisibility, and crime: Towards a critical race theory of desistance*. Routledge.

Goff, P. A., Jackson, M. C., Di Leone, B., Culotta, C. M., & DiTomasso, N. A. (2014). The essence of innocence: Consequences of dehumanizing Black children. *Journal of Personality and Social Psychology, 106*(4), 526–545.

Goings, R. (2017). Traditional and nontraditional high-achieving Black males' strategies for interacting with faculty at a historically Black college and university. *Journal of Men's Studies, 25*(3), 316–335.

Goings, R., & Shi, Q. (2018). Black male degree attainment: Do expectations and aspirations in high school make a difference? *Spectrum: A Journal on Black Men, 6*(2), 1–20.

Goings, R., Smith, A., Harris, D., Wilson, T., & Lancaster, D. (2015). Countering the narrative: A layered perspective on supporting Black males in education. *Perspectives on Urban Education, 12*(1), 54–63.

Goodwill, J. R., Watkins, D. C., Johnson, N. C., & Allen, J. O. (2018). An exploratory study of stress and coping among Black college men. *American Journal of Orthopsychiatry, 88*(5), 538–549.

Graham, M., & Robinson, G. (2004). "The silent catastrophe": Institutional racism in the British educational system and the underachievement of Black boys. *Journal of Black Studies, 34*(5), 653–671.

Greer, T. M., & Brown, P. (2011). Minority status stress and coping processes among African American college students. *Journal of Diversity in Higher Education, 4*(1), 26–38.

Griffith, D. M., Ellis, K. R., & Allen, J. O. (2013). An intersectional approach to social determinants of stress for African American men: Men's and women's perspectives. *American Journal of Men's Health, 7*(4, Supplement), 19S–30S.

Grimmett, M. A., Beckwith, A., Lupton-Smith, H., Agronin., & Englert, M. (2017). A community counseling center model for multicultural and social justice counselor education. *Journal of Counselor Leadership and Advocacy, 4*(2), 161–171.

Hardeman, H. (2018, September 24). Temple Rhodes scholar: I'm proof that your circumstances don't define your success. *Philadelphia Inquirer*. http://www.philly.com/philly/opinion/commentary/temple-university-rhodes-scholar-hazim-hardeman-oxford-20180924.html

Harding, D. J. (2010). *Living the drama: Community, conflict, and culture among inner-city boys*. University of Chicago Press.

Harmon, W. C., James, M. C., & Farooq, R. (2020). Ecologies of hope: Understanding educational success among Black males in an urban Midwestern city. *Journal of Multicultural Affairs, 5*(2), 1–18.

Harper, S. R. (2015). Black male college achievers and resistant responses to racist stereotypes at predominantly white colleges and universities. *Harvard Educational Review, 85*(4), 646–674.

Harper, S. R., & Davis, C. H. F., III. (2012). They (don't) care about education: A counternarrative on Black male students' responses to inequitable schooling. *Educational Foundations*, *2*(1–2), 103–120.

Harris, P. C. (2014). The sports participation effect on educational attainment of Black males. *Education and Urban Society*, *46*(5), 507–521.

Harris, P. C., Hines, E. M., Kelly, D. D., Williams, D. J., & Bagley, B. (2014). Promoting the academic engagement and success of Black male student-athletes. *High School Journal*, *97*(3), 180–195.

Harrison, C. K., Bukstein, S., Mottley, J., Comeaux, E., Boyd, J., Parks, C., & Heikkinen, D. (2010). Scholar-baller: Student athlete socialization, motivation, and academic performance in American society. In P. Peterson, E. Baker, & B. McGaw (Eds.), *International Encyclopedia of Education* (vol. 1, pp. 860–865). Elsevier.

Hartman, S. (1997). *Scenes of subjection: Terror, slavery and self-making in nineteenth-century America.* Oxford University Press.

Hill, M. L. (2016). *Nobody: Casualties of America's war on the vulnerable, from Ferguson to Flint and beyond.* Atria Books.

Hines, E. M., Cooper, J. N., & Corral, M. (2019). Overcoming the odds. First-generation Black and Latino male collegians' perspectives on pre-college barriers and facilitators. *Journal for Multicultural Education*, *13*(1), 51–69.

Holland, N. E. (2011). The power of peers: Influences on postsecondary education planning and experiences of African American students. *Urban Education*, *46*(5), 1029–1055.

Holzman, M. (2008). *Given half a chance: The Schott 50 state report on public education and Black males.* Schott Foundation for Public Education.

hooks, b. (1994). *Teaching to transgress: Education as the practice of freedom.* Routledge Kegan Paul.

hooks, b. (1995). *Killing rage: Ending racism.* Henry Holt.

hooks, b. (2004). *We real cool: Black men and masculinity.* Routledge.

Hotchkins, B. K. (2016). African American males navigate racial microaggressions. *Teachers College Record*, *118*(6), 1–36.

Howard, L. C. (2012). Performing masculinity: Adolescent African American boys' response to gender scripting. *Journal of Boyhood Studies*, *6*(1), 97–115.

Howard, L. C., Rose, J. C., & Barbarin, O. A. (2013). Raising African American boys: An exploration of gender and racial socialization practices. *American Journal of Orthopsychiatry*, *83*(2–3), 218–230.

Howard, T. C. (2008). Who really cares? The disenfranchisement of African American males in preK–12 schools: A critical race theory perspective. *Teachers College Record*, *110*(5), 954–985.

Howard, T. C. (2013). How does it feel to be a problem? Black male students, schools, and learning in enhancing the knowledge base to disrupt deficit frameworks. *Review of Research in Education*, *37*(1), 54–86.

Howard, T. C. (2014). *Black male(d): Peril and promise in the education of African American males*. Teachers College Press.

Howard, T. C., & Associates (2017). The counter narrative: Reframing success of high achieving Black and Latino males in Los Angeles County, Los Angeles: University of California, Los Angeles, UCLA Black Male Institute.

Howard, T. C., Woodward, B., Navarro, O., Haro, B., Watson, K., & Huerta, A. H. (2019). Renaming the narrative, reclaiming their humanity: Black and Latino males descriptions of success. *Teachers College Record, 121*, 1–31.

Hrabowski, F. A., III, Maton, K. I., & G. L. Greif. (1998). *Beating the odds: Raising academically successful African American males*. Oxford University Press.

Huber, L. P. (2008). Building critical race methodologies in educational research: A research note on critical race *testimonio*. *Florida International University Law Review, 4*(1), 159–173.

Hucks, D. (2014). *New visions of collective achievement: The cross-generational schooling experiences of African-American males*. Sense.

Huerta, A. (2015). "I didn't want my life to be like that": Gangs, college, or the military for Latino male high school students. *Journal of Latino/Latin American Studies*, *7*(2), 119–132.

Huerta, A. H., McDonough, P. M., & Allen, W. R. (2018). "You can go to college": Employing a developmental perspective to examine how young men of color construct a college-going identity. *Urban Review, 50*, 713–734.

Huerta, A. H., & Rios-Aguilar, C. (2021). Treat a cop like a god: Exploring the relevance and utility of funds of gang knowledge among Latino male students. *Urban Education*, *56*(8), 1239–1268.

Hurd, N. M., Stoddard, S. A., & Zimmerman, M. A. (2013). Neighborhoods, social support, and African American adolescents' mental health outcomes: A multilevel path analysis. *Child Development*, *84*(3), 858–874.

Hurtado, S., Alvarado, A. R., & Guillermo-Wann, C. (2015). Creating inclusive environments: The mediating effect of faculty and staff validation on the relationship of discrimination/ bias to students' sense of belonging. *Journal Committed to Social Change on Race and Ethnicity, 1*(1), 60–81.

Hypolite, L. I. (2020). People, place, and connections: Black cultural center staff as facilitators of social capital. *Journal of Black Studies*, *51*(1), 37–59.

Jack, A. A. (2018). *The privileged poor: How elite colleges are failing disadvantaged students*. Harvard University Press.

James, C. E. (2012). Students "at risk": Stereotypes and the schooling of Black boys. *Urban Education*, *47*(2), 464–494.

James, M. C. (2010). Never quit: The complexities of promoting social and academic excellence at a single-gender school for urban African American males. *Journal of African American Males in Education*, *1*(3), 167–195.

James, M. C., & Lewis, C. W. (2014). Villains or virtuousos: An inquiry into Blackmaleness. *Journal of African American Males in Education*, *5*(2), 105–109.

James, S. (Director). (1994). *Hoop dreams* [Film]. Criterion Collection.

Jayakumar, U., Vue, R., & Allen, W. (2013). Pathways to college for young Black scholars: A community cultural wealth perspective. *Harvard Educational Review, 83*(4), 551–579.

Jenkins, T. S. (2006). Mr. Nigger: The challenges of educating Black males within American society. *Journal of Black Studies, 37*(1), 127–155.

Jett, C. C. (2016). Ivy league bound: A case study of a brilliant African American male mathematics major. *Spectrum: A Journal on Black Men, 4*(2), 83–97.

Jett, C. C. (2019). "I have the highest GPA, but I can't be valedictorian?": Two Black males' exclusionary valedictory experiences. *Race Ethnicity and Education*, 1–19. https://doi.org/10.1080/13613324.2019.1599341

Joe, S., Scott, M. L., & Banks, A. (2018). What works for adolescent Black males at risk of suicide: A review. *Research on Social Work Practice, 28*(3), 340–345.

Johnson, J. M. (2002). In-depth interviewing. In J. Gubrium & J. Holstein (Eds.), *Handbook of interview research: Context and method* (pp. 103–119). Sage.

Johnson, J. M. (2017). Choosing HBCUs: Why African Americans choose HBCUs in the twenty-first century. In M. Brown & T. E. Dancy (Eds.), *Black colleges across the Diaspora: Global perspectives on race and stratification in postsecondary education* (pp. 151–169). Emerald Group Publishing.

Johnson, M. S. (2013). Strength and respectability: Black women's negotiation of racialized gender ideals and the role of daughter–father relationships. *Gender & Society, 27*(6), 889–912.

Johnson, O. (2018). "Expressive cool" and the paradox of Black and white males' neighborhood socialization toward education. *Youth & Society, 50*(3), 299–327.

Johnson, P., & Philoxene, D. (2018). It makes me feel like a monster: Navigating notions of damage in this work. In N. S. Nasir, J. R. Givens, & C. P. Chatmon (Eds.), *"We dare say love": Supporting achievement in the educational life of Black boys* (pp. 68–80). Teachers College Press.

Johnson, P. D. (2016). Somebodiness and its meaning to African American men. *Journal of Counseling and Development, 94*, 333–343.

Johnson, R. M. (2015). Measuring the influence of juvenile arrest on the odds of four-year college enrollment for Black males: An NLSY analysis. *Spectrum: A Journal on Black Men, 4* (1), 49–72.

Johnson, S. (2019). *Curriculum of the mind: A Blackcrit, narrative inquiry, hip-hop album on anti-Blackness & freedom for Black male collegians at historically white institutions* [Unpublished doctoral dissertation]. University of Oklahoma Electronic Theses and Dissertations.

Johnson, W. E., Pate, D. J., & Givens, J. (2010). Big boys don't cry, Black boys don't feel: The intersection of shame and worry on community violence and the social construction of masculinity among urban African American males: The case of Derrion Albert. In C. Edley, Jr., & J. Ruiz de Velasco (Eds.), *Changing places: How communities will improve the health of boys of color* (pp. 462–492). University of California Press.

Johnson-Ahorlu, R. N. (2013). "Our biggest challenge is stereotypes": Understanding stereotype threat and the academic experiences of African American undergraduates. *Journal of Negro Education, 82*(4), 382–392.

Johnston-Guerrero, M. P. (2016). The meanings of race matter: College students learning about race in a not-so-postracial era. *American Educational Research Journal, 53*(4), 819–849.

Jones, N. (2010). *Between good and ghetto: African American girls and inner-city violence*. Rutgers University Press.

Kendi, I. X. (2016). *Stamped from the beginning: The definitive history of racist ideas in America.* Nation Books.

King, J. E. (1992). Diaspora literacy and consciousness in the struggle against miseducation in the Black community. *Journal of Negro Education, 61*(3), 317–340.

King, J. E. (2005). *Black education*. Routledge.

Kiyama, J. M. (2010). College aspirations and limitation: The role of educational ideologies and funds of knowledge in Mexican American families. *American Educational Research Journal, 47*(2), 330–356.

Knight, M., & Marciano, J. (2013). *College ready: Preparing Black and Latina/o youth for higher education—A culturally relevant approach*. Teachers College Press.

Knight, M. G., Norton, N. E. L., Bentley, C. C., & Dixon, I. R. (2004). The power of Black and Latina/o counterstories: Urban families and college-going processes. *Anthropology & Education Quarterly, 35*(1), 99–120.

Kumah-Abiwu, F. (2019). Urban education and academic success: The case of higher achieving Black males. *Urban Education*, 1–27. https://doi.org/10.1177/0042085919835284

Kumah-Abiwu, F. (2020). Media gatekeeping and portrayal of Black men in America. *Journal of Men's Studies, 28*(1), 64–81.

Kunjufu, J. (2004). *Countering the conspiracy to destroy Black boys*. African American Images.

Kunjufu, J. (2013). *Changing school culture for Black males*. African American Images.

Ladson-Billings, G. (1998). Just what is critical race theory and what's it doing in a nice field like education? *International Journal of Qualitative Studies in Education, 11*(1), 7–24.

Ladson-Billings, G. (2000). Racialized discourses and ethnic epistemologies. In N. Denzin & Y. Lincoln (Eds.), *Handbook of qualitative research* (2nd ed., pp. 257–277). Sage.

Ladson-Billings, G. (2006). From the achievement gap to the education debt: Understanding achievement in U.S. schools. *Educational Researcher, 35*(7), 3–12.

Ladson-Billings, G. (2011). Boyz to men? Teaching to restore Black boys' childhood. *Race Ethnicity and Education, 14*(1), 7–15.

Ladson-Billings, G., & Tate, W. F. (1995). Toward a critical race theory of education. *Teachers College Record, 97*(1), 47–68.

Laing, T. (2017). Black masculinities expressed through, and constrained by, brotherhood. *Journal of Men's Studies, 25*(2), 168–197.

Lane, T. B., & Id-Deen, L. (2020). Nurturing the capital within: A qualitative investigation of Black women and girls in STEM summer programs. *Urban Education*, 1–29. https://doi.org/10.1177/0042085920926225

Langtiw, C. L., & Heidbrink, L. (2016). Removal, betrayal, and resistance: Comparative analysis of Black youth in the U.S. and Haitian-decent youth in the Dominican Republic. *Community Psychology in Global Perspective, 2*(2), 40–55.

Laymon, K. (2018). *Heavy: An American memoir*. Bloomsbury.

Leake, D. O., & Leake, B. L. (1992). Islands of hope: Milwaukee's African American immersion schools. *Journal of Negro Education, 61*, 4–11.

Lewis-McCoy, R. (2016). Boyz in the "burbs": Parental negotiation of race and class in raising Black males in suburbia. *Peabody Journal of Education, 91*(3), 309–325.

Lindsay, K. (2018). *In a classroom of their own: The intersection of race and feminist politics in all-Black male schools*. University of Illinois Press.

Lindsey, T. B. (2018). Ain't nobody got time for that: Anti–Black girl violence in the era of #SayHerName. *Urban Education, 53*(2), 162–175.

Linley, J. L. (2018). Racism here, racism there, racism everywhere: The racial realities of minoritized peer socialization agents at a historically white institution. *Journal of College Student Development, 59*(1), 21–36.

Lofton, R. (2021). Plessy's tracks: African American students confronting academic placement in a racially diverse school and African American community. *Race Ethnicity and Education*, 1–20. https://doi.org/10.1080/13613324.2021.1924141

Lofton, R., & Davis, J. E. (2015). Toward a Black habitus: African Americans navigating systemic inequalities within home, school, and community. *Journal of Negro Education, 84*(3), 214–230.

Love, B. L. (2016). Anti-Black state violence, classroom edition: The spirit murdering of Black children. *Journal of Curriculum and Pedagogy, 13*(1), 22–25.

Love, B. L. (2019). *We want to do more than survive: Abolitionist teaching and the pursuit of educational freedom*. Beacon Press.

Luedke, C. L. (2017). Person first, student second: Staff and administrators of color supporting students of color authentically in higher education. *Journal of College Student Development, 58*(1), 37–52.

Lynn, M. (2002). Critical race theory and the perspectives of Black men teachers in the Los Angeles public schools. *Equity & Excellence in Education*, *35*(2), 119–130.

Lynn, M. (2006). Education for the community: Exploring the culturally relevant practices of Black male teachers. *Teachers College Record*, *108*(12), 2497–2522.

Lynn, M., & Dixson, A. D. (Eds.). (2013). *Handbook of critical race theory in education*. Routledge.

Lynn, M., & Parker, L. (2006). Critical race studies in education: Examining a decade of research on U.S. schools. *Urban Review*, *38*(4), 257–290.

Martin, B., Harrison, C., & Bukstein, S. (2010). "It takes a village" for African American male scholar-athletes. *Journal of the Study of Sports and Athletes in Education*, *4*(3), 277–295.

May, R. A. (2007). *Living through the hoop: High school basketball, race, and the American dream*. New York University Press.

Mazyck, J. E. (2013, November 24). Campus conversations about race now heating up the Twitterverse. *Diverse Issues in Higher Education*. https://diverseeducation.com/article/57642/

McClain, K. S., & Perry, A. (2017). Where did they go: Retention rates for students of color at predominantly white institutions. *College Student Affairs Leadership*, *4*(1), 3–10.

McClain, S., Beasley, S. T., Jones, B., Awosogba, O., Jackson, S., & Cokley, K. (2016). An examination of the impact of racial and ethnic identity, impostor feelings, and minority status stress on the mental health of Black college students. *Journal of Multicultural Counseling and Development*, *44*(2), 101–117.

McClain, S., & Cokley, K. (2017). Academic disidentification in Black college students: The role of teacher trust and gender. *Cultural Diversity and Ethnic Minority Psychology*, *23*(1), 125–133.

McCready, L. (2010). *Making space for diverse masculinities: Difference, intersectionality, and engagement in an urban high school*. Peter Lang.

McGee, E. O. (2013). Threatened and placed at risk: High achieving African American males in urban high schools. *Urban Review*, *45*(4), 448–471.

McGee, E. O., & Martin, D. B. (2011). "You would not believe what I have to go through to prove my intellectual value!": Stereotype management among academically successful Black mathematics and engineering students. *American Education Research Journal*, *48*(6), 1347–1389.

McGowan, B. L. (2017). Visualizing peer connections: The gendered realities of African American college men's interpersonal relationships. *Journal of College Student Development*, *58*(7), 983–1000.

McGowan, B. L., & Pérez, D. (2020). "A community built just for me": Black undergraduate men bridging gaps to community cultural wealth. *Journal of the First-Year Experience & Students in Transition*, *32*(1), 43–57.

McKittrick, K. (2011). On plantations, prisons, and a Black sense of place. *Social & Cultural Geography, 12*(8), 947–963.

Michael-Chadwell, S. (2014). A framework for Black males in P–12 urban school districts. In F. A. Bonner II (Ed.), *Building on resilience: Models and frameworks of Black male success across the P-20 pipeline* (pp. 13–24). Stylus.

Miller, R. J. (2021). *Halfway home: Race, punishment, and the afterlife of mass incarceration*. Little, Brown.

Mills, C. (1997). *The racial contract.* Cornell University Press.

Milner, H. R., IV. (2007). African American males in urban schools: No excuses—teach and empower. *Theory Into Practice*, 46(3), 239–246.

Mincy, R. (2006). *Black males left behind.* Urban Institute.

Mirza, H. S. (2006). "Race," gender and educational desire. *Race Ethnicity and Education*, 9(2), 137–158.

Mirza, H. S., & Reay, D. (2000). Spaces and places of Black educational desire: Rethinking Black supplementary schools as a new social movement. *Sociology, 34*(3), 521–544.

Mitchell, A. B., & Stewart, J. B. (2013). The efficacy of all-male academies: Insights from critical race theory (CRT). *Sex Roles*, 69, 382–392.

Mobley, S. D., Jr. (2017). Seeking sanctuary: (Re)claiming the power of historically Black colleges and universities as places of Black refuge. *International Journal of Qualitative Studies in Education*, 30(10), 1036–1041.

Mobley, S. D., Jr., & Johnson, J. M. (2015). The role of HBCUs in addressing the unique needs of LGBT students. *New Directions for Higher Education, 170*, 79–89.

Moore, J. L., III, & Lewis, C. L. (2014). *African American male students in PreK–12 schools: Informing research, policy, and practice*. Emerald.

Moore, J. L., III, Madison-Colmore, O., & Smith, D. M. (2003). The prove-them-wrong syndrome: Voices from unheard African-American males in engineering disciplines. *Journal of Men's Studies, 12*(1), 61–73.

Moore-Thomas, C., & Day-Vines, N. L. (2010). Culturally competent collaboration: School counselor collaboration with African American families and communities. *Professional School Counseling, 14*(1), 53–63.

Morris, M. W. (2015). *Pushout: The criminalization of Black girls in schools.* New Press.

Moten, F. (2013). Blackness and nothingness (mysticism in the flesh). *South Atlantic Quarterly, 112*(4), 737–780.

Moustakas, C. (1994). *Phenomenological research methods.* Sage.

Muhammad, K. G. (2011). *The condemnation of Blackness: Race, crime, and the making of modern urban American.* Harvard University Press.

Mustaffa, J. B. (2017). Mapping violence, naming life: A history of anti-Black oppression in the higher education system. *International Journal of Qualitative Studies in Education*, 30(8), 711–727.

Mutua, A. D. (2006). Theorizing progressive Black masculinities. In A. D. Mutua (Ed.), *Progressive Black masculinities* (pp. 3–42). Routledge.

Nelson, J. D. (2016). Relational teaching with Black boys: Strategies for learning at a single-sex middle school for boys of color in New York City. *Teachers College Record, 118*(6), 25–47.

Noguera, P. A. (2003). The trouble with Black boys: The role and influence of environmental and cultural factors on the academic performance of African American males. *Urban Education, 38*(4), 431–459.

Noguera, P. A. (2008). *The trouble with Black boys: . . . And other reflections on race, equity, and the future of public education.* Jossey-Bass.

O'Connor, C. (2020). 2019 Wallace foundation distinguished lecture: Education research and the disruption of racialized distortions: Establishing a wide angle view. *Educational Researcher, 49*(7), 470–481.

O'Connor, C., Lewis, A., & Mueller, J. (2007). Researching "Black" educational experiences and outcomes: Theoretical and methodological considerations. *Educational Researcher, 36*(9), 541–552.

Oeur, F. B. (2016). Recognizing dignity: Young Black men growing up in an era of surveillance. *Socius: Sociological Research for a Dynamic World, 2*, 1–15.

Oeur, F. B. (2018). *Black boys apart: Racial uplift and respectability in all-male public schools.* University of Minnesota Press.

Oliver, W. (2006). "The streets": An alternative Black male socialization institution. *Journal of Black Studies, 36*(6), 918–937.

Ovink, S. M. (2016). *Race, class, and choice in Latino/a higher education: Pathways in the college-for-all era.* Palgrave Macmillan.

Owens, D., Lacey, K., Rawls, G., & Holbert-Quince, J. (2010). First-generation African American male college students: Implications for career counselors. *Career Development Quarterly, 58*(4), 291–300.

Palmer, R. T., Davis, R. J., & Hilton, A. A. (2009). Exploring challenges that threaten to impede the academic success of academically underprepared Black males at an HBCU. *Journal of College Student Development, 50*(4), 429–445.

Palmer, R. T., & Gasman, M. (2008). "It takes a village to raise a child": The role of social capital in promoting academic success of African American men at a Black college. *Journal of College Student Development, 49*(1), 52–70.

Palmer, R. T., Maramba, D. C., & Lee, J. M. (2010). Investigating Black students' disinclination to consider and attend historically Black colleges and universities (HBCUs). *National Association of Student Affairs Professionals Journal, 13*(1), 23–45.

Palmer, R. T., & Strayhorn, T. L. (2008). Mastering one's own fate: Non-cognitive factors associated with the success of African American males at an HBCU. *NASAP Journal, 11*(1), 126–143.

Palmer, R. T., & Wood, J. L. (Eds.). (2012). *Black men in college: Implications for HBCUs and beyond.* Routledge.

Parker, L. (2015). Critical race theory in education and qualitative inquiry: What each has to offer each other now? *Qualitative Inquiry, 21*(3), 199–205.

Parker, L., & Lynn, M. (2002). What's race got to do with it? Critical race theory's conflict with and connections to qualitative research methodology and epistemology. *Qualitative Inquiry*, 8(1), 7–22.

Pate, D. J., Jr. (2012, April 28). Education vs. the lure of pro basketball. *CNN*. https://www.cnn.com/2012/04/28/opinion/pate-sports-education/index.html

Pattillo, M. (2012). *Black picket fences: Privilege and peril* (2nd ed.). University of Chicago Press.

Patton, D. U., Miller, R. J., Garbarino, J., Gale, A., & Kornfeld, E. (2016). Hardiness scripts: High-achieving African American boys in a Chicago charter navigating community violence and school. *Journal of Community Psychology, 44*(5), 638–655.

Patton, L. D. (2016). Disrupting postsecondary prose: Toward a critical race theory of higher education. *Urban Education, 51*(3), 315–342.

Perry, D. M., Tabb, K. M., & Mendenhall, R. (2015). Examining the effects of urban neighborhoods on the mental health of adolescent African American males: A qualitative systemic review. *Journal of Negro Education, 84*(3), 254–268.

Polite, V. C., & Davis, J. E. (1999). *African American males in school and society: Practices and policies for effective education.* Teachers College Press.

Porter, M. (1997). *Kill them before they grow: Misdiagnosis of African American boys in American classrooms*. African American Images.

Posey-Maddox, L. (2017). Race in place: Black parents, family–school relations, and multi-spatial microaggressions in a predominantly white suburb. *Teachers College Record, 119*(11), 1–42.

Purifoye, G. Y. (2015). Nice-nastiness and other raced social interactions on public transport systems. *City & Community, 14*(3), 286–310.

Quigley, M. W., & Mitchell, A. B. (2018). "What works": Applying critical race praxis to the design of educational and mentoring interventions for African American males. *Journal of African American Males in Education*, 9(2), 74–102.

Rajack-Talley, T., & Brooms, D. R. (Eds.). (2018). *Living racism: Through the barrel of the book.* Lexington.

Rankin, B. H., & Quane, J. M. (2002). Social contexts and urban adolescent outcomes: The interrelated effects of neighborhoods, families, and peers on African-American youth. *Social Problems, 49*(1), 79–100.

Reed, D., & Adams, R. D. (2020). Risk and protective factors specific to African American youth and adolescents: A systematic review. *Journal of Family Strengths, 20*(2), 1–31.

Reid, M. J., & Moore, J. L., III. (2008). College readiness and academic preparation for postsecondary education: Oral histories of first-generation urban college students. *Urban Education*, *43*(2), 240–261.

Rendón, M. G. (2014). "Caught up": How urban violence and peer ties contribute to high school noncompletion. *Social Problems*, *61*(1), 61–82.

Reynolds, R. (2010). "They think you're lazy," and other messages Black parents send their Black sons: An exploration of critical race theory in the examination of educational outcomes for Black males. *Journal of African American Males in Education*, *1*(2), 144 163.

Richardson, J. B., Jr. (2009). Men do matter: Ethnographic insights on the socially supportive role of the African American uncle in the lives of inner-city African American male youth. *Journal of Family Issues*, *30*(8), 1041–1069.

Richardson, J. B., Jr., & St. Vil, C. (2015). Putting in work: Black male youth joblessness, violence, crime, and the code of the street. *Spectrum: A Journal on Black Men*, *3*(2), 71–98.

Richardson, J. B., Jr., & St. Vil, C. (2016). "Rolling dolo": Desistance from delinquency and negative peer relationships over the early adolescent life-course. *Ethnography*, *17*(1), 47–71.

Richardson, J. B., Jr., Van Brakle, M., & St. Vil, C. (2014). Taking boys out of the hood: Exile as a parenting strategy for African American male youth. *New Directions in Child Adolescent Development*, *143*, 11–31.

Rios, V. M. (2006). The hyper-criminalization of Black and Latino male youth in the era of mass incarceration. *Souls*, 8(2), 40–54.

Rios, V. M. (2011). *Punished: Policing the lives of Black and Latino boys*. New York University Press.

Roberts, N. (2015). *Freedom as marronage*. University of Chicago Press.

Robertson, R. V., & Chaney, C. (2017). "I know it [racism] still exists here:" African American males at a predominantly white institution. *Humboldt Journal of Social Relations*, 39, 260–282.

Robertson, R. V., & Mason, D. (2008). What works? A qualitative examination of the factors related to the academic success of African American males at a predominately white college in the south. *Challenge: A Journal of Research on African American Men*, *14*(2), 67–89.

Robinson, S. A. (2017). "Me against the world": Autoethnographic poetry. *Disability & Society*, *32*(5), 748–752.

Robinson, W. L., Paxton, K. C., & Jonen, L. P. (2011). Pathways to aggression and violence among African American adolescent males: The influence of normative beliefs, neighborhood, and depressive symptomatology. *Journal of Prevention and Intervention in the Community*, 39(2), 132–148.

Rogers, L. O., & Brooms, D. R. (2020). Ideology and identity among white male teachers in an all-Black, all-male high school. *American Educational Research Journal*, 54(2), 440–470.

Rogers, L. O., & Way, N. (2016). "I have goals to prove all those people wrong and not fit into any one of those boxes": Paths of resistance to stereotypes among Black adolescent males. *Journal of Adolescent Research, 31*, 263–298.

Rowley, L. L., & Bowman, P. J. (2009). Risk, protection, and achievement disparities among African American males: Cross-generation theory, research, and comprehensive intervention. *Journal of Negro Education, 78*(3), 305–320.

Sampson, R. J. (2012). *Great American city: Chicago and the enduring neighborhood effect*. University of Chicago Press.

Sealey-Ruiz, Y., & Greene, P. (2015). Popular visual images and the (mis)reading of Black male youth: A case for racial literacy in urban preservice teacher education. *Teaching Education, 26*(1), 55–76.

Scheurich, J. J., & Young, M. (2004). Coloring epistemologies: Are our research epistemologies racially biased. *Educational Researcher, 26*(4), 4–16.

Schott Foundation for Public Education. (2004). *Public education and Black male students: A state report card*. Author.

Schott Foundation for Public Education. (2015). *Black lives matter: The Schott 50 state report on public education and Black males*. Author.

Serrano, U. (2020). "Finding home": Campus racial microclimates and academic homeplaces at a Hispanic-Serving Institution. *Race Ethnicity and Education*, 1–20. https://doi.org/10.1080/13613324.2020.1718086

Sexton, J. (2011). The social life of social death: On Afro-pessimism and Black optimism. *InTensions*, 5, 1–47.

Sharpe, C. (2016). *In the wake: On blackness and being*. Duke University Press.

Shedd, C. (2015). *Unequal city: Race, schools, and perceptions of injustice*. Russell Sage Foundation.

Smith, C. D., & Smith Lee, J. R. (2020). Advancing social justice and affirming humanity in developmental science research with African American boys and young men. *Applied Developmental Science, 24*(3), 208–214.

Smith, W. A., Allen, W. R., & Danley, L. L. (2007). "Assume the position . . . you fit the description": Psychosocial experiences and racial battle fatigue among African American male college students. *American Behavioral Scientist, 51*(4), 551–578.

Smith, W. A., Hung, M., & Franklin, J. D. (2011). Racial battle fatigue and the miseducation of Black men: Racial microaggressions, societal problems, and environmental stress. *Journal of Negro Education*, 80(1), 63–82.

Smith, W. A., Mustaffa, J. B., Jones, C. M., Curry, T. J., & Allen, W. R. (2016). "You make me wanna holler and throw up both my hands!": Campus culture, Black misandric microaggressions, and racial battle fatigue. *International Journal of Qualitative Studies in Education*, 29(9), 1189–1209.

Snyder, S. (2018, December 19). From North Philly to Oxford. *Philadelphia Inquirer*. https://www.inquirer.com/education/a/hazim-hardeman-rhodes-scholar-temple-north-philly-20181219.html

Solórzano, D. G., Ceja, M., & Yosso, T. J. (2000). Critical race theory, racial microaggressions, and campus racial climate: The experiences of African American college students. *Journal of Negro Education*, *69*(1–2), 60–73.

Solórzano, D. G., & Delgado Bernal, D. (2001). Examining transformational resistance through a critical race and LatCrit theory framework: Chicana and Chicano students in an urban context. *Urban Education*, *36*(3), 308–342.

Solórzano, D. G., & Yosso, T. J. (2002). Critical race methodology: Counter storytelling as an analytical framework for education research. *Qualitative Inquiry*, *8*(1), 23–44.

Spencer, M. B., Dupree, D., Cunningham, M., Harpalani, V., & Munoz-Miller, M. (2003). Vulnerability to violence: A contextually-sensitive, developmental perspective on African American adolescents. *Journal of Social Issues*, *59*(1), 33–49.

Squire, D. D., Williams, B. C., & Tuitt, F. (2018). Plantation politics and neoliberal racism in higher education: A framework for reconstructing anti-racist institutions. *Teachers College Record*, *120*(14), 1–19.

Stack, C. (1974). *All our kin: Strategies for survival in a Black community*. Harper & Row.

Stewart, E. A., Schreck, C. J., & Simons, R. L. (2006). "I ain't gonna let no one disrespect me": Does the code of the street reduce or increase violent victimization among African American adolescents? *Journal of Research in Crime and Delinquency*, *43*(4), 427–458.

Stewart, E. B., Stewart, E. A., & Simons, R. L. (2007). The effect of neighborhood context on the college aspirations of African American adolescents. *American Educational Research Journal*, *44*(4), 896–919.

Strauss, A., & Corbin, J. (1998). *Basics of qualitative research: Techniques and procedures for developing grounded theory*. Sage.

Strayhorn, T. L. (2008). The role of supportive relationships in facilitating African American males' success in college. *NASPA Journal*, *45*(1), 26–48.

Strayhorn, T. L. (2014). Making a way to success: Self-authorship and academic achievement of first-year African American students at historically Black colleges. *Journal of College Student Development*, *55*(2), 151–167.

Strayhorn, T. L. (2017). Factors that influence the persistence and success of Black men in urban public universities. *Urban Education*, *52*(9), 1106–1128.

Strayhorn, T. L. (2018). *College students' sense of belonging: A key to educational success* (2nd ed.). Routledge.

Suskin, R. (1998). *A hope in the unseen: An American odyssey from the inner city to the Ivy League*. Broadway.

Swanson, D. P., Cunningham, M., & Spencer, M. B. (2003). Black males' structural conditions, achievement patterns, normative needs, and "opportunities." *Urban Education*, *38*(5), 608–633.

Terry, C. L., Flennaugh, T. K., Blackmon, S. M., & Howard, T. C. (2014). Does the "Negro" *still* need separate schools? Single-sex educational settings as critical race counterspaces. *Urban Education*, *49*(6), 666–697.

Thelamour, B., George Mwangi, C., & Ezeofor, I. (2019). "We need to stick together for survival": Black college students' racial identity, same-ethnic friendships, and campus connectedness. *Journal of Diversity in Higher Education*, *12*(3), 266–279.

Thompson, G. L., & Allen, T. G. (2012). Four effects of the high-stakes testing movement on African American K–12 students. *The Journal of Negro Education*, *81*(3), 218–227.

Tichavakunda, A. A. (2020). Studying Black student life on campus: Toward a theory of Black placemaking in higher education. *Urban Education*, 1–28. https://doi.org/10.1177/0042085920971354

Tichavakunda, A. A. (2021). *Black student life: Campus communities and experiences of Black engineering majors*. SUNY Press.

Tichavakunda, A. A., & Galan, C. (2020). The summer before college: A case study of first-generation, urban high school graduates. *Urban Education*, 1–20. https://doi.org/10.1177/0042085920914362

Tierney, W. G., & Venegas, K. M. (2006). Fictive kin and social capital: The role of peer groups in applying and paying for college. *American Behavioral Scientist*, *49*(12), 1687–1702.

Tillman, L. C. (2002). Culturally sensitive research approaches: An African American perspective. *Educational Researcher*, *31*(9), 3–12.

Toldson, I. A. (2008). *Breaking barriers: Plotting the path to academic success for school-age African American males*. Congressional Black Caucus Foundation.

Toldson, I. A. (2011). *Breaking barriers: Plotting the path away from juvenile detention and toward academic success for school-age African-American males*. Congressional Black Caucus Foundation.

Toldson, I. A. (2015). Why we believe! Getting over the fact that Black boys are brilliant (Editor's commentary). *Journal of Negro Education*, *84*(2), 105–106.

Toldson, I. A., & Johns, D. J. (2016). Erasing deficits. *Teachers College Record*, *118*(6), 1–7.

Tyson, K. (2003). Notes from the back of the room: Problems and paradoxes in the schooling of young Black students. *Sociology of Education*, *76*(4), 326–343.

Venzant Chambers, T. T., & McCready, L. T. (2011). "Making space" for ourselves: African American student responses to their marginalization. *Urban Education*, *46*(6), 1352–1378.

Wallace, D. (2018). Safe routes to school? Black Caribbean youth negotiating police surveillance in London and New York City. *Harvard Educational Review*, *88*(3), 261–288.

Warde, B. (2008). Staying the course: Narratives of African American males who have completed a baccalaureate degree. *Journal of African American Studies*, *12*(1), 59–72.

Warmington, P. (2014). *Black British intellectuals: Race, education and social justice*. Routledge.

Warren, S. (2005). Resilience and refusal: African-Caribbean young men's agency, school exclusions, and school-based mentoring programmes. *Race Ethnicity and Education*, *8*(3), 243–259.

Washington, A. R. (2010). Professional school counselors and African American males: Using school/community collaboration to enhance academic performance. *Journal of African American Males in Education*, *1*(1), 26–39.

Washington, A. R. (2018). Integrating hip-hop culture and rap music into social justice counseling with Black males. *Journal of Counseling & Development*, *96*, 97–105.

Washington, A. R., & Henfield, M. S. (2019). What do the AMCD multicultural social justice counseling competencies mean in the context of Black Lives Matter. *Journal of Multicultural Counseling and Development*, *47*(3), 148–160.

Watkins, D. C. (2006). The depressive symptomology of Black college men: Preliminary findings. *California Journal of Health Promotion*, *4*(3), 187–197.

Watkins, D. C., Green, B. L., Goodson, P., Guidry, J. J., & Stanley, C. A. (2007). Using focus groups to explore the stressful life events of Black college men. *Journal of College Student Development*, *48*(1), 105–118.

Watkins, D. C., Walker, R. L., & Griffith, D. M. (2010). A meta-study of Black mental health and well-being. *Journal of Black Psychology*, *36*(3), 303–330.

Weiston-Serdan, T. (2017). *Critical mentoring: A practical guide*. Stylus.

White, J. L., & Cones, J. H. (1999). *Black man emerging: Facing the past and seizing a future in America*. Routledge.

Whiting, G. W. (2006). From at risk to at promise: Developing scholar identities among Black males. *Journal of Secondary Gifted Education*, *17*(4), 222–229.

Wilder, C. S. (2013). *Ebony and ivy: Race, slavery, and the troubled history of America's universities*. Bloomsbury Publishing USA.

Wilkerson, I. (2020). *Caste: The origins of our discontents*. Penguin Random House.

Williams, B. C., Squire, D. D., & Tuitt, F. A. (2021). *Plantation politics and campus rebellions: Power, diversity and the emancipatory struggle in higher education*. SUNY Press.

Williams, K. L., Burt, B. A., Clay, K., & Bridges, B. K. (2019). Stories untold: Counter-narratives to anti-Blackness and deficit-oriented discourse concerning HBCUs. *American Educational Research Journal*, *56*(2), 556–599.

Williams, P. (1987). Spirit-murdering the messenger: The discourse of fingerpointing as the law's response to racism. *University of Miami Law Review*, *42*, 127–157.

Wilson, W. J. (1987). *The truly disadvantaged: The inner city, the underclass, and public policy*. University of Chicago Press.

Wilson, W. J. (2010). *More than just race: Being Black and poor in the inner city*. W. W. Norton.

Wood, J. L. (2014). Apprehension to engagement in the classroom: Perceptions of Black males in the community college. *International Journal of Qualitative Studies in Education, 27*(6), 785–803.

Wood, J. L., Harris, F., III, & Howard, T. C. (2018). *Get out! Black male suspensions in California public schools*. Community College Equity Assessment Lab and the UCLA Black Male Institute.

Wood, J. L., Newman, C. B., & Harris, F., III. (2015). Self-efficacy as a determinant of academic integration: An examination of first-year Black males in the community college. *Western Journal of Black Studies, 39*(1), 3–17.

Wood, J. L., & Turner, C. S. V. (2012). Black males and the community college: Student perspectives on faculty and academic success. *Community College Journal of Research and Practice, 35*(1–2), 135–151.

Wood, J. L., & Williams, R. C. (2013). Persistence factors for Black males in the community college: An examination of background, academic, social, and environmental variables. *Spectrum: A Journal on Black Men, 1*(2), 1–28.

Woodson, A. (2017). "Being Black is like being a soldier in Iraq": Metaphorical expressions of Blackness in an urban community. *International Journal of Qualitative Studies in Education, 30*(2), 161–174.

Woodson, C. G. (2011). *The mis-education of the Negro*. Tribeka Books. (Original work published 1933)

Wright, B., & Counsell, S. (2018). *The brilliance of Black boys: Cultivating success in the early grades*. Teachers College Press.

Wright, C., Maylor, U., & Becker, S. (2016). Young Black males: Resilience and the use of capital to transform school "failure." *Critical Studies in Education, 57*(1), 21–34.

Wright, C., Pickup, T., & Maylor, U. (2020). *Young British African and Caribbean men achieving educational success*. Routledge.

Wright, C. Y., Standen, P., & Patel, T. (2010). *Black youth matters: Transitions from school to success*. Routledge.

Wun, C. (2016). Unaccounted foundations: Black girls, anti-Black racism, and punishment in schools. *Critical Sociology, 42*(4–5), 737–750.

Wynter, S (1994). No humans involved: An open letter to my colleagues. *Knowledge on Trial, 1*(1), 42–74.

Yancy, G. (2008). *Black bodies, white gazes: The continuing significance of race*. Rowman & Littlefield.

Yosso, T. J. (2005). Whose culture has capital? A critical race theory discussion of community cultural wealth. *Race Ethnicity and Education, 8*(1), 69–91.

Young, A. A. (2004). *The minds of marginalized Black men: Making sense of mobility, opportunity, and future life chances*. Princeton University Press.
Young, A. A. (2018). *Are Black men doomed?* Wiley.

Index

www.ingramcontent.com/pod-product-compliance
Lightning Source LLC
Chambersburg PA
CBHW031401270326
41929CB00010BA/1284

* 9 7 8 1 4 3 8 4 8 6 5 4 3 *